Preschool Education Programs for Children with Autism

SECOND EDITION

Edited by
Jan S. Handleman
and
Sandra L. Harris

8700 Shoal Creek Boulevard
Austin, Texas 78757-6897
800/897-3202   Fax 800/397-7633
www.proedinc.com

© 2001, 1994 by PRO-ED, Inc.
8700 Shoal Creek Boulevard
Austin, Texas 78757-6897
800/897-3202 Fax 800/397-7633
www.proedinc.com

Library of Congress Cataloging-in-Publication Data

Preschool education programs for children with autism / edited by Jan S. Handleman and Sandra L. Harris.—2nd ed.
   p. cm.
   Includes bibliographical references.
   ISBN 0-89079-850-8 (softcover : alk. paper)
   1. Autistic children—Education (Preschool)—United States—Case studies.   2. Classroom management—United States—Case studies.   I. Harris, Sandra L.   II. Handleman, Jan S.

LC4718 .p74   2000
371.94—dc21   99-086984

This book is designed in New Century Schoolbook and Italia.

Production Manager: Chris Anne Worsham
Production Coordinator: Karen Swain
Managing Editor: Chris Olson
Art Director: Thomas Barkley
Designer: Jason Crosier
Print Buyer: Alicia Woods
Preproduction Coordinator: Martin Wilson
Project Editor: Debra Berman
Staff Copyeditor: Becky Shore
Publishing Assistant: Jason Morris

Printed in the United States of America

1   2   3   4   5   6   7   8   9   10   04   03   02   01   00

Contents

Preface

The impetus for this second edition comes from our nearly 30 years of work at the Douglass Developmental Disabilities Center, New Brunswick, New Jersey, and parallel efforts by many colleagues in the field. All of us who created this book did so to share our efforts with parents and professionals seeking answers to the many remaining questions about the education of young children with autism.

As we enter the millennium, we continue to see a number of fads and fancies of treatment for autism come and go. Some people have made their fame or fortune offering the latest in a series of "cures" or revolutionary philosophical views about the treatment of autism. Often these individuals leave behind a trail of brokenhearted parents who had hoped for that bit of magic that would transform their child. The discriminating professional may also be confused about a growing range of options for treatment, some data based and some not.

Sadly, in spite of all the claims, the cure for autism is not yet known. Nonetheless, dedicated clinicians, educators, and scientists continue to labor to develop and refine data-based procedures of proven efficacy for the treatment of autism. This steady, ongoing empirical effort continues to lead to substantial gains in the ability to educate children with autism. One area where this improvement is most notable is in the education of very young children.

The educational strategies used today for preschool-aged children with autism are quite different from those of years past. However, disseminating information about these techniques has lagged behind their development. As a result, many classrooms still rely on strategies more appropriate to the early 1980s than to the turn of the century. This lack of widespread sharing of information about procedures of demonstrated value makes it urgent to ensure that information about preschool education is readily available. It is hoped that this second edition of our book will help to further clarify the many important issues and questions that are raised by parents and professionals alike.

We are grateful to the contributors to both the first and second editions of this volume who have shared in some detail a description of their classrooms. This edition focuses particularly on advances during the last 5 years. Each program described relies on data-based procedures to create its curriculum and to evaluate its impact on students. We believe such rigor is the hallmark of effective education.

We wish to thank our colleagues at the Douglass Developmental Disabilities Center and the Graduate School of Applied and Professional Psychology at Rutgers University for their ongoing support. We especially appreciate the help of Maria Arnold, Jean Burton, Lew Gantwerk, Peter Gerhardt, Rita Gordon, Barbara Kristoff, Ruth Schulman, Mary Jane Weiss, and the staff of the preschool, who continue to offer wise counsel. Nadine Byczkowski has also provided countless hours preparing this edition. We also are forever indebted to those parents who have entrusted us with the education of their children. We could ask for no higher compliment than their confidence in our program. Closer to home, Lauren Handleman continues to teach her father the power of love between children and parents.

Jan S. Handleman and Sandra L. Harris

Preschool Programs for Children with Autism

Jan S. Handleman and Sandra L. Harris

L ovaas's (1987) report of the impressive gains demonstrated by some children with autism in response to behavioral instruction prompted confirmation by others of the effectiveness of early intervention (e.g., Birnbrauer & Leach, 1993). Lovaas (1987) reported that nearly half of the young children with autism who received intensive behavior modification in his project reached normal intellectual and educational functioning at follow-up. In another important set of studies, Strain, Odom, and their colleagues documented that young children with autistic behavior can benefit socially and educationally from exposure to normal peers in an integrated preschool program (e.g., Odom, Hoyson, Jamieson, & Strain, 1985; Odom & Strain, 1986; Strain, Hoyson, & Jamieson, 1985). In addition, we found, in a study conducted at the Douglass Developmental Disabilities Center in New Brunswick, New Jersey, a nearly 19-point increase in IQ for children with autism after one year of intensive work in a segregated preschool class (Harris, Handleman, Gordon, Kristoff, & Fuentes, 1991). These and other independent reports of measurable behavior changes in preschool-aged children with autism document more substantial benefits than were thought possible a decade ago.

As a result of the encouraging data about early intervention, a variety of preschool projects have been developed and many educators are considering the establishment of similar programs in their own school systems. In spite of our enthusiasm, we are concerned about the lack of easily available information about the organization and operation of these classes and the wide variation that is likely to develop among programs.

Communication among professionals is important so that they can compare the outcomes from the various approaches and assess which methods are best under which conditions. Because there is a serious risk of drift away from data-based treatment models toward ones founded on administrative

1

convenience, intuition, or misinterpretation, communication among educators and administrators must be kept at an optimum level and program effectiveness accurately documented. It would be a particular tragedy to offer ineffective services at a time when the educational technology is available to provide substantial benefit to some children.

As in the first edition, we invited distinguished service providers in 10 different settings for young children with autism to describe their programs in some detail. Five authors were original contributors and five additional providers were asked to supplement this edition. Each author was asked to follow the same general outline, while being encouraged to embellish upon those areas of special relevance to his or her model. This structure offers the reader an opportunity to compare the various programs of a number of dimensions, while also giving the author the opportunity to highlight special features of the individual program.

Table 1.1 summarizes a number of important features characterizing the preschool programs described in this book. The reader will find both the differences and the similarities important in comparing programs and selecting features of potential use in creating a new preschool program. Although the level of detail in this book will not enable the reader to replicate precisely an existing program, it should serve to sensitize one to the variables that must be considered in the creation of a classroom, possible solutions to thorny problems, and methods of measuring progress to document the efficacy of one's intervention. Although many of the methods described in the chapters that follow are data based, the reader will nonetheless need to measure the impact of these methods in his or her own classroom. Such accountability is an integral component on ethical educational practice.

As noted in Table 1.1, the programs showcased in this book are located in a variety of settings, including public schools, private special education schools, and universities. Some of the classrooms described have been in existence for quite a while and others are relatively new. Schopler (Chapter 9), for example, started the TEACCH program in 1972, whereas Weiss (Chapter 2) established her program in 1995. This diversity of settings and range of experiences should enable the reader to find one or more programs that are a good fit with his or her administrative context.

All of the programs in this edition offer a rich ratio of adults to children. That intensity appears to be essential to the education of young children with autism. To meet that need, most of the preschool programs described buttress their full-time staff with graduate or undergraduate students from nearby colleges and universities. This is a valuable and inexpensive potential resource that every program should consider. Not only do the children benefit from the presence of energetic undergraduates, but the college students benefit as well through the opportunity for "hands-on" learning. In our own day school at Rutgers University (Chapter 10), scores of undergraduates have remained in the field of developmental disorders after their experience at our center.

Table 1.1
Summary of Program Features

	Author or Lead Author								
	Weiss	Smith	Romanczyk	Rogers	Meyer	McGee	McClannahan	Marcus	Harris
Chapter	2	3	4	5	6	7	8	9	10
Location	University	Various	University	University	Private	University	Private	Public	Various
University Training	Yes	Yes	Yes	Yes	Yes	Yes	Yes	Yes	Yes
Target Population	Aut	Aut	Aut/Mixed	Aut	Aut	Aut	Aut	Aut/CH	Aut
Opportunity for Integration	Yes	Yes	Yes	Yes	Yes	Yes	Yes	Yes	Yes
Parent Training	Yes	Yes	Yes	Yes	Yes	Yes	Yes	Yes	Yes
Transitional Planning	Yes	Yes	Yes	Yes	Yes	Yes	Yes	Yes	Yes
Assessment Instruments Used									
CARS	Yes	No	No	Yes	Yes	Yes	No	Yes	Yes
IQ	Various	Various	Slosson	Various	Binet	Bayley Binet	Binet	Bayley	Various
DSM-IV	Yes	Yes	Yes	Yes	Yes	Yes	Yes	Yes	Yes
Vineland	Yes	Yes	Yes	Yes	Yes	Yes	Yes	Yes	Yes
LAP/ELAP	No	No	No	No	No	Yes	No	No	No

Note. Aut = autism; Mixed = various diagnoses; LD = learning disability; CH = communication handicapped; CARS = *The Childhood Autism Rating Scale* (Schopler et al., 1988); Denver = *Denver Developmental Screening Test* (Frankenburg, Dodd, & Fandal, 1973); Slosson = *Slosson Intelligence Test for Children and Adults* (Armstrong & Jensen, 1981); Binet = *The Stanford–Binet Intelligence Scale* (Thorndike et al., 1986); Bayley = *Bayley Scales of Infant Development–Second Edition* (Bayley, 1993); DSM = *Diagnostic and Statistical Manual of Mental Disorders–Fourth Edition* (American Psychiatric Association, 1994); Vineland = *Vineland Adaptive Behavior Scales* (Sparrow et al., 1984); LAP/ELAP = *Learning Accomplishment Profile* (Sanford & Zelman, 1981).

Although all of the programs were selected for this book because they serve children with autism, some include other populations as well, including typical children and children with pervasive developmental disorder not otherwise specified or learning disabilities. All of the programs provide opportunities for integration with normally developing children, but the degree and intensity of integration varies from those that fully integrate children with autism from the early days of schooling to those that do this later, or on a less intensive or limited basis. Some programs integrate children in classes within their own physical setting, and others take the children to different facilities in the community to accomplish this goal. Each approach has its own benefits and challenges. Integration within one's own setting permits optimal flexibility and control over the experience, but integration in other settings may sometimes provide a more realistic sense of the natural environment in which the child must ultimately function. It is noteworthy that every program is attentive to the process of transition from school to the child's next educational experience. This universal concern for transitional planning highlights the importance of this aspect of program development.

Topics Authors Were Asked To Address

Structure and Context

This book is intended to give an educator or administrator planning to create a new classroom, or to reorganize an existing program, a sense of the range of options currently being employed by others. We have asked the contributors to translate into relatively concrete terms what it means for their program to be "behaviorally based," "developmentally sequenced," "integrated," or "segregated." In reading the descriptions one will wish to ask such questions as these: How much do the models resemble or differ from one another along these dimensions? To what extent do current data inform the operation of these programs? Given that our database falls short of the needs for inclusive programming, how do various models fill in the knowledge gaps?

We were also interested in what these prominent service providers view as important research questions that need to be addressed before we can fully evaluate the benefits of our models for serving children with autism. We asked them what they believe are the most pressing questions confronting the field. Their responses to that question may inspire those who are creating new programs to establish them in a way that will address some of these urgent issues. The reader will surely come away from the discussion with an appreciation of how much he or she has yet to learn about the education of the preschool-aged child with autism and with a healthy skepticism about any "easy cures."

Each chapter begins with an overview of the structure and context of the program. Where is it located? How long has it been in existence? How is it funded? How much does it cost to operate? This information about context helps the reader orient to the specific program and the kinds of resources available in that setting. Operating in a public school, a university campus, a hospital, or a private school may carry different implications about the structure of one's classroom (Handleman, 1988). Programs in the public schools may be required to serve every child who meets admissions criteria, whereas those in private or university settings may be able to be more selective about whom they admit. Each setting has potential benefits. For example, McGee, Morrier, and Daly (Chapter 7) and Harris, Handleman, Arnold, and Gordon (Chapter 10) operate university-based programs that have brought the normally developing peers on campus in a kind of "reverse" mainstreaming, as opposed to the use of community settings by the programs for children with autism.

Diagnosis and Assessment

We asked each of our contributors to provide considerable detail about the children being served by the program. It is often difficult to know whether the children attending one program are similar to those in another. This information helps in determining to what extent differences in treatment outcome may be affected by differences in population as opposed to treatment model. The complexities of defining autism have historically led to the inclusion of a rather heterogeneous group under this heading. The greater specificity professionals can bring to this task, the better the communication that will follow.

The diagnosis of autism has been a subject of debate for half a century. Following Kanner's (1943) initial description of infantile autism, there have been a variety of alternative definitions of precisely what constitutes autism (Schopler & Mesibov, 1988). That debate is not ended, and each recent *Diagnostic and Statistical Manual of Mental Disorders* (DSM) has offered somewhat different criteria for diagnosis (American Psychiatric Association, 1980, 1987, 1994). This ambiguity makes it essential that we communicate as fully as possible with one another about whom we are treating. As the reader will note in Table 1.1, all but two of the programs described in this book use the *DSM-IV* criteria, and many also use *The Childhood Autism Rating Scale* to accept children into their programs (CARS; Schopler, Reichler, Devellis, & Daly, 1988). The CARS was developed by the TEACCH program staff in North Carolina. By virtue of its age and size, the TEACCH program (described in Chapter 9) has served more children with autism and related disorders than any of the other programs in this book, and the authors' discussion of the complexities of diagnostic assessment is based on that rich and extensive background.

In addition to the challenge of diagnosis, there is the question of how one assesses the various dimensions of the child's functioning, including behavior, affect, social skills, cognition, speech–language, and so forth. Although assessment of children with autism has long been recognized as difficult (Browder, 1991; Powers & Handleman, 1984), it is also clear that the use of appropriate instruments and strategies makes it possible to conduct a meaningful, valid assessment of these youngsters (Schopler & Mesibov, 1988).

A variety of approaches can be used to assess the child with autism. One of these is the use of norm-based psychometric tests including intelligence tests, tests of developmental abilities, and speech–language assessments. For example, as evident in Table 1.1, most of the programs use the *Stanford–Binet Intelligence Scale–Fourth Edition* (Binet) (Thorndike, Hagen, & Sattler, 1986) and the *Vineland Adaptive Behavior Scales* (Sparrow, Balla, & Cicchetti, 1984) as norm-based assessment devices.

Behavioral assessment of the child's skills, deficits, and behavior problems is another important strategy employed in many settings (Powers & Handleman, 1984). Assessments may be based on direct observation in the classroom, home visits, community observations, parent reports, teacher reports, and videotapes. The contributors to this volume were asked to describe their approach to this individualized assessment process.

Staffing and Administration

The creation of a classroom for children with autism requires a teaching staff and an administrative structure. We asked each author to describe the staff who participate in their program in terms of credentials and responsibilities. Special education teachers, speech–language specialists, and psychologists are universally involved in these programs, as are teacher assistants. Other specialists such as occupational or physical therapists may be part of the regular staff, or may be consulted for those children who require their services. Family coordinators or parent trainers are specifically designated in some programs, such as the Rutgers Autism Program (Chapter 2).

The authors were also asked to describe the kinds of training and supervision they provide for their staff. Given the continuing changes in educational strategies for children with autism, inservice education is crucial in maintaining an effective program. McClannahan and Krantz describe in detail their systematic approach to staff training (Chapter 8).

Curriculum

Curriculum development for young children with autism is an intricate task (Handleman, 1992). Selecting appropriate goals and objectives, determining accurate levels of instruction, and identifying and creating suitable materials often present challenges for the teacher. A well-balanced and -orchestrated curriculum is typically the result of careful planning and the systematic organization of educational experiences (Handleman & Harris, 1986). The computerized approach to data collection, record keeping, and specialized assessment developed by Romanczyk, Lockshin, and Matey will be of special interest to many readers (Chapter 4).

An important component of each chapter of this book is an overview of the curriculum for the program. This includes the general philosophy that drives the curriculum, the major areas in the curriculum, and sources of materials used in the classroom. Sample curriculum items from the domains of social, affective, cognitive, speech–language, and self-help are described to help the reader understand specific examples of what the children are taught. A sample daily schedule is included to give one a sense of the flow of activities through the school day. Methods of assessing each child's progress are described. The reader will find considerable variation among the teaching approaches described in this book. For example, McGee, Morrier, and Daly (Chapter 7) focus on the use of incidental teaching to a greater degree than any of the other programs represented here. This work, started at the University of Massachusetts and now continuing at Emory University, sets this program in contrast to many others.

Integration

The development of preschool classes for children with autism and the striking progress these children have made through early intervention programs has led to an active exploration of the value of integrating these youngsters with their normally developing peers in the classroom. Strain and Odom have been especially important in exploring this dimension of treatment (e.g., Odom & Speltz, 1983; Strain, 1983). Their work and that of others raised important questions that we believed needed to be addressed in the present volume: To what extent is exposure to normally developing peers viewed as essential to the child's education? If integration or mainstreaming is provided, at what point does this occur? Are children mainstreamed all day, every day from their first day in school? Is there a gradual transition? Who are the peer children? What effect does integration have on the peers? Each of the programs has its own approach to this problem. For example, McGee and colleagues (Chapter 7) present a model that integrates children from their initial admission to the preschool program, whereas Harris and colleagues (Chapter 10) provide most of their students with 1 year of intensive segregated instruction followed by an integrated experience. Smith, Donahoe, and Davis (Chapter 3) describe a variety of opportunities in their model.

Use of Aversives

Another potentially controversial issue each author was asked to address was the use of behavior management procedures for very young children. The use of "aversive" techniques has been a topic of major debate in the treatment of life-threatening or dangerous behavior for people with autism (e.g., Harris & Handleman, 1990; Repp & Singh, 1990). We asked each contributor to describe his or her philosophy concerning the use of management techniques for preschool-aged children and to indicate which specific techniques are employed when dealing with behavior problems. Most of the interventions with preschool-aged children involve very mild aversive interventions, with a primary focus on functional assessment and teaching of appropriate alternative behaviors. The relatively brief learning history of very young children offers a sense of optimism for intervening effectively with most of their behavior problems.

Family Involvement

For more than 20 years, we have known that parent and family involvement is an important factor in maintaining the behavior changes achieved by children with autism (Lovaas, Koegel, Simmons, & Long, 1973; Schopler & Reichler, 1971). Research in the 1970s and 1980s documented that parents can master a full range of intervention techniques and use them to facilitate their child's mastery of language, social, self-help, and related skills (e.g., Harris, 1983; Howlin, 1981). More recently, concern has been expressed about the kinds of support resources necessary to maintain optimal family functioning and ensure that the family context remains appropriate to the needs of all of its members (e.g., Harris, 1994). The most intensive home-based program in this book is that of Weiss and Piccolo and their coworkers (Chapter 2) at Rutgers University who provide intensive in-home treatment programs.

In recognition of the role that families can play in treatment, the contributors to this book were asked to consider the role of parents as teacher and the level of family involvement and support. What do they expect of parents and what kind of support do they provide for families? How intimately involved are parents expected to be in their child's education? Is the program home based? School-based? Who trains parents? Must they participate?

Outcome

To the extent that such data are available, each author was asked to describe outcome data concerning children who have completed the program. These include initial placement data and any systematic follow-up information the author can provide. Where have the children gone after they have left the preschool class? How have they done in those new placements? Are there any standardized measures of change for the children from admission to graduation?

Recommendations

Each chapter concludes with recommendations from the author concerning areas of special concern that he or she believes should be addressed by educators and researchers in the future. What are the limits of available intervention methods and what should we be planning to do next?

Conclusion

We hope this book will enable established service providers to communicate more clearly with one another about their models of intervention. We also hope it will enable the newcomer to identify those approaches most consistent with his or her classroom goals and to adopt a teaching model most consistent with those objectives. Many of the contributors to this volume are available for consultation, and the person creating a new service or revamping an old one may find dialogue with one or more of these authors a useful step in the process of change.

References

American Psychiatric Association, (1980). *Diagnostic and statistical manual of mental disorders (3rd ed.).* Washington, DC: Author.

American Psychiatric Association. (1987). *Diagnostic and statistical manual of mental disorders (3rd ed., rev.).* Washington, DC: Author.

American Psychiatric Association. (1994). *Diagnostic and statistical manual of mental disorders (4th ed.).* Washington, DC: Author.

Armstrong, R. J., & Jensen, J. A. (1981). *Slosson Intelligence Test for Children and Adults.* East Aurora, NY: Slosson Educational.

Bayley, N. (1993). *Bayley Scales of Infant Development–Second Edition.* San Antonio: Psychological Corp.

Birnbrauer, J. S., & Leach, D. J. (1993). The Murdock Early Intervention Program after 2 years. *Behavior Change, 10,* 63–74.

Browder, D. M. (Ed.). (1991). *Assessment of individuals with severe disabilities: An applied behavior approach to life skills assessment.* (2nd ed.) Baltimore: Brookes.

Frankenburg, W. K., Dodd, J. B., & Fandal, A. W. (1973). *Denver Developmental Screening Test.* Denver, CO: Ladora Project and Publishing Foundation.

Handleman, J. S. (1988). Educational services in the schools: Beyond the student–teacher dyad. In M. D. Powers (Ed.), *Expanding systems of service delivery for persons with developmental disabilities* (pp. 217–229). Baltimore: Brookes.

Handleman, J. S. (1992). Assessment for curriculum planning. In D. Berkell (Ed.), *Autism: Identification, education and treatment* (pp. 77–88). Hillsdale, NJ: Erlbaum.

Handleman, J. S., & Harris, S. L. (1986). *Educating the developmentally disabled: Meeting the needs of children and families.* San Diego: College Hill.

Harris, S. L. (1983). *Families of the developmentally disabled: A guide to behavioral intervention.* Elmsford, NY: Pergamon Press.

Harris, S. L. (1994). Treatment of family problems in autism. In E. Schopler & G. B. Mesibov (Eds.), *Behavioral issues in autism* (pp. 161–175). New York: Plenum.

Harris, S. L., & Handleman, J. S. (Eds.). (1990). *Aversive and nonaversive interventions.* New York: Springer.

Harris, S. L., Handleman, J. S., Gordon, R., Kristoff, B., & Fuentes, F. (1991). Changes in cognitive and language functioning of preschool children with autism. *Journal of Autism and Developmental Disorders, 21,* 281–290.

Howlin, P. A. (1981). The results of a home-based language training program with autistic children. *British Journal of Disorders of Communication, 16,* 73–88.

Kanner, L. (1943). Autistic disturbances of affective contact. *Nervous Child, 2,* 217–240.

Lovaas, O. I. (1987). Behavioral treatment and normal education and intellectual functioning in young autistic children. *Journal of Consulting and Clinical Psychology, 55,* 3–9.

Lovaas, O. I., Koegel, R. L., Simmons, J. Q., & Long, J. S. (1973). Some generalization and follow-up measures on autistic children in behavior therapy. *Journal of Applied Behavior Analysis, 6,* 131–165.

Odom, S. L., Hoyson, M., Jamieson, B., & Strain, P. S. (1985). Increasing handicapped preschoolers' peer social interactions: Cross-setting and component analysis. *Journal of Applied Behavior Analysis, 18,* 3–16.

Odom, S. L., & Speltz, M. L. (1983). Program variations in preschools for handicapped and nonhandicapped children: Mainstreamed vs. integrated special education. *Analysis and Intervention in Developmental Disabilities, 3,* 89–103.

Odom, S. L., & Strain, P. S. (1986). A comparison of peer-initiation and teacher-antecedent interventions for promoting social interactions of autistic preschoolers. *Journal of Applied Behavior Analysis, 19,* 59–71.

Powers, M. D., & Handleman, J. S. (1984). *Behavioral assessment of severe developmental disabilities.* Rockville, MD: Aspen Systems.

Repp, A. C., & Singh, N. N. (Eds.). (1990). *Perspectives on the use of nonaversive and aversive interventions for persons with developmental disabilities.* Sycamore, IL: Sycamore Publishing.

Sanford, A. R., & Zelman, J. G. (1981). *The learning accomplishment profile.* Winston-Salem, NC: Kaplan.

Schopler, E., & Mesibov, G. B. (Eds.). (1988). *Diagnosis and assessment in autism.* New York: Plenum.

Schopler, E., & Reichler, R. (1971). Parents as co-therapists in the treatment of psychotic children. *Journal of Autism and Childhood Schizophrenia, 1,* 87–102.

Schopler, E., Reichler, R. J., Devellis, R. F., & Daly, K. (1988). *The Childhood Autism Rating Scale.* Los Angeles: Western Psychological Services.

Sparrow, S. S., Balla, D. A., & Cicchetti, D. V. (1984). *Vineland Adaptive Behavior Scales: Interview edition. Survey form manual.* Circle Pines, MN: American Guidance Service.

Strain, P. S. (1983). Generalization of autistic children's social behavior change: Effects of developmentally integrated and segregated settings. *Analysis and Intervention in Developmental Disabilities, 3,* 23–34.

Strain, P. S., Hoyson, M., & Jamieson, B. (1985). Normally developing preschoolers as intervention agents for autistic-like children: Effects on class deportment and social interaction. *Journal of the Division for Early Childhood, 9,* 105–115.

Thorndike, R. L., Hagen, E. R., & Sattler, J. M. (1986). *The Stanford–Binet Intelligence Scale (4th ed.).* Chicago: Riverside.

The Rutgers Autism Program 2

Mary Jane Weiss and Ellen Piccolo

T he Rutgers Autism Program was founded in 1994 as a division of the Center for Applied Psychology at the Graduate School of Applied and Professional Psychology at Rutgers, The State University of New Jersey. The program was founded in response to the growing need for appropriate educational programs for children with autism and other pervasive developmental disorders. The mission of the Rutgers Autism Program is to help families develop a home-based program to enable their children to realize their fullest potential. To assist in the attainment of this mission, parents and other instructors are conceptualized as team members who have an integral and essential role in the education and development of the child.

The Rutgers Autism Program also consults with schools and other agencies to develop intensive educational and behavioral programs for children with autism and other pervasive developmental disorders based on applied behavior analysis and empirically supported teaching methods. Agency or district staff receive intensive and ongoing training and are provided with the tools needed to be accountable for their students' learning. Ongoing consultation with the Rutgers Autism Program is coupled with systematic data collection to help ensure that each student is provided with an effective education.

Service delivery is a long-term commitment; those children who receive the Rutgers Autism Program's consultative services typically require 2 to 3 years of intensive intervention. The ultimate goal is to facilitate a successful transition into a less restrictive educational environment.

Program Information: Rutgers Autism Program, Rutgers University, Center for Applied Psychology, 41 Gordon Road, Suite A, Piscataway, NJ 08854; 732/445-7778

Philosophy

The Rutgers Autism Program interventions are based upon the broad spectrum of methods derived from the principles of applied behavior analysis. These treatment principles are developed from over three decades of published empirical research (Carr & Durand, 1985a, 1985b; Lovaas, 1987; Skinner, 1957). The Rutgers Autism Program applies this empirical research to address the individual needs of the child with autism.

Although the principles of applied behavior analysis guide our programming efforts and activities, each child is seen as unique. High levels of consistency, repeated and consistent presentations of material, individually selected and strategically used motivators, careful use of prompting procedures, and systematic planning for generalization are needed to establish and maintain a positive learning environment. We also recognize that flexibility must be exercised to create an environment that is maximally effective for each child. The program is comprehensive and aimed at enhancing skills in a variety of developmental domains including communication, social skills, behavioral functioning, cognition, and school readiness. We strive to organize learning experiences that will lead to enduring positive changes in functioning over time and across all settings, including the home and the community.

Service

We individually tailor our service delivery model to the needs of each child and family. Our array of consultative services includes 2- or 3-day initial workshops, follow-up workshops, phone consultations, and video reviews. The initial workshop highlights those principles of applied behavior analysis that lay the foundation for our teaching model. Following that foundation, an overview of discrete trial instruction, our primary method of teaching, is provided. As we demonstrate the techniques, strategies for enhancing compliance and managing challenging behaviors are discussed and modeled. Recommendations for the identification and implementation of effective reinforcers are also included. The majority of the workshop time is spent modeling instructional techniques and observing the implementation of these techniques by participants. Upon completion of the initial workshop, families are given a set of programs that are tailored to the child's specific educational needs.

At follow-up workshops, progress is assessed in all curricular areas. Modifications in programming and new strategies for teaching skills are identified and new goals for instruction are developed. As needed, challenging behaviors are also addressed and intervention plans are developed. Team members are observed implementing programs with the child and are given feedback to improve their skills. Staff members who are team leaders are also supported in their roles of providing on-site training to other members of the team.

Population Served

The Rutgers Autism Program serves children with autism and other pervasive developmental disorders. Our mission is to serve young children in a highly intensive model. Currently, newly accepted students must be age 4 years or younger at the start of intervention. Furthermore, children must receive from 30 to 40 hours per week of systematic one-to-one applied behavior analysis instruction. (Families are strongly encouraged to provide 40 hours of instruction.)

The Rutgers Autism Program serves children in over 10 states. Many of the children we serve are in New Jersey or in adjacent or regional states. We also serve children in the upper Northeast and in the Midwest. In these areas, there are often no appropriate school-based programs for the family to consider. The provision of a home-based applied behavior analysis program may be the only way to create an appropriate educational environment.

Professional Staff

Staff at the Rutgers Autism Program include two doctoral level supervisors, a program coordinator, and four behavior specialists. The supervisors are responsible for clinical oversight, supervision, and ongoing training. Supervisors provide weekly individual and group supervision to all Rutgers Autism Program staff. Team meetings are designed to explore challenging issues and review current research and technology. We are committed to incorporating the newest empirically developed methodology in our interventions. Four behavior specialists provide training to families and instructors in discrete trial instruction. They also provide an individualized curriculum for each child with autism whom they serve. The program coordinator provides administrative support and serves as the liaison to those individuals requesting and receiving services, including family members, school districts, and agencies. Rutgers Autism Program staff have published extensively in the field and are frequent presenters at regional and national conferences in the areas of autism and applied behavior analysis.

Assessment Procedure

All children considered for services must have a diagnosis of an autism spectrum disorder by an independent professional. Following our preliminary review of the child's medical and educational records, we ask the family to complete our intake information forms. In many cases, a videotape of the child is also requested for review. All of these materials are reviewed by senior staff and by the clinician assigned to the case. Prior to intervention,

The *Childhood Autism Rating Scale* (Schopler, Reichler, & Renner, 1988) and the *Vineland Adaptive Behavior Scales* (Sparrow, Balla, & Cicchetti, 1984) are typically administered. One of the most important issues in selecting children for the Rutgers Autism Program is the family's commitment to an intensive model of applied behavior analysis intervention. Families must make a commitment to a minimum of 30 hours of applied behavior analysis intervention weekly. Furthermore, they must agree to a pure implementation of applied behavior analysis. In other words, it is imperative that families understand the need for consistency in instructional technique and in contingency management. If another intervention is in use (e.g., speech therapy), it must be consistent with the basic tenets of the applied behavior analysis program. Ongoing assessment is a hallmark characteristic of applied behavior analysis programs. All children receiving services from the Rutgers Autism Program receive ongoing follow-up visits, in which specific assessment of progress is a major focus.

Home Instruction

Home instructional teams comprise individuals hired by the families. Most of the staff are undergraduate or graduate students in psychology or special education. Instruction takes place in the homes of the children. All instructors are required to attend the initial training. If new instructors join the team after the initial training, the new staff member is paired with an experienced instructor for 18 hours of additional training before working individually with the child. The first 6 of these hours usually involve observation of a competent instructor. The next 6 hours involve modeling by the experienced staff member, followed by implementation by the new instructor. The novice instructor is provided with extensive feedback and coaching during this period. The final 6 hours comprise instruction by the new instructor, with continuous observation by and supervision from the experienced member of the staff.

The children served by the Rutgers Autism Program generally receive 6 hours of instruction per day, 6 or 7 days per week. (There is some variability in the exact length of sessions and in scheduling, but this is the most common arrangement.) The 6 hours of daily instruction are generally divided into two 3-hour sessions. During the work sessions, instructional demands are interspersed with periods of free play. Generally, children work for 5 to 20 trials, and then play for 1 to 3 minutes. This pattern is repeated throughout the session.

Discrete trial instruction is a highly structured, data-based approach that constitutes the primary initial teaching method of the Rutgers Autism Program. Programmed instruction involves a breakdown of skills into a series of hierarchical steps, each building toward the next. All skills are initially presented in isolation (without distracters and not mixed with previously mastered items) and are introduced with prompts. A most to least prompt hierarchy is used to maximize success and to reduce errors. For many children, an instructional "no" is incorporated for incorrect responses after acquisition has been established. This is a "no" spoken in a neutral tone. Two consecutive incorrect responses set the occasion for a prompted trial. When a prompted trial is done, a most to least strategy is used. Thus, through the use of a more intrusive prompt, success is ensured. New items in programs are introduced after the target item is mastered in expanded trials (i.e., after mastery in discrimination with previously mastered items). As soon as the child's performance on an item meets mastery criteria (90% in expanded trials with two instructors in two consecutive sessions), the next item is introduced.

Alternatively, some children are taught via an errorless teaching paradigm. This is used particularly with children who are prone to repeated errors and with children who do not respond consistently to the use of an instructional "no." It is important for the instructional model to be well matched to the child's learning style and characteristics.

For each child served, an individualized curricular progression is outlined. General long-term progressions are developed at follow-up visits, to ensure the continual introduction of material. The introduction of material depends upon a hierarchical system of skill development. Detailed attention is given to the development of foundation skills and to the assessment of appropriate prerequisite skills.

Follow-up visits generally occur every 4 to 8 weeks. Interim contact includes weekly phone consultations with the consultant. In addition, video reviews generally occur at least once between visits. These interim supports afford additional opportunities for problem identification, troubleshooting, and curricular updates. In addition, instructional teams meet weekly to review programs and address concerns. These meetings are often coordinated with the consultant, who may be available by phone during the meeting.

Parental Involvement

The Rutgers Autism Program model requires a tremendous commitment on the part of the family. It is usually necessary for one parent to be at home, coordinating the program on a full-time basis. Furthermore, we generally request that parents devote a minimum of 6 to 10 hours a week to intervention. In some families, a parent opts to do some instructional hours (e.g., two 3-hour sessions per week); other families spend 6 to 10 hours per week in active generalization training.

In all families, there is a need to organize and oversee the program. Scheduling of hours, coordination of team meeting times, and ensuring adequate communication across staff are critical roles that typically fall to a parent. In some cases, an experienced lead instructor can assume some of these responsibilities. High levels of parental involvement, however, are always necessary. Parents are required to attend the initial workshop and all follow-up workshops, and to have phone contact with the consultant between visits.

Sibling Involvement

In many families of children with autism, there are siblings whose needs and concerns should be recognized and addressed. When instruction is going on in the home, there is a unique set of issues for siblings. Siblings may be confused about the instruction. They may worry that their brother or sister is working too diligently. Alternately, they may be jealous of the attention intrinsic to the intensive teaching model. (Their brother or sister has special adult friends who come to see and play with only him or her.) Depending on age, siblings can be involved in the program in a number of ways. For some children, observing sessions can reduce the mystery and provide vital information about what occurs during instruction. Other children may be asked to join small group learning activities (e.g., "mock" circle times). Older children might be interested in learning some of the instructional techniques and in serving as assistants to the instructor. The critical element in these decisions about sibling participation is ensuring that participation is welcome and voluntary.

Behavior Management

The Rutgers Autism Program approaches behavior management in the same way that it approaches skill acquisition. The focus is on the use of behavior analytic methodology, individual assessment, and tailored intervention. A thorough and appropriate functional assessment precedes intervention. In this way, an attempt is made to understand the functional nature of the behavior, that is, why it persists. Functional assessment techniques used include indirect methods, such as checklists and rating scales, including the Motivation Assessment Scale (Durand, 1990). Descriptive methods are also used. These provide direct observation of behaviors. Examples include ABC (Antecedent Behavior Consequence) analyses and scatterplots. Structural or antecedent functional analyses involve direct observation and the manipulation of antecedent events. Experimental analyses involve direct observation and the manipulation of both antecedent and subsequent events. All of these methods (indirect methods, descriptive methods, structural functional analyses, and experimental analyses) are used in the assessment of challenging behaviors.

A number of ecological and programmatic variables are also examined in functional assessments. Factors examined might include task complexity, novelty of materials used, changes in instructors, change in the daily schedule, adequacy of lighting, ventilation, noise, and crowding (O'Neill, Horner, Albin, Storey, & Sprague, 1990). Efforts to intervene with challenging behaviors always incorporate skill acquisition programs, in an effort to teach adaptive, alternative responses. Functional communication training is an essential component of behavior intervention plans (Carr & Durand, 1985a, 1985b; Durand, 1990).

It is important in the assessment of challenging behaviors to identify highly preferred stimuli and activities. Systematic preference assessments are critically important and ensure that rewards offered are serving as reinforcers. Highly preferred stimuli produce higher response rates than less preferred stimuli, when provided contingent on task completion. Thus, the choice of stimuli offered for rewards has significant educational implications. The most commonly used preference assessment procedures at the Rutgers Autism Program are those of Pace, Ivancic, Edwards, Iwata, and Page (1985), Fisher et al. (1992), and DeLeon and Iwata (1996).

Curricular Areas of Focus

Curricular emphases are comprehensive and designed to meet the needs of children who vary widely in developmental levels and learning styles. Initially, we focus on creating foundation skills in several critical areas. These are the building blocks for the subsequent learning of more complex skills. Extensions from the foundation skills are highly individualized. The same skills are taught with a variety of instructional adaptations based on each child's learning characteristics. We use the child's strengths to build skills in areas of relative weakness. Table 2.1 provides a sample of early imitation skills targeted. Table 2.2 summarizes the foundation skills for each child which are compliance, manding, matching, imitative behavior, and receptive language. As shown in Table 2.3, extensions of the curriculum include, among others, the development of expressive language, abstract concepts, and school readiness skills.

Advanced Curricular Strategies and Inclusion Experiences

As children develop more skills, the programmatic emphasis changes. Considerably more attention is paid to the broad generalization of skills and to

Table 2.1

Sample of Early Imitation Programs

Object Manipulation

Discriminative Stimulus: "Do this"

Response: Child imitates an action with an object

Sample items: Roll car on table, put block in bucket, put ring on stacker, put spoon in baby doll's mouth, put person in car

Two-Step Object Manipulation

Discriminative Stimulus: "Do this"

Response: Child imitates a sequence of actions with an object (related chains) or with objects (unrelated chains)

Sample related chains: put person in car and push car, pick up bottle and put in baby's mouth, put car in garage and close garage door, put person in swing and make it go, pick up paper and throw it away

Sample unrelated chains: put person in car and put block in bucket, roll car and bang block, put ring in bucket and put person on swing

Nonverbal Imitation

Discriminative Stimulus: "Do this"

Response: Child imitates action modeled

Sample gross motor items: clap hands, tap legs, stamp feet, raise arms

Sample mobile gross motor items: jump, turn around, walk around chair, touch toes

Sample fine motor items: thumbs up, interlock fingers, make a fist, touch index fingers

Sample oral motor items: smile, blow kiss, stick out tongue, click tongue

the development of social skills. The instructional emphasis shifts from discrete trial instruction to other behavioral methods. Methods used might include incidental teaching and fluency training. Commercially available curricular materials are also used, provided that they are empirically derived and data based. Increasingly, skills important to group instructional experiences are emphasized. These include sharing teacher attention, following instructions given to the group, and taking turns appropriately in a group context.

As children enter regular education settings, they often require the assistance of a shadow (an individual who uses systematic prompting and reinforcement to support a student's participation in a more inclusive, less restrictive environment). The provision of this support can be critical for the student's success. (See Table 2.4 for information about shadowing.)

Table 2.2

Foundation Skills

Compliance: Includes tolerance to the instructional situation, following simple requests, and extinguishing interfering behaviors.

Manding: Emphasizes the skill of requesting desired items, often utilizing *The Picture Exchange Communication System* (Frost & Bondy, 1994).

Matching: Includes matching identical and nonidentical objects, pictures, colors, symbols, and shapes. Also includes making discriminations among multiple items.

Imitative Behavior: Includes the imitation of bodily actions as well as actions with objects that are modeled by the instructor. Eventually the child is taught to imitate sequences of actions. As generalized imitation is central to later learning, this curricular skill is particularly emphasized.

Receptive Language: Includes the labeling of objects, actions, functions of objects, and characteristics of objects.

Table 2.3

Curriculum Extensions

Expressive Language: Includes verbal imitation of sounds and words, expressive labeling, and using vocal expressive language to request. Later goals include expanding length of utterance, increasing spontaneity, and development of more complex language such as conversational skills. *The Picture Exchange Communication System* (Frost & Bondy, 1994) may be used to develop skills in requesting, labeling, and sustaining conversation.

Abstract Concepts: Includes colors, shapes, prepositions, categorization, and other descriptive information.

School Readiness: Includes letter and number recognition, prewriting skills, early math skills, and prereading skills.

Play Skills: Include appropriate use of toys, play imitation, sustained play with a wide range of toys, pretend play skills, and cooperative play.

Classroom Preparation: Includes coloring, cutting, attending to group instruction, circle time skills, and calendar skills.

Self-Help Skills: Includes eating, toileting, dressing, self-care, and bathing. Feeding programs are developed when needed, particularly for problems with food selectivity.

Socialization: Includes learning and understanding game rules, social responsiveness, and initiating and maintaining social interaction with peers and adults.

Safety Skills: Includes the discrimination of familiar people and strangers, distinguishing safe and dangerous behavior, learning to cross a street, and negotiation of other potentially hazardous situations.

Perspective Taking: Includes comprehending the experiences and feeling of others.

Generalization: Includes transfer of skills across settings, across staff, across peers, across instructions, and across behaviors.

Rule-Governed Behavior: Includes responding to conditional and absolute rules and internalizing rules as a means to guide behavior.

Table 2.4
Shadowing

Broad Issues

- Shadows recognize that the first few months are a critical transition period and present multiple challenges for the target student.

- Shadows are keen observers of the target student in all skill domains and within all educational settings.

- Shadows strive to provide feedback and guidance in as *least* intrusive a manner as possible.

- Shadows recognize the boundaries of their job responsibilities and respect the authority of the classroom teacher.

- Shadows are aware of the need to constantly assess and evaluate the effectiveness of potential reinforcers. Shadows appreciate the ongoing and essential nature of this task.

Overall Objectives

- To provide feedback in a manner that minimizes prompt dependency.

- To promote the transfer of skills previously learned in a one-to-one instructional setting to the school environment.

- To promote the learning of *new* skills within a school environment that may be dramatically *different* from the one-to-one instructional setting.

- To enhance the student's socialization with classroom peers during both group work and social activities (e.g., groups).

- To facilitate learning from peers.

- To promote transitions across classroom activities with minimal disruptive behavior.

- To promote appropriate, independent activities.

- To minimize and prevent challenging behaviors.

The transition to school must be carefully orchestrated and coordinated with the home program staff. It is important for the classroom teacher to be adept in the instructional approach to facilitate the child's success. Examples of individualization strategies include the use of familiar language, visual cueing strategies, an individual motivational system, or altered instructional materials. Tremendous emphasis must be placed on developing the skills of sustained attention and independence. For example, children must learn to sustain their efforts through the completion of an activity.

Outcome Data

Outcome data have been collected for a group of 20 children served by the Rutgers Autism Program (Weiss, 1999). These children were assessed with *The Childhood Autism Rating Scale* (CARS) (Schopler et al., 1988) and the Survey form of the *Vineland Adaptive Behavior Scales* (Sparrow et al., 1984) at the start of intervention and approximately 2 years into treatment. The CARS, which contains 15 subscales based on specific behavioral characteristics, has good interrater reliability and discriminant validity (Parks, 1983; Sevin, Matson, Coe, Fee, & Sevin, 1991). The *Vineland Adaptive Behavior Scales* are widely used to assess developmental competencies in four domains: communication, socialization, daily living skills, and motor skills. Data on school placement 2 years into treatment were also collected.

Autistic Behaviors

Prior to intervention, all 20 children scored in the severely autistic range on the CARS ($M = 45.9$, range 37.5−58, $SD = 5.30$). Postintervention scores on the CARS indicated differential outcomes. Nine participants scored in the nonautistic range (i.e., below 30) and clearly did not exhibit signs of autism. Four additional children scored in this nonautistic range but did exhibit some mild manifestations of autism. Thus, 13 of the 20 children scored in the nonautistic range. Four children scored in the medium−moderate range of autism (30−36), and 3 scored in the severe range (37−60). The mean postintervention CARS score was 27.2 (range 16.5−42.5, $SD = 8.74$).

Adaptive Behavior

The preintervention range of the adaptive behavior composite standard scores on the *Vineland Adaptive Behavior Scales* (Sparrow et al., 1984) was 38 to 63 ($M = 49.85$, $SD = 7.84$). This is well below the average score of 100, with the entire range falling more than two standard deviations below the average score (Sparrow et al., 1984). Postintervention scores were variable ($M = 83.6$, range 41–125, $SD = 28.28$). Eight of the 20 participants scored over 100 on this measure, and 3 children scored in the 90s. The remaining 9 participants' scores included one in the 70s, two in the 60s, four in the 50s, and two in the

40s. (See Table 2.5 for information on the children's CARS and Vineland scores.)

School Placement

Two years into treatment, the children were placed in a variety of educational placements. Seven of the 20 participants were placed in full-time regular education without support. Three additional children were enrolled in full-time regular education but had some support (e.g., some related services or a part-time instructional assistant). None of these 3 children received any individual instruction in their classroom settings. A total of 10 participants, therefore, were receiving full-time regular education services. These 10 children were participating in group instruction and were acquiring skills within a typical classroom environment.

The remaining 10 participants still required individualized instruction. Five of these 10 children were placed full time in regular education but still required one-to-one discrete trial instruction from aides for part of the school

Table 2.5
CARS and Vineland Score Data

Child	CARS			Vineland		
	Pre treatment	Post treatment	Change	Pre treatment	Post treatment	Change
1	43.5	19.0	−24.5	48	101	+53
2	41.0	16.5	−24.5	52	113	+61
3	41.0	16.5	−24.5	50	113	+63
4	43.0	16.5	−26.5	50	110	+60
5	53.5	34.5	−19.0	39	41	+2
6	37.5	24.0	−13.5	47	94	+47
7	45.5	27.5	−18.0	39	91	+52
8	43.5	26.0	−17.5	46	110	+64
9	47.5	39.5	−8.0	48	50	+2
10	46.5	27.0	−19.5	45	54	+9
11	42.0	23.0	−19.0	55	78	+23
12	47.0	23.5	−23.5	61	95	+34
13	52.0	42.5	−9.5	63	64	+1
14	38.5	24.0	−14.5	63	109	+46
15	58.0	40.5	−17.5	38	42	+4
16	43.0	15.5	−27.5	49	113	+64
17	41.0	19.0	−22.0	60	125	+65
18	50.0	32.0	−18.0	43	59	+16
19	49.0	35.5	−13.5	57	60	+3
20	50.5	36.0	−14.5	44	50	+6

day. All 5 of these children also needed full-time instructional assistants to facilitate their participation in group instructional activities. The final 5 participants were placed in special education. Two of these 5 students were receiving one-to-one discrete trial instruction for at least 30 hours per week. Three of the 5 received a combination of one-to-one instruction and small group instruction. (See Table 2.6 for information on school placement.)

Summary of Outcome Data

The outcome data are indicative of variable outcomes. The data also suggest that an intensive applied behavior analysis program can have a very significant effect on children with autism. Half of the sample were placed in regular education with no support, or with minimal support, 2 years into treatment. Over half (13 of 20) scored in the nonautistic range on the CARS. Eight of the 20 participants scored above the average score on a test of adaptive skills. These findings are generally consistent with those reported by other researchers (e.g., Anderson, Avery, DiPietro, Edward, & Christian, 1987; Birnbrauer & Leach, 1993; Fenske, Zalenski, Krantz, & McClannahan, 1985; Harris, Handleman, Gordon, Kristoff, & Fuentes, 1991; Lovaas, 1987; Perry, Cohen, & DeCarlo, 1995).

Future Directions

There are several important directions to pursue in the future. The first is to conduct more outcome research. It is important to continue to collect the type of data we have been collecting (e.g., adaptive behavior profiles, severity of

Table 2.6
Classroom Placement After 2 Years of Treatment

Number of Children	Classroom Placement
7	Full-time regular education with no support
3	Full-time regular education with minimal support
5	Regular education with full-time aides and with discrete trial instruction for part of day
5	Full-time special education (2 of 5 receiving 30 hours one-to-one)

autistic characteristics). It is also important, however, to expand the measures to include indices of intelligence and of specific cognitive skills. Perhaps most important, it is essential to follow the children on a long-term basis. As children continue in the elementary school years, the outcome profile may shift. Social functioning may be the most important variable to assess over time, as social demands increase in complexity as children age.

Another important direction is the development of effective inclusion strategies. The vast majority of children we serve are entering the educational mainstream. Often, they are encountering educators who have little knowledge of and experience with the unique accommodations necessary for children with autism. Appropriate supports need to be provided to children with autism in these settings. Effective training protocols for educators must be developed. Furthermore, for children who require the assistance of a shadow, a comprehensive training program for shadows is essential. Preparing the future educational environments to adequately serve the needs of children with autism may be our most formidable challenge. It may also be the task that most directly determines the success of the educational placement.

References

Anderson, S. R., Avery, D. L., DiPietro, E. K., Edward, G. L., & Christian, W. P. (1987). Intensive home-based early intervention with autistic children. *Education and Treatment of Children, 10*, 352–366.

Birnbrauer, J. S., & Leach, D. J. (1993). The Murdock early intervention after 2 years. *Behaviour Change, 10*, 63–74.

Carr, E. G., & Durand, V. M. (1985a). Reducing behavior problems through functional communication training. *Journal of Applied Behavior Analysis, 18*, 111–126.

Carr, E. G., & Durand, V. M. (1985b). The social–communicative basis of severe problems in children. In S. Reiss & R. Bootzin (Eds.), *Theoretical issues in behavior therapy* (pp. 219–254). New York: Academic.

DeLeon, I. G., & Iwata, B. A. (1996). Evaluation of a multiple-stimulus presentation format for assessing reinforcer preferences. *Journal of Applied Behavior Analysis, 29*, 519–533.

Durand, V. M. (1990). *Severe behavior problems: A functional communication training approach.* New York: Guilford Press.

Fenske, E. C., Zalenski, S., Krantz, P. J., & McClannahan, L. E. (1985). Age at intervention and treatment outcome for autistic children in a comprehensive intervention program. *Analysis and Intervention in Developmental Disabilities, 5*, 49–58.

Fisher, W., Piazza, C. C., Bowman, L. G., Hagopian, L. P., Owen, J. C., & Slevin, I. (1992). A comparison of two approaches for identifying reinforcers for persons with severe and profound disabilities. *Journal of Applied Behavior Analysis, 25*, 491–498.

Frost, L. A., & Bondy, A. S. (1994). *The Picture Exchange Communication System: Training Manual.* Cherry Hill, NJ: Pyramid.

Harris, S. L., Handleman, J. S., Gordon, R., Kristoff, B., & Fuentes, F. (1991). Changes in cognitive and language functioning of preschool children with autism. *Journal of Autism and Developmental Disorders, 2*, 281–290.

Lovaas, O. I. (1987). Behavioral treatment and normal educational and intellectual functioning in young autistic children. *Journal of Consulting and Clinical Psychology, 55*, 3–9.

O'Neill, R. E., Horner, R. H., Albin, R. W., Storey, K., & Sprague, J. R. (1990). *Functional analysis of problem behavior: A practical assessment guide*. Pacific Grove, CA: Brooks/Cole.

Pace, G. M., Ivancic, M. T., Edwards, G. L., Iwata, B. A., & Page, T. J. (1985). Assessment of stimulus preference and reinforcer value with profoundly retarded individuals. *Journal of Applied Behavior Analysis, 18*, 249–255.

Parks, S. (1983). The assessment of autistic children: A selective review of available instruments. *Journal of Autism and Developmental Disorders, 13*, 255–266.

Perry, R., Cohen, I., & DeCarlo, R. (1995). Case study: Deterioration, autism, and recovery in two siblings. *Journal of the American Academy of Child and Adolescent Psychiatry, 34*, 232–237.

Schopler, E., Reichler, R. J., & Renner, B. R. (1988). *The Childhood Autism Rating Scale*. Los Angeles: Western Psychological Services.

Sevin, J. A., Matson, J. L., Coe, D. A., Fee, V. E., & Sevin, B. M. (1991). A comparison and evaluation of three commonly used autism scales. *Journal of Autism and Developmental Disorders, 21*, 417–430.

Skinner, B. F. (1957). *Verbal behavior*. Acton, MA: Copley.

Sparrow, S. S., Balla, D. A., & Cicchetti, D. V. (1984). *Vineland Adaptive Behavior Scales*: Interview Edition. Survey form manual. Circle Pines, MN: American Guidance Service.

Weiss, M. J. (1999). Differential rates of skill acquisition and outcomes of early intensive behavioral intervention for autism. *Behavioral Interventions, 14*, 3–22.

The UCLA Young Autism Project · 3

Tristram Smith, Patricia A. Donahoe, and Billie Jo Davis

The treatment model developed at the University of California at Los Angeles (UCLA) Young Autism Project is designed to maximize cognitive, adaptive, and socioemotional functioning in preschool-aged children with autism so that they can take better advantage of educational opportunities available in their communities later in life. The model is based on research by Ivar Lovaas and colleagues, as well as studies from other applied behavior analytic (ABA) treatment programs worldwide.

From 1962 to 1969, Lovaas and colleagues conducted research and treatment with children with autism who were inpatients at the UCLA Neuropsychiatric Hospital. During this period, they published some of the first studies showing that children with autism derived clinically important benefits from ABA treatment (e.g., Lovaas, Berberich, Perloff, & Schaeffer, 1966). However, they also identified a number of limitations (Lovaas, Koegel, Simmons, & Long, 1973). First, benefits often were specific to the hospital setting where treatment took place and did not generalize to new settings or to individuals in those settings. Second, gains in one area such as language did not by themselves lead to gains in other areas such as peer interaction. Rather, gains tended to be specific to the particular skills addressed in treatment. Finally, children remained substantially delayed in development, particularly if they began treatment past the age of 5 years.

In 1970, in an effort to improve treatment efficacy, Lovaas and colleagues began providing services in children's homes and communities as opposed to hospitals, and sought the help of individuals in those settings (parents, teachers, and peers) instead of relying exclusively on therapists. They also focused on treating as many behavior problems as possible rather than seeking a central

Program Information: Department of Psychology, Washington State University, P.O. Box 644820, Pullman, WA 99164-4820; 509/335-7750.

problem that, when remediated, would bring about widespread improvement in other areas. In addition, they concentrated on early intervention, beginning treatment with children under 4 years old. Research continued on enhancing language (Lovaas, 1977) and attention (Lovaas, Koegel, & Schreibman, 1979), as well as ameliorating maladaptive behaviors (e.g., Carr, Newsom, & Binkoff, 1976; Epstein, Taubman, & Lovaas, 1985). As described in more detail later in this chapter, outcome evaluations indicated that some children with autism made substantial gains with treatment and by age 7 appeared to function like typically developing children in many respects, although other children unfortunately made only small improvements (Lovaas, 1987; McEachin, Smith, & Lovaas, 1993).

Because of the favorable outcomes achieved by some children, one emphasis of current research is on whether independent investigators can obtain similar outcomes and whether the treatment is effective for populations beyond that studied by Lovaas (1987). In addition to these replication efforts, studies are being conducted on how to enhance treatment effectiveness (e.g., Smith, 1994), particularly for those children who derive little benefit from existing interventions.

Several sources of financial support are available to families seeking this form of treatment. Many families currently receive funding for this program from their local school districts, whereas others seek funding from private sources such as insurance companies. Fees vary across treatment sites, but average approximately $3,000 to $3,500 per month, per child.

Population Served

The UCLA treatment model is designed to serve preschool-aged children with autism. At this writing, 11 sites throughout the United States and two in Europe are implementing the model. Six sites are located in university settings, 5 in private agencies, and 2 in public agencies. Approximately 90 children with autism are enrolled in a study on outcomes achieved by children in the UCLA treatment model supported by the National Institute of Mental Health (NIMH) (Multisite Young Autism Project; MYAP). The principal investigators are Tristram Smith at Washington State University and Lovaas at UCLA. Children in MYAP are under 3½ years old at intake, have an independent diagnosis of autism, are free of major medical conditions other than autism, and live within 60 kilometers (37 miles) of a replication site. Additionally, workshop consultations are provided to families of children with autism who are ineligible for the study, either because they are older than 3½ years (sites accept children aged 5 years or younger) or because they reside outside the catchment area of a site. Both clinic-supervised treatment (as provided to families in the NIMH-supported investigation) and family-directed treatment (as implemented by families receiving workshop consultations) are based on the same treatment manual (Lovaas, 1981). However, procedures for assessing children and delivering services differ in important respects, as discussed in the next sections.

Assessment Procedures

Clinic-Supervised Treatment

Assessments in MYAP are carried out for three purposes: (1) as a baseline against which to compare later functioning, (2) as predictive measures of how an individual child will respond to treatment, and (3) as a tool to aid in treatment planning. For a baseline evaluation, a number of standardized tests are administered at pretreatment and yearly thereafter. Examiners are master's or doctoral level personnel who have received training from psychologists in the MYAP on assessing children with autism and who have demonstrated reliability, as specified in Table 3.1. At pretreatment, examiners use Freeman's (1976) techniques for maximizing children's attention and motivation. At later assessments, they adhere to the standard procedures outlined in the test manuals. By optimizing children's performance at pretreatment, but not at later assessments, examiners produce conservative estimates of children's improvement.

The standardized tests (listed in Table 3.2) assess a variety of domains such as intelligence, general cognitive ability, language, and adaptive behavior (how effectively these children function in everyday situations). Procedures for more comprehensive evaluation of socioemotional functioning are currently under development. In addition to child measures, parent measures assess family functioning and satisfaction with services.

For prediction of treatment response, we have been investigating a measure that we have developed, the Early Learning Measure (ELM), which is a behavior observation instrument that samples how quickly children acquire new skills during the first 6 months of treatment in four areas: imitating gross motor actions, such as raising arms up; following simple instructions, such as "stand up" or "wave"; imitating speech sounds, such as "m" or "a"; and expressively labeling objects. We hope to use the ELM to concentrate services on those children most likely to benefit and to identify those for whom we need to investigate how to provide more effective interventions.

To guide treatment planning, behavior observations are recorded continually during treatment and are kept in a logbook. These observations include data on children's acquisition of new skills; antecedent–behavior–consequence charts of disruptive behaviors (if applicable); and informal, written notes on children's behavior (e.g., spontaneous communication or play activity, mood during treatment sessions, level of interest in the skills being taught, response to going on outings). Such notes assist in monitoring a child's progress in treatment and functioning in everyday settings.

Table 3.1

Procedures for Certification in Assessment and Treatment in the MYAP

Assessment

The examiner administers the *Bayley Scales of Infant Development–Second Edition* (Bayley, 1993) to children with autism at pretreatment. A psychologist (Jacqueline Wynn or Tristram Smith) independently retests the same children within 1 month of the initial administration. The examiner must obtain a mental age within 2 months of that obtained by the psychologist for three consecutive children.

Treatment

Level I Certification (Staff Therapist)

1. Obtain a minimum of 60 hours of experience conducting one-to-one treatment under the supervision of a Level II therapist.

2. Take a course, Fieldwork in Behavior Modification, and obtain a passing score, as graded by a reviewer on the MYAP.

3. After completing certification requirements 1 and 2, submit a 15-minute videotape of the therapist conducting one-to-one treatment with a client with whom the applicant has worked for a minimum of 10 hours. The Level II therapist who supervises the client selects one program that is currently in acquisition for the child, in each of the following areas: (a) verbal imitation (if the child has not yet begun verbal imitation, select a nonverbal imitation program; if the child has passed all verbal imitation programs, select a conversation program—i.e., a program with a verbal discriminative stimulus and a verbal response); (b) receptive language; and (c) expressive language. (If the child has not begun expressive language programs, select a nonverbal imitation program [if one was used in (a), this should be a second nonverbal imitation program—e.g., if (a) was imitation of facial expressions, this may be imitation of drawing or blockbuilding].) The applicant is videotaped as he or she conducts each program for 5 minutes. Only the applicant, the client, and the videotaper are present during these sessions, and the videotaper refrains from making any comments on the therapist's performance until after the completion of the videotaping. The completed videotape is scored by a reviewer for the MYAP. Scoring is based on the measure developed by Koegel, Russo, and Rincover (1977).

Level II Certification (Supervisory Therapist)

1. Complete a 9-month, full-time internship supervised by a Level II therapist. For at least 3 of these months, the applicant must be engaged in training novice therapists (i.e., therapists who have not yet obtained Level I certification).

2. Obtain Level I certification.

3. Complete assigned readings on applications of learning theory and obtain a satisfactory grade on a test based on these readings.

4. Obtain satisfactory ratings from the Level II supervisor and from the novice therapists trained by the applicant.

(continues)

Table 3.1 *Continued*

5. After completing requirements 1 through 4, submit a 20-minute videotape of the applicant conducting one-to-one treatment with a client with whom the therapist has never worked. Based on a review of the child's records, the applicant sets up programs that are new to the client in each of four areas: (a) verbal imitation (if the child has not yet begun verbal imitation, select a nonverbal imitation program; if the child has passed all verbal imitation programs, select a conversation program—i.e., a program with a verbal SD and a verbal response); (b) receptive language; (c) expressive language; and (d) interactive play. Only the applicant, the child, and the videotaper are present during these sessions, and the videotaper refrains from making any comments on the therapist's performance until after the completion of the videotaping. The completed videotape is scored by a reviewer for the MYAP.

6. Obtain recertification every 2 years by submitting a videotape as described above.

Parent-Directed Treatment

Because children in parent-directed treatment usually live at a distance from a site, it is not possible to conduct as uniform or thorough an assessment as with children in clinic-supervised treatment. However, it remains important to obtain objective data on children's functioning. Therefore, prior to the first workshop, families are asked to provide diagnostic evaluations and results of standardized testing of intelligence and adaptive behavior, as conducted by a licensed physician, psychologist, or other mental health practitioner who is independent of the Multisite Project and has expertise in developmental disabilities. The standardized testing is repeated yearly as long as the child is receiving workshops. In addition, the ELM, *Parenting Stress Index* (Abidin, 1990), and *Workshop Evaluation Questionnaire* (Lovaas and Wynn, 1995) are given at each workshop, along with recommendations on how to record data in the child's logbook.

Teaching and Administrative Staff

Clinic-Supervised Treatment

In clinic-supervised treatment, there are four levels of service providers: student therapists, senior therapists, case supervisors, and project directors. Student therapists provide the majority of the one-to-one behavioral treatment. A prerequisite for becoming a student therapist is to obtain a high grade in a college level course on learning theory, behavior analysis, or both. New

Table 3.2

Schedule of Assessments

		Time of Assessment		
Measures	Intake	12 Months	24 Months	Age 7 Years
1. *Autism Diagnostic Interview–Revised* (Lord, Rutter, & LeCouteur, 1994)	x			
2. *Bayley Scales of Infant Development–II* (Mental Development Index; Bayley, 1993)		x		
3. *Wechsler Preschool and Primary Scale of Intelligence–Revised* (Wechsler, 1989)[a] or *Wechsler Intelligence Scale for Children–III* (Wechsler, 1991)[a]	x	x	x	
4. *Merrill–Palmer Scale of Mental Tests* (Stutsman, 1948)	x	x	x	x
5. *Wechsler Individualized Achievement Test* (Wechsler, 1992)				x
6. *Reynell Developmental Language Scales* (Reynell, 1990)	x	x	x	x
7. *Vineland Adaptive Behavior Scales* (Sparrow, Balla, & Cicchetti, 1984)	x	x	x	x
8. *Child Behavior Checklist for Ages 4–18* (Achenbach, 1995a) and *Teacher Report Form* (Achenbach, 1995b)				x
9. Parent Satisfaction Questionnaire [b]				x
10. Family Background Questionnaire [b]	x			
11. Early Learning Measure [b]	x			

[a] If the child does not achieve a basal, the Bayley is administered.
[b] Measures developed by investigators in the MYAP.

student therapists work alongside experienced therapists for about 25 hours, until observations by senior personnel indicate that they are able to conduct sessions themselves. Treatment teams of approximately five student therapists are assigned to each family, with each student therapist working a minimum of 5 hours a week. Additionally, each student therapist must attend a weekly 1-hour clinic meeting with the child, parents, senior therapist, and case supervisor.

After a minimum of 6 months as student therapists, those who excel are eligible to become senior therapists. Senior therapists are selected from the pool of student therapists based on their outstanding performance. Senior therapists oversee a treatment team and work closely with the case supervisor. Case supervisors are selected from the group of senior therapists, based on having accumulated a minimum of 1,500 supervised hours of treatment experience and having demonstrated outstanding skill. The criteria for these positions are discussed in more detail later in this section.

Project directors are doctoral level personnel who have been licensed in a mental health profession, usually psychology. To become a project director, one must have completed a 9-month internship at UCLA and have acquired considerable expertise in the background of behavioral treatment and its application to children with autism. The project director has daily contact with all case supervisors, as well as weekly contact with all other treatment personnel, clients, and families.

Supervisors and project directors meet weekly with each child, as well as the child's parents, student therapists, and senior therapist to review the child's progress. They inspect data in the child's logbook and ask student therapists to demonstrate programs during the meeting to ensure that the therapists are clear on procedures and receive feedback regarding their performance. They also respond to questions from parents or therapists. Based on the information obtained during this meeting, they modify the child's curriculum (e.g., introduce new instructional programs when the child has mastered existing ones, alter the format of instructional programs when the child's progress is slow).

To ensure treatment quality and consistency across sites, we have developed two levels of certification, as shown in Table 3.1. To achieve Level I certification, therapists must pass an examination on the information covered in the treatment manual (Lovaas, 1981) and a videotaped evaluation focusing on their skill in implementing discrete trials. Level I therapists can work proficiently under supervision, but are not authorized to provide supervision themselves. Level II certification distinguishes case supervisors from student and senior therapists. To achieve Level II certification, a therapist must pass an examination covering scholarly articles concerning autism, ABA, and ABA treatment (with an emphasis on studies pertaining to the UCLA program). Additionally, they must obtain satisfactory ratings from trainees, supervisors, and parents, and they must pass a videotape evaluation in which they select and introduce instructional programs to children. Level II certification does not qualify individuals to enter independent practice, which requires knowledge of a wide range of additional topics (e.g., legal and ethical issues, diagnosis and assessment, problems that other family members may have, evaluation of new research on autism treatment). However, it does indicate that, within the MYAP, the individual can design children's curricula, train new therapists, and discuss treatment with families. Currently, the scoring criteria for Level II certification are being validated.

Case-supervised treatment allows for extensive staff training and daily monitoring of children's treatment. However, it is highly labor intensive. For example, a senior therapist who works full time can properly train new student therapists and oversee treatment for a maximum of three children. A clinic supervisor can oversee three to four senior therapists. A project director can effectively supervise approximately 15 children at once. Because of these limitations, a site can enroll only a small number of children in clinic-supervised treatment.

Parent-Directed Treatment

Parent-directed treatment was initiated in an attempt to make the UCLA treatment available to a larger number of families. Parents recruit therapists, who are typically college students, and obtain workshop training. Consultants for these workshops are case supervisors whom project directors have individually selected. Consultants complete 25 hours of training that focuses specifically on the implementation of workshops, and they then receive weekly supervision from project directors. Parents are responsible for overseeing their child's program, with ongoing assistance from the workshop consultant.

The family, child, and student therapists attend the first workshop, which lasts 3 days, 6 hours per day. The goal of this workshop is to teach the parents and therapists how to implement behavioral treatment techniques with the child. The workshop consultant demonstrates treatment procedures, and the parents and student therapists practice these procedures. Additionally, to prepare the family to supervise the child's program between workshops, the consultant discusses topics such as hiring and training students to serve as therapists, collecting data on the child's performance, participating in school placement meetings, monitoring the child's progress, and seeking additional consultation as needed. Following the workshop, the consultant sends an 8- to 15-page report that summarizes points made during the workshop and describes the programs in the child's curriculum.

Subsequently, the family and student therapists attend 1- to 2-day follow-up workshops every 3 months. During these consultations, the parents and student therapists discuss the child's progress and, along with the workshop leader, update the child's programs. Additionally, they continue to practice treatment procedures that are demonstrated by the workshop leader. The consultant provides the family with a report similar in format to that written for the first workshop. Between workshops, the parents and student therapists conduct therapy with the child. The workshop consultant is available for telephone or videotape consultations to address questions or concerns that may arise. It is strongly recommended that families call at least once per month.

By delegating much of the responsibility for treatment to parents in parent-directed treatment, consultants can increase the number of families they serve. By relying on paraprofessionals, they can keep costs down. Even so, factors such as extensive demands on parents, infrequent training from consultants, reliance on therapists who may have little background in learning theory and ABA, and high staff turnover may reduce treatment effectiveness, relative to clinic-supervised treatment. Hence, we are currently investigating outcomes in parent-directed treatment.

Curriculum

Typically developing children appear to learn from their environment all of their working hours, 7 days a week, 365 days a year, by exploring, playing creatively, modeling, conversing, and so on (Bredekamp & Copple, 1997). Unfortunately, children with autism have little skill or inclination to learn in this manner. Therefore, to match the richness of typically developing children's learning opportunities, we provide intensive intervention to children with autism. Most children in clinic-supervised treatment receive 40 hours per week of one-to-one ABA intervention. This level of intensity is also recommended for most children in parent-directed treatment. However, in both forms of treatment, lower levels of intensity may be appropriate for (a) children under 3 years old, who often start with only 20 hours per week; (b) children near the end of treatment, for whom the number of treatment hours is gradually reduced; and (c) children for whom 40 hours per week is counterindicated for other reasons (e.g., medical limitations, slow progress with 40 hours).

Much research has shown that children with autism fail to understand communicative efforts that well-meaning adults successfully use to communicate to their typically developing children (Spradlin & Brady, 1999). Because of this failure, such children have encountered continual frustration in learning situations and understandably react to such frustration with tantrums and other attempts to escape or avoid future failures. Consequently, in the UCLA program, every effort is made to construct teaching situations that maximize children's success and minimize failures. During the first year of treatment, therapists rely primarily on a discrete trial format, characterized by (a) one-to-one interaction with a therapist, (b) short and clear instructions from the therapist, (c) carefully planned procedures for prompting children to follow instructions and for fading such prompts, and (d) immediate reinforcement for each correct response made by children. As children progress, therapists gradually decrease the use of this format and increase their emphasis on naturalistic instruction, much of which takes place in group settings.

Treatment usually lasts approximately 3 years, although the precise length is determined on a case-by-case basis. In a 40-hour per week program, therapists provide 2- to 3-hour treatment sessions 5 to 7 days per week. Session times are arranged by the treatment team and parents, based on three considerations: (1) children's needs (e.g., some are most receptive to treatment if they have sessions every day; others do better with a day or two off), (2) family preferences (e.g., some may want their children to have certain days or times free), and (3) therapist schedules. To maintain children's motivation, sessions include frequent opportunities for successes (perhaps as many as 12 per minute in discrete trial training), individually selected reinforcements for these successes, and a diverse set of instructional programs (focusing on communication, academic skills, self-help, play, motor activities, etc.). In discrete trial training, children usually spend 2 to 5 minutes at a time working on an instructional program such as imitating actions performed by a thera-pist, with 1- to 2-minute breaks between sessions. Also, children receive a 10-to 15-minute break at the end of every hour and a 1- to 2-hour break in the middle of the day. If a child regularly naps, an additional break may occur for naptime.

A treatment manual (Lovaas, 1981) and associated videotapes (Lovaas & Leaf, 1981) outline particular instructional programs as well as ways to indi-vidualize programs for particular children. Large individual differences exist in children's rates of progress. Nevertheless, one may identify goals that tend to be addressed in each year of treatment. At the beginning of the first year, therapists work on establishing rapport with the child by engaging in activi-ties such as games that the child is familiar with and enjoys. Additionally, they request actions that the child is likely to perform successfully (e.g., putting a block in a bucket or sitting down in a chair). As noted, given their history of failure in teaching situations, children may attempt to escape or avoid the teaching situation (e.g., by having a tantrum or running away). By reinforcing successful completion of tasks and withholding reinforcement for escape or avoidance behavior, therapists increase attentiveness and motiva-tion in the teaching situation while reducing interfering behaviors.

After this initial phase of treatment, which usually requires 2 to 4 weeks, treatment focuses on teaching skills that help children learn effectively. Chil-dren are taught to follow simple instructions (e.g., "stand up," "come here," "clap"), imitate basic gross and fine motor actions (e.g., waving, stomping feet, and rubbing tummy), and match identical objects to each other. Thera-pists then help children extend their newly acquired imitative skills to model appropriate play activities with toys such as blocks. Later in the first year, children are taught to imitate speech sounds. These sounds are then chained together to teach the child to imitate syllables, words, and eventually sen-tences. Also during the first year, children are taught self-help skills such as dressing, eating with utensils, and putting away toys and other belongings.

Teaching communicative language, abstract concepts, and interactive play is the focus of the second year of treatment. Children are taught to label both objects and actions receptively (e.g., by pointing to the object or a picture of an action labeled by the therapist) and expressively (e.g., by responding to ques-tions such as "What is it?" or "What is she doing?"). If a child has limited vocal speech, an augmentative communication system is likely to be introduced, such as the *Picture Exchange Communication System* (Bondy & Frost, 1994).

Building on their labeling skills, children are taught sentences, beginning with simple structures (e.g., "I want," "I have," "I see") and progressing to more complex ones (e.g., describing present and past events, using future tense, telling stories). Further, children are taught a variety of descriptors, such as colors, shapes, opposites (big–little, hot–cold, etc.), prepositions, pronouns, and emotions. They also learn to respond to conversational questions (e.g., "What's your name?") and make statements on a topic (e.g., "I like pizza," "I like ice cream"). Children are taught imaginary play skills, such as pretending to be something (e.g., airplane, animal) or using objects creatively (e.g., making believe that a string is a snake). In addition to communication and play skills, treatment is aimed at expanding self-help skills (e.g., toileting, brushing teeth, closing fasteners on clothing).

During the third year of treatment, the focus is on socialization and adjustment to school and other community settings. Children receive instruction on how to learn by observing people around them, even when they are not interacting directly with those people (e.g., learning a new play skill by watching a game that others are playing). Additionally, they are taught how to role-play with another person (e.g., teacher–student) and play games with rules (e.g., Lotto). They also practice joining an ongoing conversation, starting or stopping a conversation, and asking and responding to questions. Further, they may receive instruction on how to carry out tasks independently. For example, they may learn to self-monitor by identifying and stating the goal of a task, the steps necessary to achieve this goal, and the extent to which they achieved this goal.

School Placement and Peer Interaction

When treatment begins, it takes place in children's homes rather than at school. We view home as developmentally appropriate because, at treatment onset, most children in the UCLA Program have language and social skills comparable to that of a typically developing 1-year-old. However, we emphasize school entry and peer interaction later in treatment, after children have acquired skills that help them function in group settings. Such skills include imitating nonverbal and verbal behaviors, speaking in short phrases, cooperating with verbal requests from others, playing appropriately with toys, and using self-care skills such as dressing and toileting. The time required to master these skills varies greatly across children, though a year into treatment may be a rough average.

Research has shown that integrated school settings tend to provide more encouragement for social interaction, more appropriate peer models, and higher academic expectations than do self-contained settings (e.g., McGee, Paradis, & Feldman, 1993; Strain, 1983). Therefore, we enter children into preschool classes for typically developing students. We aim to have children remain in such classes when they go on to elementary school, but recognize that some may be better served in a special education setting, where they may participate in more individualized curricula. School entry occurs gradually, with continual monitoring of children's functioning and the appropriateness of the classroom placement for them. The precise steps involved in helping children adapt to school and assessing their progress are tailored to the individual child, but generally include the following.

About 3 months prior to enrolling in school, the child begins to practice common preschool tasks such as drawing, cutting and pasting, and counting. The child also engages in activities such as sitting in a circle for storytime, raising hands, lining up, and passing food at snacktime. In addition, play dates are arranged in which one typically developing peer visits the child's home for 30 to 60 minutes, with a therapist or parent facilitating interaction between the two. The child and peer are taught games such as "Follow the Leader" and "Hide-and-Seek" that they both may enjoy. Further, the child spends short periods of time in group activities such as gymnastics or mommy-and-me classes.

When the child starts preschool, a full-time aide accompanies him or her. The aide is a therapist who has worked in the child's home program. The aide prompts the child to use skills previously mastered at home, assists the child in following the classroom routine, and observes the child to identify skills that can be taught to enhance school functioning. Initially, the child may attend class for only 30 minutes a day. As he or she progresses, this length is increased slowly to full time. At that point, treatment focuses on having the child respond more to the classroom teacher and peers, and less to the aide. An emphasis is placed on teaching observational learning and independent work skills (as described in the preceding section), arranging for peers from the class to participate in play dates at the child's home, and working with the teacher to identify specific tasks he or she will ask the child to perform without assistance from the aide (e.g., making transitions between activities). Then, as the child becomes less reliant on the aide, the aide is gradually faded out. For example, the aide may be assigned partly to the child with autism and partly to classmates, or may attend only part time.

Throughout, parents, aides, and teachers closely monitor the child and collaborate to help the child be successful and reduce the risk of ostracism. From this collaboration, the treatment team identifies additional skills to teach at home and generalize to school to enhance the child's adjustment. They also identify and evaluate behavior management systems and incentive programs (e.g., token economies) to assist the child. If, despite these interventions, serious problems arise, such as peer rejection or disruptive behavior, the child may be removed from the class and given a fresh start in a different class.

At age 5, children proceed to a kindergarten class for typically developing children if they display most of the skills that their classmates do (see Bredekamp & Copple, 1997) and are ready to begin fading the aide. Otherwise, they repeat preschool to be with peers closer to their developmental level and to have additional time to adjust to the school setting, and they continue receiving one-to-one instruction at home. This extra year enables many children to catch up to typically developing children who are entering kindergarten, as evidenced by skills such as engaging in extensive sociodramatic play, cooperating in small groups, having a vocabulary of over 5,000 words, and speaking in complex sentences (Bredekamp & Copple, 1997). For such children, the process of fading the aide and enhancing socialization is complex (see Lovaas & Buch, 1997). However, our research indicates that most of these children function without an aide by the end of kindergarten and remain in regular classes for many years without special assistance (McEachin et al., 1993).

If, after repeating preschool, children continue to be delayed relative to their classmates, our research indicates that they are likely to need ongoing special services (Lovaas, 1987). Therefore, we evaluate alternative placement options, seeking ones in which (a) teachers are willing to collaborate with us (most are quite willing, but a few are not); (b) peers model appropriate, adaptive skills for the child with autism; and (c) the class has a clear structure and rules. Potential placements include ABA elementary school programs for children with autism, other special education classes, or classes with typically developing children in which the child with autism receives assistance from an aide. In any of these placements, it is often important to supplement classroom instruction with one-to-one discrete trial instruction (10 hours per week is common), as children may still learn most efficiently in this format. Therapists from the home program assist in making the transition to these placements. Because of the complex issues associated with identifying appropriate placements for children who continue to have special needs, such children may be at greater risk for losing skills, developing new maladaptive behaviors, or having other difficulties than are children who are fully integrated into regular classes. Therefore, project directors discuss this risk with parents and service providers, and are available for periodic follow-up consultations, as needed.

Behavior Management

While the primary emphasis of the UCLA treatment is on enhancing adaptive behaviors, the treatment also addresses maladaptive behaviors. If children display highly dangerous or disruptive behavior at intake (e.g., self-injury), this behavior is addressed immediately in all settings where it occurs. Otherwise, maladaptive behaviors are initially addressed in the context of one-to-one treatment sessions, then in everyday situations in the home, and then in school and community settings. In this way, behavior management efforts occur in increasingly complex situations.

As discussed, the first stage of treatment emphasizes establishing rapport with the children. Because children with autism have a long history of being unsuccessful in teaching situations, they may initially emit a variety of escape behaviors, such as tantrummimg, attempting to leave, or refusing to respond. These behaviors diminish greatly during the initial phase of treatment, and children are generally eager to participate in sessions for the remainder of treatment. However, as with any other intervention, escape or avoidance behaviors may still arise from time to time. Examples of these behaviors include refusing to come to therapists when called, attempting to end sessions early, crying, or not responding to therapists' instructions.

Based on data in the logbook and observations made at team meetings, the treatment team conducts a functional analysis of the behaviors. Such an analysis may reveal that some instructional programs are too easy or hard for children, and that therefore the treatment team needs to revise the curriculum. It may indicate that the reinforcers offered to a particular child are ineffective for him or her. Thus, the treatment team may need to identify more potent reinforcers, become more enthusiastic when administering them, or change the format of the sessions (e.g., use materials that the child favors, allow the child to select reinforcers prior to each session, or take turns so that the child has an opportunity to give instructions). The functional analysis may also implicate contextual factors, such as too many distractions in the treatment setting, problems with sleeping or eating that lower the child's attentiveness, or insufficient breaks from treatment during the day. If behavior observations and log notes fail to identify the functions of behavior, or if an intervention fails to reduce the behavior, a more formal functional analysis procedure may be used (e.g., Iwata, Dorsey, Slifer, Bauman, & Richman, 1982).

Because parents participate as therapists in the treatment (as described in the next section), they often find that they become much more successful than before in obtaining cooperation from their child in everyday situations around the home. However, they may still find that children follow some directions when given in treatment but not in everyday situations, and may have other problems such as irregular sleep habits, excessively narrow food preferences, aggression toward siblings, and reckless behaviors such as climbing on high furniture or throwing objects. Thus, the parents may require assistance from the treatment team in generalizing their child's skills at following instructions and in conducting a functional analysis of other problems (e.g., Durand, 1998, on sleeping; Munk & Repp, 1994, on eating; Carr, 1994, on aggression). Interventions derived from this analysis always involve teaching adaptive, alternative behaviors (e.g., appropriate play or leisure activities that may replace the disruptive behaviors). This teaching is often combined with extinction, time-out, or response cost for engaging in the disruptive behaviors.

After a child has mastered skills in treatment as well as in everyday situations at home, it is important that the treatment team and the parents work together to generalize these skills to public settings. Within community settings, children begin to develop and practice a variety of social skills in their interactions with other adults, such as teachers, as well as other children. However, some children exhibit disruptive behaviors (e.g., wandering or running away on crowded streets, tantrumming, noncompliance). To address these difficulties, the parents and the treatment team re-create a variety of community settings such as crosswalks, grocery stores, restaurants, and schools in the home for children to role-play appropriate behaviors. To reinforce these appropriate behaviors when they occur in public, they also establish some type of reward system (e.g., a token economy). In some cases, it is necessary to combine reinforcement procedures with reductive procedures derived from a functional analysis of the disruptive behavior.

Parental and Family Involvement

Clinic-Supervised Treatment

Parents are viewed as integral parts of their children's treatment teams. Prior to enrolling their children into the Young Autism Project, they have a 1-hour interview with the project director. In this meeting, the project director becomes acquainted with families, obtains information on children's medical and developmental history, and gives parents an opportunity to ask questions. The project director also asks parents to view a videotape on the UCLA treatment (Anderson & Aller, 1987), gives them recent publications on outcomes achieved by children in the program (e.g., McEachin et al., 1993), and offers them the opportunity to accompany a case supervisor to observe another child's treatment program. The parents are then given an informed consent form, which outlines the treatment their children will receive, the parents' role in that treatment, and the range of outcomes that children achieve following treatment (some making substantial progress but others deriving little or no benefit).

Throughout treatment, parents attend all treatment meetings and approve in advance any intervention procedures to be used with their child. Also, for the first 3 to 4 months of treatment, parents are asked to work alongside an experienced therapist for 5 hours per week. During this time, the therapist and parents take turns implementing the child's one-to-one, discrete trial treatment programs, and they provide each other with feedback on their work. Thus, parents learn to become effective therapists for their child and are able to make informed decisions about their child's treatment. Subsequently, many parents reduce the number of hours of discrete trial training they provide, but continue to have an important role in generalizing and expanding skills that children acquire in treatment. For example, they implement incidental teaching procedures to encourage their children to use communication skills in everyday settings, incorporate self-help skills into children's daily routines, and arrange for situations that enable children to develop their skills (e.g., outings where children can learn new names for objects or events). Parents also find peers in the community to participate in play dates with their child, set up play dates by coordinating with the peers' parents, and often oversee the play dates. In addition, they contact school districts about placements for their child, visit the placements that are offered, and communicate with children's teachers about children's progress in those placements.

Siblings are often eager and able to serve as models for play and conversation skills. In many instances, before the parents find a peer in the community, it may be beneficial for siblings to participate in play dates with the child. Extended family members such as grandparents also may participate in treatment, particularly by generalizing and expanding on children's skills.

Parent-Directed Treatment

In addition to the responsibilities that parents have in clinic-supervised treatment, parents in parent-directed treatment recruit consultants and treatment teams, and control the amount and length of treatment. Between visits from the consultant, they may also train new therapists. Further, they organize weekly clinic meetings, monitor their child's progress in the program, and implement changes in programs as suggested by the consultant. Thus, they have a very substantial role in their children's treatment.

Outcome Measures and Research

Lovaas (1987) studied 19 children with autism who received 40 hours per week of treatment for 2 or more years, as well as two control groups ($n = 40$) of similar children who received minimal behavioral treatment (10 hours per week or less). The intensively treated group of children increased its mean intelligence quotient (IQ) from 63 at pretreatment to 83 at age 7. In contrast, the mean IQ of the 40 children in the two minimally treated control groups remained almost unchanged. Nine of the 19 intensively treated children (47%) were described as "normal functioning" because they obtained average IQs and were performing satisfactorily in school placements for typically developing children by the age of 7. By contrast, only 1 of the 40 minimally treated children (3%) achieved such a favorable outcome.

In 1993, McEachin et al. conducted a follow-up of these children at an average age of 12 years. The study revealed not only that the intensively treated children had maintained their intellectual and academic gains from age 7 but that they had achieved an average IQ 31 points higher than that of the control group (85 vs. 54). A particularly rigorous assessment was conducted with the 9 children previously classified as normal functioning to evaluate whether they displayed any residual problems that had been overlooked in the previous assessments. Measures of intelligence, personality, and adaptive functioning indicated that 8 of the 9 children were functioning well in all these areas and thus continued to display normal functioning.

The children classified as normal functioning accounted for most of the gains in IQ and other measures. For example, the 9 intensively treated children with this classification at age 7 displayed an average IQ increase of 37 points, compared to an average increase of 3 points for the other 10 intensively treated children. Therefore, although the large gains made by some children were highly encouraging, the relatively small gains made by other children indicated the need for continued efforts to improve the treatment.

Lovaas (1987) excluded from his study children with autism if they performed in the range of severe or profound mental retardation at pretreatment. However, Smith, Eikeseth, Klevstrand, and Lovaas (1997) compared 11 such children who received 30 hours per week of treatment to 10 similar children who received minimal treatment. They reported that, although the gains made by these children were smaller on average than those made by the higher functioning children studied by Lovaas (1987), they did appear clinically important. For example, intensively treated children had a higher mean IQ at age 7 than minimally treated children (36 vs. 24) and were more likely to have communicative speech (10 of 11 vs. 2 of 10), although the groups did not significantly differ in the number of behavior problems that children displayed.

Interim reports from two studies suggest that other groups of children may benefit from the UCLA treatment. In a study with fully randomized assignment to intensive treatment (30 to 40 hours per week of treatment for 2 or more years) or parent training (5 hours per week of in-home parent training for 3 to 9 months), Smith, Wynn, Groen, and Lovaas (1996) reported outcomes after 1 year for 32 children with mild to moderate mental retardation (14 with a diagnosis of autism, 18 without). The 16 children who were intensively treated gained an average of 13 to 18 IQ points after 1 year of intensive treatment, whereas the 16 children in parent training declined on most measures. Eikeseth (1996) reported that 14 children who were 3½ to 6 years old at treatment onset and were high functioning (as evidenced by an intake IQ above 50) gained a mean of 19 IQ points after 1 year of treatment. However, because these studies are in progress and have not yet undergone peer review, the results must be viewed with caution. One published outcome study yielded negative results: Smith, Klevstrand, and Lovaas (1995) found that children with Rett's disorder unfortunately did not benefit from the UCLA treatment.

Issues for Future Research

The UCLA Young Autism Project is one of several ABA treatment programs that have reported highly favorable outcomes from early intervention for children with autism (Smith, 1999). A top priority for future research is to examine whether independent investigators, using rigorous research methodologies, can obtain equally favorable outcomes. Accordingly, we are studying children who are receiving the UCLA treatment from a variety of sites in the United States and Europe (MYAP; NIMH Grant 1 R01 MH 48863). The MYAP has three goals: (1) to replicate the UCLA diagnostic, assessment, and treatment procedures across sites; (2) to increase intellectual, academic, language, adaptive, and socioemotional functioning in the children with autism who receive the treatment; and (3) to predict which identified subjects will achieve best outcomes based on a pretreatment assessment. While the MYAP focuses on clinic-supervised treatment, we are also investigating parent-directed treatment, which is a model of service delivery that, as described, differs in many respects from clinic-supervised treatment and hence may yield less favorable results. Our current investigations include more comprehensive pretreatment and follow-up assessments than previous studies so that we can appraise children's outcomes more thoroughly and assess the impact of treatment on the family.

We anticipate that one product of our ongoing research will be objective, validated criteria for identifying individuals who are proficient to implement the UCLA treatment. Such criteria will help assess the comparability of treatment across sites in the MYAP. Further, they may assist families who are seeking consultants for parent-directed treatment. At present, professionals with a wide range of qualifications are offering workshop consultations on home-based ABA treatment for children with autism, and parents have few guidelines for choosing among these professionals. Thus, empirically validated criteria for making such choices are needed.

Another product of our ongoing investigations may be the development of procedures for predicting which children will benefit most from the UCLA treatment and which children need improved services. Efforts are already under way to enhance interventions for children who are slow to acquire receptive and expressive language. Interestingly, clinical observations suggest that some of these children are responsive to instruction in the use of reading and writing to communicate. Therefore, we are currently studying the effects of such instruction. In addition, some children seem to discriminate more readily between multiword instructions (e.g., "put the hat on" vs. "jump the frog") than single-word instructions (e.g., "hat" vs. "frog"). Such patterns of responding suggest the possibility of neurological impairments in children's ability to differentiate between auditory stimuli, despite strong skills in other areas. Hence, we are investigating the use of physiological measures, particularly evoked potentials, to determine whether children's brain activity responds to changes in auditory stimuli. We are optimistic that investigations such as these will expand the range of children for whom we can provide effective services.

References

Abidin, R. R. (1990). *Manual for the Parenting Stress Index* (3rd ed.). Odessa, FL: Psychological Assessment Resources.

Achenbach, T. M. (1995a). *Child Behavior Checklist for Ages 4–18.* Burlington: University of Vermont Department of Psychiatry.

Achenbach, T. M. (1995b). *Teacher Report Form.* Burlington, University of Vermont Department of Psychiatry.

Anderson, E. L. (Producer), & Aller, R. (Director). (1987). *Behavioral treatment of young autistic children* [Film]. Huntington Station, NY: Focus International.

Bayley, N. (1993). *Bayley Scales of Infant Development* (2nd ed.). San Antonio: Psychological Corp.

Bondy, A. S., & Frost, L. A. (1994). The picture exchange communication system. *Focus on Autistic Behavior, 9,* 1–19.

Bredekamp, S., & Copple, C. (Eds.). (1997). *Developmentally appropriate practice in early childhood programs* (rev. ed.). Washington, DC: National Association for the Education of Young Children.

Carr, E. G. (1994). Emerging theory in the functional analysis of problem behavior. *Journal of Applied Behavior Analysis, 27,* 393–399.

Carr, E. G., Newsom, C. D., & Binkoff, J. A. (1976). Stimulus control of self-destructive behavior in a psychotic child. *Journal of Abnormal Child Psychology, 4,* 139–153.

Durand, V. M. (1998). *Sleep better: A guide to improving sleep for children with special needs.* Baltimore: Brookes.

Eikeseth, S. (1996, May). Intensive behavioral treatment for 3½–7 year old children with autism. In O. I. Lovaas (Chair), *Replications of the UCLA Young Autism Project,* symposium conducted at the annual meeting of the Association for Behavior Analysis, San Francisco.

Epstein, L. J., Taubman, M. T., & Lovaas, O. I. (1985). Changes in self-stimulatory behaviors with treatment. *Journal of Abnormal Child Psychology, 13,* 281–294.

Freeman, B. J. (1976). Evaluating autistic children. *Journal of Pediatric Psychology, 1,* 18–21.

Iwata, B. A., Dorsey, M. F., Slifer, K. J., Bauman, K. E., & Richman, G. S. (1982). Toward a functional analysis of self-injury. *Analysis and Intervention in Developmental Disabilities, 2,* 3–20.

Koegel, R. L., Russo, D. C., & Rincover, A. (1977). Assessing and training teachers in the generalized use of behavior modification. *Journal of Applied Behavior Analysis, 10,* 197–205.

Lord, C., Rutter, M., & LeCouteur, A. (1994). Autism Diagnostic Interview Revised: A revised version of a diagnostic interview for caregivers of individuals with possible developmental disorders. *Journal of Autism and Developmental Disorders, 24,* 659–686.

Lovaas, O. I. (1977). *The autistic child: Language training through behavior modification.* New York: Irvington.

Lovaas, O. I. (1981). *Teaching developmentally disabled children: The Me book.* Austin, TX: PRO-ED.

Lovaas, O. I. (1987). Behavioral treatment and normal educational and intellectual functioning in young autistic children. *Journal of Consulting and Clinical Psychology, 55,* 3–9.

Lovaas, O. I., & Buch, G. (1997). Intensive behavioral intervention for young children with autism. In N. N. Singh (Ed.), *Prevention and treatment of severe behavior problems: Models and methods in developmental disabilities* (pp. 61–86). Pacific Grove, CA: Brooks/Cole.

Lovaas, O. I., Berberich, J. P., Perloff, B. F., & Schaeffer, B. (1966). Acquisition of imitative speech by schizophrenic children. *Science, 151*, 705–707.

Lovaas, O. I., Koegel, R., & Schreibman, L. (1979). Stimulus overselectivity in autism: A review of research. *Psychological Bulletin, 86*, 1236–1254.

Lovaas, O. I., Koegel, R. L., Simmons, J. Q., & Long, J. S. (1973). Some generalization and follow-up measures on autistic children in behavior therapy. *Journal of Applied Behavior Analysis, 6*, 131–166.

Lovaas, O. I., & Leaf, R. B. (1981). *Five video tapes for teaching developmentally disabled children*. Baltimore: University Park Press.

Lovaas, O. I., & Wynn, J. W. (1995). *Workshop Evaluation Questionnaire*. Los Angeles: Office of Behavioral Research and Education.

McEachin, J., Smith, T., & Lovaas, O. I. (1993). Long-term outcome for children with autism who received early intensive behavioral treatment. *American Journal of Mental Retardation, 97*, 359–372.

McGee, G. G., Paradis, T., & Feldman, R. S. (1993). Free effects of integration on levels of autistic behavior. *Topics in Early Childhood Special Education, 13*, 57–67.

Munk, D. D., & Repp, A. C. (1994). Behavioral assessment of feeding problems of individuals with severe disabilities. *Journal of Applied Behavior Analysis, 27*, 241–250.

Reynell, J. K. (1990). *Reynell Developmental Language Scales*. Los Angeles: Western Psychological Association.

Smith, T. (1994). Improving memory to promote maintenance of treatment gains in children with autism. *The Psychological Record, 44*, 459–473.

Smith, T. (1999). Early intervention for children with autism. *Clinical Psychology: Research and Practice, 6*, 33–49.

Smith, T., Eikeseth, S., Klevstrand, M., & Lovaas, O. I. (1997). Intensive behavioral treatment for preschoolers with severe mental retardation and pervasive developmental disorder. *American Journal on Mental Retardation, 102*, 228–237.

Smith, T., Klevstrand, M., & Lovaas, O. I. (1995). Behavioral treatment of Rett's disorder: Ineffectiveness in three cases. *American Journal on Mental Retardation, 100*, 317–322.

Smith, T., Wynn, J. W., Groen, A. D., & Lovaas, O. I. (1996, May). Intensive behavioral treatment for children with mild to moderate mental retardation. In O. I. Lovaas (Chair), *Replications of the UCLA Young Autism Project*, symposium conducted at the annual meeting of the Association for Behavior Analysis, San Francisco.

Sparrow, S. S., Balla, D. A., & Cicchetti, D. V. (1984). *Vineland Adaptive Behavior Scales*. Circle Pines, MN: American Guidance Service.

Spradlin, J. E., & Brady, N. C. (1999). Early childhood autism and stimulus control. In P. M. Ghezzi, W. L. Williams, & J. E. Carr (Eds.), *Autism: Behavior analytic perspectives* (pp. 49–65). Reno, NV: Context.

Strain, P. S. (1983). Generalization of autistic children's behavior change: Effects of developmental integrated and segregated settings. *Analysis and Intervention in Developmental Disabilities, 3*, 23–34.

Stutsman, R. (1948). *Guide for administering the Merrill–Palmer Scale of Mental Tests*. New York: Harcourt, Brace & World.

Wechsler, D. (1989). *Wechsler Preschool and Primary Scale of Intelligence–Revised*. San Antonio: Psychological Corp.

Wechsler, D. (1991). *Wechsler Intelligence Scale for Children–Third Edition*. San Antonio: Psychological Corp.

Wechsler, D. (1992). *Wechsler Individual Achievement Test*. San Antonio: Psychological Corp.

The Children's Unit for Treatment and Evaluation

4

Raymond G. Romanczyk, Stephanie B. Lockshin, and Linda Matey

T he Children's Unit for Treatment and Evaluation (hereafter called Unit) serves children (12 months through 12 years of age) with autism spectrum disorders, as well as children with developmental and emotional disorders. This chapter focuses upon the preschool component of the Unit for children with autism and related disorders. The Unit is one of the three direct service components of the Institute for Child Development. It is located on the State University of New York (SUNY) at Binghamton campus. The Unit was established in 1975 and granted special status in 1977 through an act of the New York State Legislature (Senate Bill 5911-A), which allowed the Unit to exist with a dual status as a fully certified New York State Education Department private school and at the same time as organizationally part of SUNY at Binghamton. The bill permits school districts and other state agencies to contract directly with the Unit.

The preschool and school-age programs differ primarily by the age of the children served rather than structure or specific activities. The preschool program is conducted between 9:00 a.m. and 2:30 p.m. 5 days per week, 12 months per year. Children may be admitted and discharged at any time throughout the calendar year. Referrals originate from a wide range of sources, including school districts, physicians, social services, family court, mental health professionals, and parents.

Funding for student placement is obtained in two ways. For those children below 3 years of age, the placement decision is approved and funded by the county's department of health. The tuition is paid for by the county in which the child resides (for 1997–1998, the 12-month tuition was $29,339).

Program Information: The Children's Unit for Treatment and Evaluation, State University of New York at Binghamton, Binghamton, NY 13902-6000; 607/777-2829.

For children between the ages of 3 and 5, each school district's committee for preschool special education approves placement with a member of the county health department as an ad hoc member of the committee. Tuition for these children also is paid by the county in which the child resides.

As a New York State Education Department–certified private school, the Unit must comply with regulations of the State Education Department with respect to child–staff ratios, age distribution, and programmatic and operational regulations, including such items as periodic on-site evaluations and external fiscal auditing. The program is also implicitly evaluated by the university with respect to the substantial physical plant that it occupies and other resources allocated to it.

Philosophy

The following is an excerpt from our program brochure:

> Our guiding philosophy is to employ intensive, child-centered, empirically validated educational and clinical procedures. Children who manifest developmental, learning, or emotional disorders impact not only upon themselves, but also their families and their communities, and this challenge must be met by a reciprocal intensity, quality, and precision of services. We firmly believe that providing a caring, warm, supportive environment that respects the dignity of individuals and celebrates their unique qualities and potential is the *minimum* starting point for services. Thus, our hallmark is the utilization, on a continuing basis, of well conducted educational and clinical research that appears in peer reviewed professional journals. Further, we utilize highly sophisticated assessment and evaluation technology.

The Unit was created to serve as one component in a continuum of services. That is, it was designed as an intensive short-term program, not as a parallel program in which children would enter and remain for many years. Its focus was to achieve an approximately 3-year duration of placement that would result in sufficient change to permit the child to function within the context of the services available within his or her local community. Because of this philosophy, the emphasis is on a focused rather than a balanced curriculum (Romanczyk & Lockshin, 1984). This focused approach, which may also be termed a deficit-oriented approach, seeks to identify the factors that are most crucial in preventing the child from benefiting fully from the continuum of services in the local community. By focusing on these deficits and problem areas, rather than attempting to provide a balanced curriculum, it is possible to provide in a brief time span the necessary intensity of services that permits the relatively speedy transition to community-based services. This model is of particular importance with respect to preschool children, as early identification permits intensive services to come to bear at a particularly opportune point in the child's development. Because of this focus on child participation in services within the local community, and the focus on individual child characteristics and skill deficits that are impeding such placement, the criteria for discharge from the program reflect a specific child–local community interaction. The Unit serves children from scores of different communities (within a 100-mile radius), from urban to suburban to rural, and the resources available in these different communities vary to an extreme degree. An absolute level of progress is not used for discharge decisions; rather, progress relative to what is required within the child's local community becomes the criteria. This approach allows maximum flexibility for families and their local school districts and service providers.

The philosophical underpinnings of the Unit are rooted in child advocacy, family involvement, use of empirically validated procedures, and the importance of training, research, and data dissemination. Our model has evolved over time, and is strengthened by research demonstrating the effectiveness of systematic behavioral interventions with difficult to treat populations. Further, the behavioral model provides a technology for effective teaching, ongoing assessment, and evaluation of treatment outcomes based on precise and continuous behavior recording and analysis. Thus, our program is committed to a comprehensive, integrated, and state-of-the-art behavioral model of service delivery. It is noteworthy to point out that our philosophy is derived from empirical research rather than a philosophy in search of research support.

Within the behavioral model, objective measurement is the focus for treatment decisions. Therefore, extensive analyses are conducted to identify appropriate goals for intervention and habilitation. In addition to the administration of standardized tests, checklists, and skill inventories, formal behavior analyses are conducted to provide information regarding the frequency, intensity, and duration of target behaviors. Additional observations are conducted to determine controlling stimuli and the effects of environmental expectations and demands. Assessment of behavior assets is also conducted to determine their relationship to the behavior excesses or deficits, their relative strength, and the degree of stimulus control necessary to elicit responding.

From an administrative perspective, the problem of efficiently collecting, organizing, interpreting, and monitoring the myriad of information needed to fully implement our model is colossal, and represents a continuing challenge.

Demographics

The Unit typically serves an enrollment of about 32 children. Over 275 children have been enrolled, with 47% entering as preschoolers. In New York, a child's educational classification determines eligibility for special education services. Educational classifications are *not* synonymous with classifications using the *Diagnostic and Statistical Manual of Mental Disorders–Fourth Edition* (DSM–IV) of the American Psychiatric Association (1994). Thus, of this preschool enrollment, as determined by DSM–IV criteria, 45% are children with autism.

The gender distribution of our preschool population of children with autism is 74% males and 26% females. The children's scores on *The Childhood Autism Rating Scale* (CARS; Schopler, Reichler, Devellis, & Daly, 1988) have an intake average 50.4 (range 31.5–58), indicating a population classified by the CARS as "severely autistic." Average age at admission is 3.4 (range 1.1 min–4.9 max), and average length of participation in the program is 3.3 years.

Staffing

Our preschool and school-aged programs have identical components. The staffing pattern described is for the entire program. Staff are not assigned to one or the other program but participate fully in both.

Administrators

The director, a full-time administrative assistant, and a part-time clerical assistant serve as the administrative staff. The responsibilities of these individuals include development, coordination, monitoring, and updating of Unit policies, procedures, and organization as is necessary to provide appropriate and effective services. This includes complying with New York State regulations for monitoring and record keeping of service provision.

Psychologists

The director and the coordinator of clinical services are doctoral level, state-licensed clinical psychologists. A full-time doctoral level school psychologist is also employed.

Typically several graduate students in the doctoral clinical program at SUNY at Binghamton serve as interns. They assist in standardized assessment, behavioral assessment, and evaluation analysis. However, their primary duties are to serve as consultants to the staff, assist in the behavioral development of the children, and conduct child therapy groups that focus on social skills and emotional expression. Clinical interns are also an integral part of the parent education program, which is discussed later in this chapter.

Teachers

The Unit typically employs eight special education teachers, including six teachers, one head teacher, and one coordinating teacher. Teachers are directly responsible for the formulation and implementation of Individualized Goal Plans (IGPs), the creation of the specific programs needed to execute the IGPs, the provision of direct educational services, and supervision of paraprofessional staff involved in program implementation. Further, they are responsible for the systematic and detailed evaluation of child progress. Teachers provide information regarding children's programs and progress to ensure systematic and complete feedback to parents.

In addition, the head teacher is responsible for serving as a role model in assessing, implementing, and developing child programs. Providing feedback to teachers, aides, and undergraduate practicum students on their classroom performance is an additional role assumed by the head teacher.

The coordinating teacher's primary responsibility is to ensure the quality of the children's programs, through direct contact with children to perform assessments and exploratory educational and behavioral programs. Responsibilities include consulting with professional staff in the development and implementation of programs, reviewing child progress, coordinating and reviewing the IGP process and all computer-assisted analyses, monitoring the daily activities of the Unit, and resource management.

Speech Therapists

Two speech pathologists are responsible for assessment, development, and supervision of speech and language programs. These individuals consult with all professional staff in performing these duties so as to create unified language programs that are conducted by the entire staff, consistent with our philosophy of integration of services.

Behavior Analyst

A doctoral level behavior analyst monitors, organizes, catalogs, retrieves, graphs, and analyzes child data in a manner that facilitates in-depth progress analysis and evaluation. A primary component of this position is to conduct observation of child behavior, in addition to that conducted by the staff, in order to provide additional information for the purpose of critical analysis of specific child behavior. This individual is responsible for approximately 1,700 individual goals and over 250 individual behavior programs throughout the school year, as well as monitoring staff to ensure that data collection, summary, and submission are completed accurately and within stated timelines.

Social Worker

The social worker assists the coordinator of clinical services in providing daily support to families and assisting with their interactions with other agencies, social services, and family court, as well as parent–staff communication.

Adaptive Physical Education Teacher

The adaptive physical education teacher is responsible for implementing state regulations concerning physical education requirements. Our program emphasizes that physical education takes place in the context of social skills and leisure skills development.

Art and Music Teacher

The art and music teacher is responsible for implementing state regulations concerning art and music education requirements. Our program emphasizes that this education takes place in the context of social skills and leisure skills development.

Teacher Aides

We typically employ 10 to 15 teacher aides, depending on enrollment. Many of the teacher aides currently have or are pursuing bachelor's and master's degrees. An explicit career ladder has enabled many aides to be promoted to teacher by taking necessary advanced coursework (tuition is subsidized by the Unit) and by demonstrating superior competence in the role of aide.

All aides attend weekly staff meetings as participating members and are encouraged to attend professional conferences. Their role extends beyond that of traditional teacher aide and includes a high degree of training, supervision, and competency demonstration.

Parent Program Assistant

The primary role of the parent program assistant is to help the coordinator of clinical services and social worker in providing daily support to families.

Duties include monitoring written notes sent daily and assisting with providing daily homework.

Nurse

The half-time nurse monitors general health status, performs routine health screening, and maintains a database of child medical history. Medications prescribed by the child's physician are administered by the nurse, and frequent contact is maintained to provide staff observations. To maintain a conservative approach to medication for behavioral and emotional problems, staff are not informed as to child medication status, and are thus "blind" to medication use, thus permitting more objective and accurate assessment of both positive and negative effects of medications.

Custodian

The half-time custodian maintains a clean and safe environment, and assists with inventory of supplies and materials.

Other Therapists

Occupational therapy and physical therapy consultants are employed monthly to observe and assess specific children on goals that are required in the various areas of their discipline. The emphasis is on training all staff to implement programs so that such objectives will be integrated into the child's daily activities.

Undergraduates

Over 1,700 undergraduates have participated in the Unit as paraprofessionals. Participation earns the student course credit. The course syllabus, in addition to an extensive sequence of skill training prior to their interaction with children, also includes reading current literature in the field and collecting, analyzing, and presenting data in a convention poster format at the end of the semester. There are two levels of undergraduates: program trainees, who are least experienced and are under supervision by professional staff members at all times, and program assistants, who serve directly as assistants to the professional staff members. These individuals, having had a minimum of 1 year of experience working at the Unit, use advanced instructional skills and focus primarily on speech and language development.

Professional Staff Training and Supervision

Initial Training

Orientation spans a week of lectures, reading, observation, demonstration, and discussion of Unit policy, philosophy, and functions. All staff are required to pass at a high level (90%) a written exam concerning Unit policies and procedures. Failure to pass results in termination. Beginning teachers and teacher aides are supported in numerous ways, including an explicit pairing of each to a mentor (an experienced staff member). A gradual increase in child-related activities and responsibilities is provided so as to enable each individual to acquire skills on a given level before assuming responsibility for more advanced activities. Videotapes are made and feedback provided on interactions with children, and are periodically continued throughout the course of staff members' involvement at the Unit.

Ongoing Supervision and Training

The coordinating teacher and head teacher rotate staff supervision on a daily basis, and provide direct observation and feedback on performance. Weekly individual supervision meetings with the coordinating teacher address written lessons and progress evaluation, and cover a current review of individual children and educational objectives. Overall performance in terms of time-lines, skill level, quality of written reports, and so forth, are discussed. In addition, two written evaluations per year are prepared for each teacher by the coordinating teacher. The first addresses the following 10 skill areas:

1. Child interaction
2. Classroom staff interaction
3. Parent, agency, visitor interaction
4. Interpersonal sensitivity
5. Lesson preparation
6. Lesson implementation
7. Child progress documentation
8. Classroom management
9. Classroom organization
10. Response to feedback

The second evaluation consists of a list of specific objectives, each of which is evaluated in two ways: (1) an evaluation of change since the initial evaluation and (2) absolute skill or performance level. Both evaluations are completed by the coordinating teacher and reviewed with the director. A meeting is held with each teacher individually to present and discuss the evaluation.

The critical component is that these evaluations are a formalization of the daily and weekly feedback given to the teachers and as such are a condensation of previously discussed issues. Thus, no information contained within the evaluation is unexpected to the teacher. In addition, the second evaluation is directly tied to the first, and change toward a goal is evaluated based on the initial evaluation, as well as absolute performance level.

As part of ongoing supervision, numerous meetings are held weekly to ensure effective communication and ongoing feedback to and between staff members. These meetings are held before child arrival or after child departure. An example of a weekly schedule is as follows:

Staff briefing—Held two times a week, attended by all staff members.

Staff meeting—Attended by all staff members and chaired by the director. The purpose is to review child progress and determine treatment strategy changes if required.

Team meeting—Staff focus on a specific subset of the children and meet with the coordinating teacher to implement staff meeting decisions and to bring suggestions and options to staff meetings.

Teacher supervision meetings—Held individually between the coordinating teacher and the special education teachers and speech pathologists.

Aide supervision meeting—Weekly supervision meeting conducted by each teacher with his or her aides.

Staff work meeting—Weekly 1-hour meeting attended by all staff. One purpose is to complete tasks that require input from numerous staff members.

Professional development meetings—Held every 6 weeks, these meetings are conducted by the coordinating teacher with each staff member to discuss issues regarding current and future professional goals, and current performance.

Undergraduate Training and Supervision

Training and supervision for undergraduates (who may participate for several semesters) have the following primary components:

1. An intensive, full-day, weekend orientation and initial training session. It is held on the first Saturday and Sunday of the first week of the semester to provide an immersion environment and provide an intensive and efficient initial training program. The weekend training covers

- An introduction to policies and procedures, and a historical overview of the development of the Unit, a description of the population served, the specifications of the service, and research and training objectives.

- An introduction to the physical environment, organizational structure, and decision-making processes. The students' paraprofessional role is discussed, as well as policies and procedures regarding confidentiality and safety, and data collection tools and procedures.

- Discussion of specific skills and behaviors concerning interactions with other staff, participation in supervision, and the type of feedback from professional staff that will be delivered in both written and oral form.

- Training and modeling of basic behavioral procedures and review of implementation videotapes.

- In vivo teaching sessions with currently enrolled children, which are observed by other trainees and a supervisor, followed by critique and feedback.

- Completion of a performance competency exam.

- Completion of a written exam (with a score of at least 90%) concerning Unit policies and procedures.

2. Weekly seminars that provide and test for specific information regarding autism and applied behavior analysis.

3. Weekly in vivo conduct of habilitative programs under the direct supervision of a staff member.

4. Continuing weekly written performance feedback.

5. Global evaluations completed and reviewed by professional staff and distributed periodically.

Assessment

Overview

Objective measurement of child performance and behavior serves numerous functions in educational settings. The term *assessment* is typically used to define the process through which professionals evaluate a child's ability levels. Assessment may be conducted in a variety of forms: standardized tests of intelligence or achievement, standardized developmental scales or checklists, criterion-based assessment, and behavioral or functional assessment.

Administration of standardized tests of intelligence and achievement is typically conducted when the purpose of assessment is to compare an individual's performance within specific content area to that of a comparable normative sample. The scores derived from the child's performance are routinely used for diagnostic and placement decisions, evaluation of treatment outcomes, and global program evaluation. However, the value of standardized testing in the process of habilitative planning has been challenged because test scores (standard scores, T-scores, age and grade equivalents, percentile ranks, etc.) and data obtained from item analysis often fail to provide sufficient specificity for the selection of appropriate target behaviors. This criticism is particularly salient when considering the assessment of young children with autism and pervasive developmental disorders because the deficits associated with these disorders are likely to intensify the negative effects of the situational, organismic, and environmental variables that often affect test performance.

Alternative methods of standardized assessment that do not rely on eliciting a child's specific response include the use of various scales and checklists. With these measures, an informant (parent, guardian, teacher, or other individual having first-hand knowledge of the child's behavior in a variety of circumstances) provides information about the child's ability to perform the behaviors in question (i.e., motor skills, social skills, concept development, expressive and receptive language, maladaptive behavior). Many of these checklists have been standardized and thus permit normative comparisons; however, as these are indirect measures, caution in interpretation is urged.

Systematic functional analysis is also an important part of the assessment process. Although this method of assessment is frequently associated with deceleration of unwanted behavior, the methodology contributes significantly to increasing the effectiveness of habilitative programs. Simply defined, functional analysis is the process through which the variables that affect behavior, performance, and learning are identified. Conducting a functional analysis requires a systematic plan for observing behavior. One generates a series of questions about the child's behavior and assesses the specific environments in which the behavior is observed. By manipulating one component of the setting at a time, it is possible to identify the variables that influence (increase, decrease, maintain, elicit) behavior patterns and thus to develop appropriate intervention strategies to effect change.

The last type of assessment discussed in this section involves monitoring child progress. In typical educational settings, routine assessment of child progress tends to occur on interval schedules (i.e., weekly spelling tests, report cards at the end of marking periods) or on ratio schedules (i.e., assessing knowledge gained at the end of a unit of instruction). Programs using applied behavior analysis strategies tend to record data on child behavior and performance on a response-by-response basis so that the data may be analyzed very precisely to evaluate progress and signal the need to investigate impediments to learning.

Protocols for Assessment for Children with Autism and Developmental Disabilities

We use the criteria of the DSM–IV to establish a diagnosis. To date, there is no generally accepted standard assessment battery for young children with autism and severe developmental disorders. The characteristics of children with autism and individual differences inherent in the population, coupled with the limitations of standardized tests of intellectual functioning and achievement, results in a lack of consensus regarding the optimal measures to be used in the assessment of young children with autism. A review of the literature (Estaban, Cochran, & Romanczyk, 1998) found extreme variation in assessment selection. Within the context of this variability, some of the more commonly used instruments are discussed next.

The CARS (Schopler et al., 1988) is used to assist in the diagnosis of autism. To assess intellectual functioning, *The Stanford–Binet Intelligence Scale–Fourth Edition* (Thorndike, Hagen, & Sattler, 1986), the *Bayley Scales of Infant Development–Second Edition* (Bayley, 1993), and the *Slosson Intelligence Test for Children and Adults* (Armstrong & Jensen, 1981) are often used. The *Vineland Adaptive Behavior Scales* (Sparrow, Balla, & Cicchetti, 1984) is commonly used for measuring child competence in activities necessary for day-to-day functioning (i.e., communication, self-help, social competence, and motor functioning). The *Peabody Picture Vocabulary Test–Revised* (Dunn & Dunn, 1981) is frequently used to assess language ability.

Assessment at the Unit

When conducting assessments, we typically select from the following list:

Vineland Adaptive Behavior Scales (Sparrow et al., 1984)

Child Behavior Checklist for Ages 4–18 (Achenbach, 1995)

The Childhood Autism Rating Scale (Schopler et al., 1988)

Autism Screening Instrument for Educational Planning–Second Edition (Krug, Arick, & Almond, 1993)

Peabody Picture Vocabulary Test–Revised (Dunn & Dunn, 1981)

Expressive Vocabulary Test (Williams, 1997)

Bayley Scales of Infant Development–Second Edition (Bayley, 1993)

Stanford–Binet Intelligence Scale–Fourth Edition (Thorndike et al., 1986)

Slosson Intelligence Test–Revised (Slosson, Nicholson, & Hibpshman, 1990)

Wechsler Intelligence Scale for Children–Third Edition (Wechsler, 1991)

Screening Test for Auditory Comprehension of Language (Carrow, 1973)

Assessments Upon Admission

In addition to instruments selected from the previous list, informal assessments are also used. Assessments using our curriculum (the Individualized Goal Selection [IGS] Curriculum, see below) are conducted throughout the initial 30-day admission period to assess the child's specific level of functioning in all developmentally appropriate areas. Assessments are conducted periodically during this period to ensure that the performance obtained is representative and not based on atypical emotional, behavioral, or social responses at any given time. In addition, baseline data are taken on identified problematic behaviors as well as adaptive skills to determine their presence, accuracy, intensity, frequency, and duration. Several parent interviews are typically conducted during this 30-day assessment period.

Also during this time, the child is exposed to and encouraged to participate in various classroom activities where group size, constitution, task, structure, setting, and duration are systematically monitored to evaluate the child's reaction and ability to benefit from each. The Individualized Goal Plan (IGP) is then developed to meet each child's needs with these parameters in mind.

We feel strongly that assessment is the starting point for habilitative planning and is a continuing and necessary component of ongoing decision making and evaluation of effectiveness. In addition to use of standardized tests, checklists, and rating scales, assessment of child performance and behavior is an ongoing process that involves frequent individualized behavioral or functional assessments.

Curriculum

Philosophy

The Unit uses the IGS Curriculum (Romanczyk & Lockshin, 1982; Romanczyk, Lockshin, & Matey, 1998), which was specifically designed for young children with autism and related developmental, learning, and emotional disabilities, and has evolved over the last 20 years. It does *not* provide a lockstep sequence of exercises but rather provides a broad guide or "road map" to development in 19 areas felt to be important for child progress. Although it is organized in a developmental sequence, it is not expected that a child would simply progress through each particular item in sequence. It serves as an assessment tool, a guide, and provides a format for setting priorities. Structurally the IGS Curriculum is composed of 19 areas of development:

1. Maladaptive behavior
2. Attentive skills
3. Speech
4. Receptive language
5. Expressive language
6. Concept formation
7. Gross motor skills
8. Self-help and daily living skills
9. Social skills
10. Reading
11. Fine motor skills
12. Written communication
13. Arithmetic
14. Cultural skills
15. General information
16. School related skills
17. Life relevant skills
18. Leisure skills
19. Emotional & self-control development

Within each area, levels of development are specified. Further, within each level, there are stages of development, and in turn within each stage, there are specific behaviorally referenced tasks. The tasks then serve as the focus for activities and intervention, and are logically grouped under stages and levels of development. This organizational structure represents a filter approach in which one can use the area delineation to specify broad goals, the levels serve to set priorities within areas, the stages represent specific deficit components within the levels of priority, and finally the tasks serve as the day-to-day activities to be conducted by staff in addressing the child's needs.

For example, in the area of expressive language, a level would be *labeling* or *descriptive speech*. The stage is used to represent a long-term goal. The task represents a short-term goal and is defined as the intermediate steps necessary to achieving the long-term goal. Thus, short-term goals are selected such that the mastery of successive short-term goals in a given stage contributes to the achievement of the long-term goal. Finally, it is not expected that functional use in many contexts will occur merely by the acquisition of individual goals. Therefore, within the IGS Curriculum, tasks exist in overlapping concepts and different stages use specific skills in various ways. This "parallel programming" is intended to ensure that the child functionally uses, generalizes, and maintains acquired skills.

The curriculum is also structured such that each of the several thousand entries has a unique code number associated with it. This code serves as the organizing principle for many activities at the Unit, from direct instruction to administrative management via a series of sophisticated computer databases. A brief excerpt appears in Table 4.1:

Curriculum Progression

The IGS Curriculum presents a number of areas for habilitation, treatment, and development. Child development and achievement are not viewed as linear. Areas of development are intertwined in a complex network of interrelationships in day-to-day life experiences. Thus, progression through the curriculum is not unidirectional. As an example, a goal of increasing a child's communication abilities will not only target goals in the areas of expressive and receptive language, but necessarily will include aspects of attentive skills, cognitive development, social skills, and content areas. In this way, communication is not an isolated task or activity but is integral to day-to-day activities in a wide range of environments and activities. Figure 4.1 illustrates a simple example of such linkages across goals.

Curriculum Organizing Principles

The process of developing an Individualized Goal Plan (IGP) to ensure breadth of acquisition is a complex effort and requires the integration of input from multiple staff members, parents, and school districts. Following parental input and preparation of a draft IGP by multiple staff members, the next step is a consultation meeting with the coordinating teacher to refine the draft. At this point the draft is distributed to both parents and school districts. Further modifications and discussions are held with the Unit staff. Only when consensus is obtained does the IGP become a working plan.

Figure 4.2 illustrates the interrelated factors that are considered in the curriculum planning and implementation process. The factors are discussed in more detail in the following text.

GRIP

GRIP, as an acronym for Growth, Relationships, Independence, and Participation, helps place perspective on the process of goal selection and prioritization. It is presented and documented as a basis for ensuring that the expectation and goals for the child includes the following:

1. Having continuing and expanding positive physical, intellectual, emotional, and behavioral *growth*.

Table 4.1
Example of IGS Curriculum Code

Area 2—Attentive Skills

Level 1. Basic Attentive Skills

Stage 1. Sitting

14040 Task 1. Remains seated when placed in chair.
When placed in chair, (Student) will remain seated with buttocks on the chair, feet on the floor, and body oriented toward the teacher.

14050 Task 2. Sits independently and remains seated.
(Student) will sit in a chair with buttocks on the chair, feet on the ground, and body oriented toward the teacher, and will remain seated for duration of activity/task.

State 2. Eye Contact

14070 Task 1. Establishes eye contact in response to command, "Look at me."
The student will establish eye-to-eye contact with the teacher in response to the instruction "Look at me."

14080 Task 2. Establishes eye contact in response to name only.
When called by name, (Student) will establish eye-to-eye contact with the teacher.

14085 Task 3. Establishes eye contact during typical interactions.
(Student) will establish periodic (at least once per minute) eye-to-eye contact with person involved in the interaction. Does not include direct requests for eye contact.

State 3. Visual Attention

14090 Task 1. Orients to materials upon teacher request.
Given the instruction, "Look at the (materials)," (Student) will orient to the materials and maintain attention for the duration of a trial or one statement interaction.

14100 Task 2. Orients to teacher/materials independently.
(Student) will independently orient to the teacher and materials following the teacher's general session initiation statement (e.g., "It's your turn" or "It's time to work") without the need for specific attending prompts.

14110 Task 3. Orients to teacher/materials independently for duration of lesson/interaction.
(Student) will independently orient to the teacher and materials following the teacher's general session initiation statement (e.g., "It's your turn" or "It's time to work") without the need for specific attending prompts, and will maintain appropriate attending for the duration of the lesson or interaction.

2. Developing and maintaining positive and sustained social and work *relationships*.

3. Developing the skills necessary to enable personal *independence*.

4. Developing the skills, motivation, and knowledge to permit active *participation* in the life of family and community.

GRIP also requires developing and enabling of the following:

a. Appropriate exercise of choice

b. Meaningful options

c. Skills of adaptation so as to minimize accommodation

d. Appropriate self-control, inhibition, and behavior control

e. Appropriate self-expression

f. Appropriate control of stress and anxiety

g. Discrimination of important aspects of the social and physical environment to promote social interaction and personal safety

h. Identification of the emotional needs and stress of parents, guardians, and service providers, as separate from the needs and abilities of the child

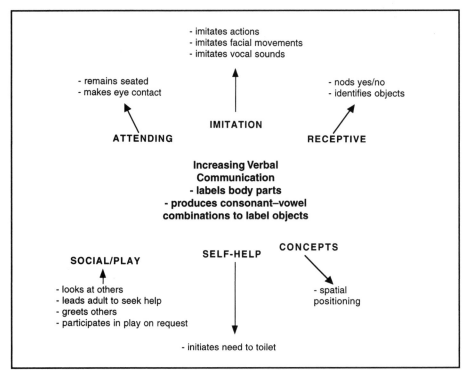

Figure 4.1. Example of interconnectedness of curriculum areas.

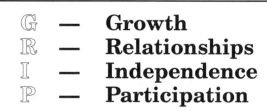

G — Growth
R — Relationships
I — Independence
P — Participation

Habilitative Domains
1. Communication
2. Behavioral–Emotional
3. Social
4. Preacademic–Academic
5. Life Skills

Instructional Level
1. Basic Skills Training
2. Integrated Skills
3. Functional Skills
4. Independent

Child

Behavioral Expectations
1. Learning Readiness
2. Social Awareness
3. Social Norms
4. Self-Regulation
5. Respect for Others
6. Sensory Awareness
7. Independent Learning

Goals
1. Explicit–Written
2. Individualized
3. Precise Data Collection
4. Rigorous Evaluation

Required Resources
1. Large group
2. Group
3. Small group
4. Individual
5. Multiple

Instructional Formats
1. Focused Instruction
2. Experiential Learning
3. Enrichment/Stimulation
4. Skill Integration Activities

IGS Curriculum
1. Maladaptive Behavior
2. Attentive Skills
3. Speech
4. Receptive Language
5. Expressive Language
6. Concept Formation
7. Gross Motor Skills
8. Self-Help and Daily Living Skills
9. Social Skills
10. Reading
11. Fine Motor Skills
12. Written Communication
13. Arithmetic
14. Cultural Skills
15. General Information
16. School-Related Skills
17. Life Relevant Skills
18. Leisure Skills
19. Emotional and Self-Control Development

Figure 4.2. The process of outcome-focused planning, priorities, goal selection, and implementation.

Habilitative Domains

The concept of a focused curriculum, from a pragmatic perspective, requires definition of what the focus of instruction should be for each child prior to goal selection. Domain prioritization is our mechanism for specifying the focus of program content. The following are the five domains:

1. Communication
2. Behavioral/Emotional
3. Social
4. Preacademic/Academic
5. Life Skills

Using assessment data to determine child need, each domain is hierarchically ordered to represent the intensity of programming needed to move the child toward acquisition of those skills needed for various environments. These priorities are not rigid, and the rank ordering of priorities changes over time to reflect changes in child progress. Many factors must be considered in determining domain priorities for each student, as the domain priorities specify not only the instructional priorities for the upcoming school year but also the amount of time allotted for instruction in each habilitative domain.

Decisions regarding prioritization of habilitative domains necessitate a review of each student's current level of functioning. Sources of this information should include the following:

1. Parent goals specified in the GRIP

2. Previous child progress

3. Standardized assessment

4. Nonstandardized assessment

5. Observation of child behavior across various settings

6. Parent reports

7. Knowledge about the subsequent educational setting in which the child will be placed

Domain priorities serve as the blueprint for the development of each child's individualized habilitative program in the following ways:

1. Domain priorities are translated directly into the proportion of instructional time allocated to each domain. In the spirit of preserving the relative importance of specific domains, the number of instructional periods is greatest for domains with the highest priority rankings. Thus, it would not be unusual for a 4-year-old child with limited receptive and expressive skills to spend 75% of instructional time working in the Communication domain (i.e.,

speech, expressive and receptive language). It also would not be unusual to find that Communication goals were being addressed during instructional periods that had a primary focus on skills associated with other domains. Continuing with the example above, if self-dressing was an instructional goal targeted for the Life Skills domain, there would be a strong emphasis on practicing language skills during self-dressing lessons.

2. Domain prioritization also serves as a guide for the development of each child's IGP. That is, both the selection of specific habilitative goals and the number of goals selected should preserve the relative emphasis of the domain priorities.

3. The habilitative priorities also provide specific guidelines for how instructional activities are scheduled throughout the school day. From a scheduling perspective, this means that habilitative goals falling within high-priority domains should be scheduled for a greater proportion of time than those designated as lower priority domains.

4. Finally, grouping habilitative goals within domains makes it possible to regularly monitor the relative emphasis of activities within a given day and to evaluate the appropriateness of time allocation within a child's program.

IGP Goal Selection

After the domain priorities have been established, the next step is to identify appropriate IGP goals to achieve the mandate of the domain priorities. Reference is made to GRIP goals and the child's current level of functioning using the sources listed previously. Given the extent of child deficits, there may be a tendency toward selecting more goals than could possibly be addressed within the limits of a year. In this context, however, it is useful to consider what we term parallel programming; that is, asking what other curriculum goals can be selected that will give the child practice in priority areas while addressing other required goals (e.g., expressive labeling in an art/gym goal).

Instructional Level

Instructional level refers to a conceptual continuum that identifies the appropriate unit of instruction for a given child relative to a specific goal. Because instructional levels are determined for each goal, it is expected that a child's habilitative program will likely include all levels of instruction. The following list depicts when each instructional level would be appropriate:

Instructional level	Child ability
Basic Skills	Limited ability in completing skill or skill components
Integrated Skills	Mastery of several component skills of complex task
Functional Skills	Ability to perform chains of component skills
Independent Skills	Ability to perform skills with minimal adult support

The *Basic Skills* level encompasses all elementary skills, such as simple attentive skills, cognitive skills (matching, sorting, sensory awareness), speech skills, language skills, and self-help skills. Instruction at the Basic Skills level involves an extensive task analysis (i.e., breaking a complex skill into its component parts) and systematically teaching the component skills to mastery criterion.

The *Integrated Skills* level of instruction may be distinguished from Basic Skills depending on whether the target involves the acquisition of a specific skill component or whether the target involves combining (chaining) of several skill components that have already been acquired to address functional usage within an appropriate environmental setting (home, school, grocery store, restaurant, etc.). The Integrated Skill level is employed after several individual components of a task sequence are mastered. At this point, the expectation for success changes; that is, the child is required to perform a series of skills (i.e., a chain of skills acquired via specific and sometimes intensive training) to achieve success. This is the process of skill integration or the process through which individual behaviors are linked together to enable the development of functional skills.

The prerequisite for instruction at the *Functional Skills* level is that the child has demonstrated the capacity to integrate a sufficient number of specific task components. The focus of instruction is on functional use of the skill within specific contexts that the child encounters each day. When all of the task components have been integrated into the skill routine, emphasis continues to be placed on the refinement of the skill until it is performed at age-appropriate levels.

The focus at the *Independent Skills* level of instruction is on age-appropriate initiation and completion of the skill. This involves teaching the child to discriminate where and when to perform the skill and to self-monitor for task completion.

Instructional Format

Whereas instructional level specifies the information taught within a given habilitative program, instructional format specifies the context for instruction. There are four instructional formats.

1. *Focused Instruction*: This format uses a discrete trial format that emphasizes the salience of verbal and visual cues, prompts, immediate external feedback, extensive practice, and careful monitoring of response patterns to adjust instructional parameters to facilitate acquisition.

2. *Experiential Learning*: This format uses learning situations that are carefully choreographed to enable students to learn via natural consequences within the learning environment (i.e., their success or failure at solving problems). An important emphasis within this instructional format is to encourage

students to persist when confronted with difficult situations or failure experiences and to generate and explore the efficacy of alternative strategies in an effort to solve problems.

3. *Enrichment/Stimulation*: This format provides a learning environment that is engineered to elicit responses that are already in the child's repertoire or to provide sufficient sensory input and motivational conditions to elicit novel or spontaneous behavior. In the area of language, for example, a child who has acquired food labels might be encouraged to play grocery store to promote use of language in a more naturalistic environment.

4. *Skill Integration*: The focus in this format is to encourage application of activities to a variety of skills. For a given group of children, this might translate to writing, planning, and performing a play or carrying out a science experiment (to practice following directions, observing changes, and reporting outcomes). For another group of children, it may involve learning to play a board game using concepts already acquired (e.g., playing "Color Bingo" once color recognition has been acquired).

Continuum of Educational Environments

Just as skills are arranged in a hierarchy from simple to complex, it may be equally important to establish hierarchies of learning environments to facilitate learning. It is possible to shape appropriate group or "classroom" behavior, attentional skills, and remediation of skill deficits by providing a continuum of learning environments. New and more complex settings are introduced systematically when the data indicate that the child has demonstrated mastery of skills and behaviors in the more simple environments.

The process of systematically shaping a child's learning environment is an important process at the Unit. A variety of learning environments are designed to accommodate individual child needs and to prepare the child for a school program within his or her community. Decisions regarding child clusters and instructional settings are based on extensive behavioral observation during the first few weeks of placement at the Unit. Data obtained from these observations and standardized tests assist the staff with the decision-making process. The following is a partial list of questions considered when determining the appropriate learning settings for a particular child:

1. What areas have been designated as habilitative priorities for the child? What are the child's functional levels in these areas?

2. Within each of the prioritized domains, what factors impede child progress?

   a. Are maladaptive behaviors an impediment to learning?

   b. What are the child's management needs to prevent harm to self or others?

c. Does the child have basic attentional skills (e.g., remaining in seat, establishing eye contact, following simple instructions in a one-to-one or small group setting)?

    d. Does the child require multiple, repetitive trials for learning to occur?

    e. Does the child require considerable physical prompting for learning to occur?

3. Does the child have the ability to remain on task for short periods of time in a small group setting?

4. What age-appropriate activities are in the child's repertoire?

5. Can the child work independently for short periods of time?

6. Does the child's behavior change as a function of task difficulty, group size, or activity level in the classroom?

Once answers to these questions have been obtained, the child's level of functioning is matched with a learning environment. There are a variety of environments to select from, ranging in small increments from a one-to-one student–teacher ratio in an individual therapy room to a large group setting comprised of eight children and one teacher.

It is important to emphasize that any one child may be involved in as many as 3 or 4 different learning environments during the school day. Group size and environmental setting may change as a function of the specific task or activity. Thus, child groupings are not static assignments, as they are intended to change as a function of the child's skill levels in all areas of development. Further, assignment to a particular setting is not constrained by arbitrary time frames, such as school year, but may change as frequently as child behavior indicates. In addition to the functional level of the group, another consideration in developing child clusters is the age range represented in the group. Age is a critical factor in that the children must participate in groups that permit age-appropriate activities to occur.

Interface Between Assessment and Goal Selection

Preparation Prior to Selecting Goals

Selecting the Individualized Education Program (IEP) goals necessary to maximize progress and achieve outcomes specified by parents in the GRIP is by no means an easy task. Decisions related to the number of goals to select and the sequence in which skills will be taught (identification of goals that are prerequisites for other goals) must be made within the context of relevant assessment data. Data central to this decision-making process include review of child progress to date, review of standardized and nonstandardized assessments, and parents' reports.

Review of Standardized Assessment Data

Review of standardized assessment data not only should involve attention to summary scores that provide information about overall levels of ability in the skill areas evaluated by the test, but also should include review of the pattern of performance on the individual scales contained within the test and on individual test items. Analysis of response patterns will provide more specific information about areas of strength and weakness.

Once areas of strength and weakness have been identified, staff use the curriculum to identify skills associated with the strengths and weaknesses and to further assess the limits of performance. The following questions guide staff in assessing variables that need to be considered prior to engaging in the goal selection process.

Does the child have the appropriate prerequisite skills for learning?

For children to learn efficiently, they must be able to maintain a level of behavioral control that enables them to participate in instruction, must adequately comprehend expectations for the task, and must demonstrate attentional skills that are adequate for task performance. Thus, it is important to target instruction in these prerequisite skills if they are absent or inadequate.

How quickly does the child acquire new information?

This affects the decision-making process in a number of areas, as follows:

1. The number of goals to select within a given domain
2. The type of instructional format (e.g., focused vs. experiential)
3. The instructional methodology necessary for acquisition to occur
4. The resources necessary for instruction

Does the child retain new information once learned?

If the child has difficulty maintaining skills acquired, the following needs to be considered:

1. Limit the number of goals selected.
2. Select a series of goals within curriculum areas that follow a logical sequence. Performance of the more advanced skill should incorporate skills taught at a lower level. An example of this can be found in teaching language skills. The child should first be taught to label objects using a single word. Teaching the child to use other language structures (e.g., labeling in a full sentence, asking questions) should use the same pool of words acquired during labeling tasks.

Does the child seem to be able to use new skills across settings, people, and situations?

If the child does not generalize the use of new skills, programming for generalization needs to be incorporated in the planning of the instructional program. If generalization is problematic, the following strategy should be considered:

1. Limit the number of goals selected within each curriculum area related to a specific skill.
2. Select similar goals from other curriculum areas that will require the child to use acquired skills in other settings.

Once the child learns a specific skill, does the child use that skill to learn new skills (e.g., counting sequentially to self-cue solutions to addition problems)?

If the child is capable of retaining and using skills in this way, goals should be selected in a sequence that allows the child to elaborate upon acquired skills. The answer to this question will influence the decision-making process in a number of areas, as follows:

1. The number of goals to select within a given domain
2. The type of instructional format (e.g., focused vs. experiential)
3. The instructional methodology necessary for acquisition to occur
4. The resources necessary for instruction

Does the acquisition of new material occur differentially for various types of material (e.g., verbal, nonverbal, reading, arithmetic)?

If so, it may be desirable to teach the child the new skill in the preferred modality first. For example, the child may need to match colors before learning to name them. Sequencing goals in this way may have a number of advantages. First, when teaching within the preferred modality, there is a higher probability of success. Many children with autism have learning histories that are fraught with failure. Early success may be helpful in generating and maintaining motivation.

Materials

Although many commercially prepared materials are available at the Unit, they are typically used along with staff-created materials on a highly individualized basis. The emphasis at the Unit is on the teaching methodology rather than materials per se. While commercially prepared materials can be of some value, the method of material presentation, prompting procedures, sequencing of tasks, and appropriate motivational strategies are by far the most important elements of an effective teaching environment. This approach extends to our use of computers in instruction; much of our software is internally developed.

Resource Management

Each child's daily schedule consists of a sequence of half-hour sessions in a variety of settings where group size, constitution, subject, instructor, and response and participation requirements vary based on the child's strengths and the requirements in each area targeted in the IGP. These schedules are printed in several forms, one of which accompanies the child throughout the day. The following are two examples.

Daily Schedule—Information Included

Day

Time

Instructor

Domain

Location

Group size

IGP task(s)

Proportion of half-hour period allocated to tasks

Goal type

Program start date

Current program step and description

Number and total amount of times the goal is scheduled per week

Total time (number of 30-minute intervals) the program is scheduled per week

Daily Schedule—Information Interpretation and Use

Provides staff schedule—location and activity of each staff member for each half-hour interval

Specifies priority distribution of domain foci

Provides accountability check for implementation of IGP priority areas

Provides visual display of distribution across the week

Specifies proportion of half-hour interval devoted to each task scheduled within a period

Allows for prioritization of goals within each half-hour session

Provides opportunities to run complementary goals simultaneously, while maintaining the relative priority of each

Provides relative distribution of time across goals

Provides assessment information about average duration of each lesson or probe

Specifies current program step

The computerized schedule program is a component of the same system that is used to manage IGP information. Therefore, schedule data, such as program title, type, start date, step, and so on, are automatically inserted by simply entering the goal number. Thus, entry is quick and consistent with the student's approved habilitative treatment program.

Multiple printout formats allow for staff, student, and location schedules. In addition, the program provides a detailed printout at any time for parents, school districts, and involved professionals, that is up to date and can be used to determine observation schedules based on purpose or need.

Least Restrictive Environment (LRE)

We first wrote on the topic of least restrictive environment (LRE) some time ago (Romanczyk & Lockshin, 1984). In the first edition of this book (Romanczyk, Matey, & Lockshin, 1994), we restated our position:

It is interesting that individuals with severe disabilities are often inordinately caught up in various political and dogmatic issues. One of these current issues is "integration versus segregation." While at one level it is of course the case that all individuals should participate in their local community in all aspects of their daily lives, it is also the case that there is a wide range of community support and services, and there is also a wide range of needs of children with autism. Therefore, it seems apparent that it is unquestionably *incorrect* to say that all children with autism should receive services outside of local community settings, just as it is unquestionably *incorrect* to say that all children should only receive services within their community settings. Part of the difficulty may be that "education" has very different meanings. For us it does not mean attending a local school, but rather means receiving the educational and clinical interventions that can maximize the child's potential. Thus, for this reason, we take a moderate approach that is tied tightly to our philosophy of assessment. The choice of type and location of service is a function of the child's needs. Terms such as "least restrictive" cannot simply be applied to "bricks and mortar."

The goal of integration into the typical school setting is unquestionably correct. However, for some children, a normalized setting, even with extensive support services, may not be the least restrictive setting. Central to the issue is one's definition of "least restrictive."

For some children, a strategy of a continuum of services, from an intense, focused, individualized, specialized setting to the more typical classroom with required support services, is the most appropriate. This allows for rapid acquisition of needed skills and for a choreographed approach to habilitation. Some children who are placed in the supposed "least restrictive" placement do not progress at a rate consistent with their potential. There can be an illusion of progress as they are "with their peers" and are present in various activities. This could be seen as in the least restrictive placement, but from a different perspective, it is highly restrictive if one is sensitive to temporal factors. If a child is in an environment where learning takes place at some fraction of the pace that is possible in a more specialized environment, then this indeed represents a restrictive environment. (p. 207, 210)

The following statement of policy was issued by the New York State Education Department in May of 1998 (Mills, 1998):

For some students, the LRE may be placement full time in a general education program with supplementary aids and services provided to the student and/or the student's teacher in that setting. For other students, the LRE may be a special class or special school. Any setting that prevents a child from receiving an appropriate education to meet his or her cognitive, social, physical, linguistic and/or communicative needs is not the LRE for that individual student. The placement decision for an individual student must be made only after the IEP is completely developed to address the full range of the student's needs. (p. 8)

Despite a sense of frustration concerning the slow pace at which change occurs in the cycles of history and the gap between well-intended philosophy and effective outcome, we are pleased with this significant and welcome change in philosophy. It reflects an individualized assessment approach rather than a one-size-fits-all approach.

Maladaptive Behavior

Because of the specialized group of children that we serve, severe maladaptive behaviors are common problems. Many of the behaviors displayed are extremely intense and of danger to the child and others. Nevertheless, the Unit has a strong philosophy of a skill development and assessment-oriented approach rather than an intervention- or technique-oriented approach. Too often the technique-oriented approach to behavioral intervention focuses on creating intervention strategies and then using the behavioral methodology to evaluate those interventions. In contrast, we advocate performing detailed assessments from which interventions are derived and then appropriately used, focusing in particular on antecedent events.

One reason the technique-oriented approach is commonly used is pragmatic. Whereas assessment can involve tremendous use of resources, a "let's try it and see if it works" strategy can be more efficient if the intervention is indeed successful. However, such an approach, while it may (and we emphasize the word *may*) be effective for highly skilled and experienced clinicians, does not serve as a good basis for a complex organization in which many different individuals participate in the delivery of services. Under such circumstances, it is prudent to use assessment procedures to produce information that can then be evaluated by supervisory and senior staff to create intervention programs for which staff are then trained to implement. Such an approach can produce frustration for both staff and parents as often the immediate request is to "do something." It is imperative, however, that the focus of intervention programs be on long-term amelioration of the behavior for the child rather than an immediate amelioration of adult anxiety and frustration.

With respect to assessment, certain basic strategies and tools are in place throughout the Unit. For example, all classrooms have videotaping facilities, and camcorders are available for staff and parents to use in home settings. A number of specialized behavior recording forms are used on a consistent basis, complemented by global rating scales designed to reflect observations over extended periods of time.

Also easily available are computer-assisted observational procedures, designed to analyze videotape records. These computer systems permit extensive, extremely rapid data analyses in various formats suitable for the different assessment questions that may be asked. For example, the programs can produce simple bar charts to indicate frequency of events, as well as conditional probability analyses to indicate the interrelatedness of various behaviors and for analyzing episodic versus frequency versus duration information.

Although it is impossible to constantly record all forms of possible behavior that a child may display, by continuously recording and analyzing a very large set of child behavior in this way, we are able to take advantage of naturally occurring variation as a method for assessing possible eliciting and maintaining factors. Also, having a large pool of collateral behavior information is useful for broadly evaluating various intervention strategies.

While we place great emphasis on behavior measurement, we also are concerned with eliciting aspects of behavior in addition to consequent events. Eliciting factors include many different variables, such as sensory modulation, social interaction, task difficulty, pacing and method of material presentation, physical internal stimuli, and conditioned arousal-inducing stimuli. In particular we are concerned with the role of arousal and anxiety in many complex behavior problems. This role has been given little attention, particularly in young children, in the professional literature and in educational settings. Recently our efforts in this area have included psychophysiological monitoring, identification of social versus task escape–motivated children, and the role of multiple determinants of individual topographies of various classes of behavior (Romanczyk & Matthews, 1998; Taylor, Ekdahl, Romanczyk, & Miller, 1994; Taylor & Romanczyk, 1994).

Decision Making and Methods of Assessing Progress

The hallmark of our program is data-based decision making (Romanczyk, 1996). To achieve, on a programmatic basis, high efficiency and cost benefit, and to provide extensive, accurate data analysis, a series of highly sophisticated, networked computer databases are used. These databases are used by all staff for tasks such as recording child performance on tasks, adaptive and maladaptive behavior, parent contacts, homework and home intervention programs, standardized assessments, scheduling of resources, and development of the IGP. Further, the IGP information is transferred to a combination word processor–database that permits staff to create explicit written protocols for each IGP goal. That is, staff are required to produce a document that can be read and implemented by any reasonably well-trained individual. This document serves as the keystone for maintaining high levels of staff consistency and communication. Because a large number of staff are employed and a large number of paraprofessionals are used, it is critical that explicit instructions be provided for each IGP goal.

The same database produces interim reports for parents and staff, and greatly facilitates preparation of end-of-year progress reports. Most important, however, the various databases provide a detailed analysis of child status and progress for review at each week's staff meeting. At staff meetings, a computer projection system provides a 4 x 6 foot image of access to all databases. This permits all staff to fully participate in analysis and interpretation without needing paper records and copies. Questions and issues can be pursued throughout the many interconnected databases rather than relying on memory or the necessarily limited paper reports and graphs that would normally be prepared. Without this comprehensive computer capability, detailed review of child progress on such a frequent basis would not be possible. Our system is interactive so that staff meeting decisions are entered into the databases as they occur. Figure 4.3 illustrates the dynamic and interrelated processes involved in our decision-making processes that are aided by our extensive computer system. This process and system have yielded significant impact on child progress (Romanczyk, 1984, 1986, 1991). For each goal targeted in each child's IGP, data are collected on an ongoing, most often daily, basis (approximately 15,000 data points are collected each day). The manner in which progress is assessed varies given the requirements of the specific objective. For reduction of maladaptive behavior objectives, each goal has a specific data collection schedule, which is rotated from week to week to ensure that sampling occurs at all periods of the week and all parts of the day. With the schedule in place, the data are collected by

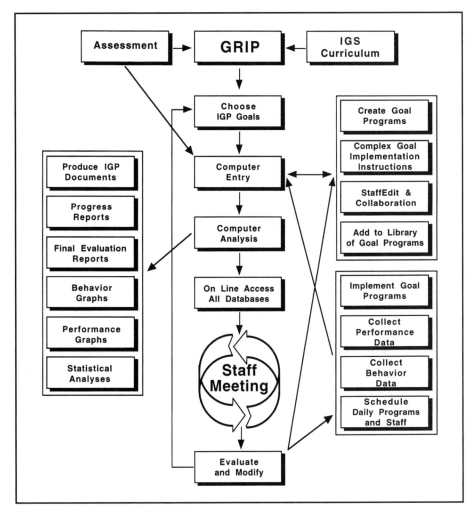

Figure 4.3. Typical staff workflow.

frequency, intensity, duration, or percent occurrence (an interval recording system where the evaluator's score is the presence or absence of the target behavior in a 15-minute interval). In addition, each goal is individually assessed to determine whether or not elicitor ratings (i.e., the presence of a specific elicitor is assumed to be responsible for the presence of the target behavior) need to be collected.

Assessment of progress in habilitative areas is accomplished via continual scoring of child responses for discrete trial programs, and summary information concerning accuracy and rate for incidental and independent learning situations. Data are collected on the accuracy and error pattern of the responses, the child's response to prompts, emission of approximations to the correct response, and notation of failure to respond. Program procedure modifications may occur on a daily basis, reflecting the child's performance.

There is a subset of goals for which a scale rating or checklist is used. Goals that are most appropriate for this type of data collection include appropriate social interaction, cooperation and play, and goals where quality, intensity, or degree of performance are the focus. Analysis of the child's performance on these goals occurs on a weekly basis.

Another form of behavior analysis that is resource intensive but necessary is the recording of children's daily behavior observations made by the teaching staff. Graphs that are then computer generated not only present the frequency of events per day, but also include a separate plot of minimum, maximum, and average for each day, and a temporal analysis showing the frequency of behavior within half-hour periods across days. This latter analysis is a system first used at the Unit in 1980 (Lockshin & Romanczyk, 1982; Romanczyk, Colletti, & Brutvan, 1982) and is similar to the scatter plot analysis proposed by Touchette, MacDonald, and Langer in 1985. However, at the Unit these computer-generated graphs and statistics are not "special" analyses conducted when a particular problem behavior is encountered, but rather have been systematized such that all child behavior is analyzed in this format on a continuing basis. This permits analysis of trends and interactions with particular tasks or staffing patterns or complex cyclical patterns.

Parent Involvement

Our philosophy at the Unit is that parent and family involvement is an integral part of the child's education and is critical to maximizing the child's ultimate level of functioning, habilitatively, socially, and emotionally. We further recognize that raising a child with autism is difficult, both emotionally and physically. For parents to be effectively involved in their child's treatment, they need to develop specific skills to affect behavior change. Parents also need emotional and practical support to help them achieve an appropriate balance of the efforts they must invest over time for their child with autism with responsibilities to other family members, careers, life pursuits, and so forth.

We also recognize that parents' ability and skill levels, as well as motivational levels, vary dramatically, and thus we offer communication, participation, training, and support services at a variety of levels to meet the needs of the wide range of individual families. Table 4.2 lists the various parent support components provided at the Unit.

An example of the importance the Unit places on parent involvement is the policy on parent visits. Parents may visit the Unit to observe the child and program unannounced, without making an appointment or informing staff of their visits. Upon arrival they have the choice of observing the child in vivo or observing through closed-circuit TV. If they choose the latter, neither staff nor children are notified of their visit, and parents may watch without informing staff of their presence. We feel that this complete freedom on the parents' part is clearly their right, and the staff accept this not as an invasion of their privacy but rather as an opportunity for the parents to view what typically occurs on a given day with their child.

Parent education at the Unit provides parents with an opportunity to learn basic techniques in working with their children, away from the distractions frequently present at home. The goals include the following:

1. Information on childhood disorders
2. Instruction in basic behavior management techniques
3. Direct supervision in implementing behavior management procedures (stating rules, planned ignoring, positive reinforcement)
4. Assessment of parent–child interactions
5. Targeting specific goals for home programs
6. Developing home programs
7. Methods of data collection
8. Direct supervision of implementation of programs

We use several manuals (Lockshin, 1985, 1998) that were designed to provide our parents with basic information and background. The inclusion of these manuals in our program enabled us to move away from a lecture format and adopt more of a seminar format during which parents and staff jointly developed programs for home implementation and reviewed child progress on specific programs. These group meetings provide parents with the opportunity to share their personal experiences and to benefit from the experiences of other parents.

Parent Services

Although the staff members are committed to active parent participation, recruiting parent participation has been a perennial challenge. Historically,

Table 4.2
Home–School Communication and Parent Support Services

Format	Purpose	Frequency
Program Orientation and Habilitative Planning		
Parent Manual	• to provide practical information needed to prepare children for school: immunizations, lunches, absences, school hours, medications, etc.	Upon enrollment with annual updates
Unit IGP Conference	• to review assessment data • to discuss priorities for instruction and intervention • to discuss strategies and philosophy • to set long-term and short-term goals	Annually
Child Progress		
Parent–Teacher Meetings	• to review child progress on a regular basis • to answer questions regarding child progress in the school • to obtain important information about child behavior and performance in the home setting	Every 10 weeks
School Observation	• to observe the child during school day activities	Any time; no appointment necessary
Report Cards	• to report on child progress and school–home communication	Every 10 weeks
Formal Unit Reports	• to summarize child progress at the end of the school year • to provide school districts with information prior to annual meetings	Annually In the spring of each year
Progress Notes	• to communicate with parents regarding program progress, program changes, and other noteworthy events	Every 3 weeks
Certificates	• to provide the student with a tangible source of reinforcement for school progress to share with parents	Every 3 weeks
Projects	• to provide a tangible product of the student's work at school (worksheet, art project, book report, etc.)	Every 3 weeks
Informational Updates		
Routine Telephone Contact	• to obtain information on child progress and behavior at home • to obtain information about changes at home • to obtain information related to home concerns and to make referrals to Unit for further discussion	Monthly

(continues)

Table 4.2 *Continued*

Format	Purpose	Frequency
Health Updates	• to provide a consistent method of updating changes in health status, medication, etc.	Monthly
Social History Updates	• to provide a consistent method of updating important changes in the home environment and support systems that may affect the children	Monthly
Unit Bulletin	• to review school activities, events, reminders, staff changes, etc.	Monthly

Collaborative (Home–School) Habilitation

Format	Purpose	Frequency
Home–School Notes	• to monitor child behavior, performance, and mood at home and at school • to serve as a means of communicating the events of the school day to the home • to provide the school with information regarding child reactions to events and activities at home	Daily; revised on a monthly basis
Homework	• to assist in maintaining skills acquired in school and to promote generalization of skills to the home setting • to address skill building: using skills learned in functional settings • Homework is developed in three curriculum areas: Life Skills, Leisure Skills, Academic/Preacademic Skills • parents are provided with written instructions to help them maximize child performance at home • parents are advised to read the Parent Information Series prior to implementing homework assignments; no specific prerequisite skills are required	Daily
Home Programs	• Home programs are the home counterparts to school programs that are implemented in the school setting. Because of the technical complexity of these programs, we require that, prior to receiving home programs, parents participate in the Parent Education Series where they learn about basic learning principles and how they are applied to developing habilitative programs for children with	As indicated

(continues)

Table 4.2 *Continued*

Format	Purpose	Frequency
Home Programs *(continued)*	developmental disabilities. Following participation in the Parent Education Series, Unit staff will consult with parents on realistic expectations for home programming, transfer of school programs to the home setting, data collection and management, and program evaluation.	
Parent Education	• *Basic Seminar Series:* This forum is designed to teach parents the basic principles of behavioral interventions to provide them with the knowledge they will need to develop and implement habilitative and behavior management programs. This seminar will use the Parent Information Series as the basis of instruction. During this seminar series, parents will be encouraged to apply the principles learned to specific behaviors observed in the home setting.	
	• *Advanced Seminar Series:* This seminar series is for parents who wish to continue developing their knowledge about behavioral principles and techniques and who wish to continue as habilitative agents. Materials include an expanded reading list. Program development, implementation, and evaluation will be the primary focus of this seminar series.	Scheduled periodically
	• *Parent Workshops*: A variety of workshops will be offered that will focus on specific topic areas (e.g., toilet training, stress and time management, increasing social skills). The Basic Seminar Series is a prerequisite for participation in those workshops focused on child habilitation.	Scheduled periodically
Home Intervention Program	• to assist parents in the development and implementation of home programs within the following domains to address specific concerns: Behavioral/emotional control, Communication, Social Skills, and Emotional Control and Self-Regulation. Examples of the types of issues addressed in this format include toilet training, speech, bedwetting, noncompliance, development of age-appropriate leisure skills, decreasing aggression, self-injury, tantrums, destructive behav-	Schedules will be determined individually

(*continues*)

Table 4.2 *Continued*

Format	Purpose	Frequency
Home Intervention Program *(continued)*	ior, and appropriate expression of anger. Parents must participate in the Parent Education Series prior to obtaining consultation related to the development of programs for home interventions.	
Intensive Home Intervention	• to assist parents in developing an intensive program (more than 40 hours per week) to facilitate development in areas of concern (i.e., speech, language, and social skills). The program involves teaching parents the skills needed to be an effective teacher for their child. Activities involve classroom instruction, reading materials, hands-on work with the children, and problem-solving meetings with staff.	Parents must be able to commit a minimum of 15 hours per week
Parent Consultation	• to meet with a staff member to discuss specific questions or concerns related to school or home	Appointments must be made in advance
	• to discuss issues related to long-term development and perspectives	
Parent Advisement	• to discuss topics that are too personal or emotional to raise in other school–home formats. Based on an assessment of need, referrals will be made to appropriate Unit services or to other agencies within the community.	Tuesday 9 to 10 a.m Thursday 1:30 to 2:30 p.m. Appointments must be made in advance
Institute for Child Development Newsletter	• to provide parents with up-to-date information on research findings and to highlight issues in the areas related to autism, learning disability, and emotional and behavioral disorders	

only a small proportion of parents have participated in the wide range of services offered.

Part of the challenge involved in providing comprehensive services to the families in a small city in upstate New York. Given the relatively small population of the immediate area, the population served by the Unit spans a geographic radius of approximately 100 miles and includes many rural areas.

The referral process is also a contributing factor; few families whose children are enrolled in the Unit are self-referred. Referrals are typically made for the children who present with severe problems and families experiencing considerable distress. Indeed, many referrals are for "difficult" families. There is no parent ability or resource requirement for child admission. Thus our population of families is characterized by a very large range, from that of highly motivated and cooperative individuals to hostile, uncooperative, and impaired individuals.

Although we strongly encourage parent participation in all parent services, participation is strictly on a voluntary basis. Making continued child enrollment contingent upon active parent participation has been considered as a way of increasing parent involvement, but then service provision to the student population in most need would be decreased significantly.

Over the years, parents have provided staff with many reasons for limited participation, some of which follow:

1. Given the geographic area served by the program, many of our families have identified travel (i.e., distance, time, and cost) and child care for other children in the family as major obstacles to participation.

2. Frequently, work schedules, particularly in single-parent families and in families where both parents work, interfere with parent involvement.

3. Many of our parents consider school personnel the "experts" and expect the staff to "treat" and "fix" the "problem." Moreover, no other educational program in our area requires the level of participation we routinely solicit.

4. Popular press regarding the efficacy of "fad" treatments influences parents' decisions regarding their level of direct involvement. Understandably, many of our families continue to search for the elusive "cause" of autism and a "magic bullet." Despite education regarding the outcome data for alternative treatments and the efficacy of applied behavior analysis, many families continue to seek treatments that have no documented efficacy, in lieu of investing their time, money, and resources into more intensive home involvement using an applied behavior analysis approach.

5. Some of our parents have personal and relationship problems that result in feelings of denial or hopelessness concerning the child.

Figure 4.4 illustrates the trend in two levels of parent participation across years.

Accommodations To Increase Parental Involvement

Although the majority of our parents opt not to participate in formal parent education programs, they continue to seek professional consultation, particularly when behavior problems arise. Treating behavior problems in the

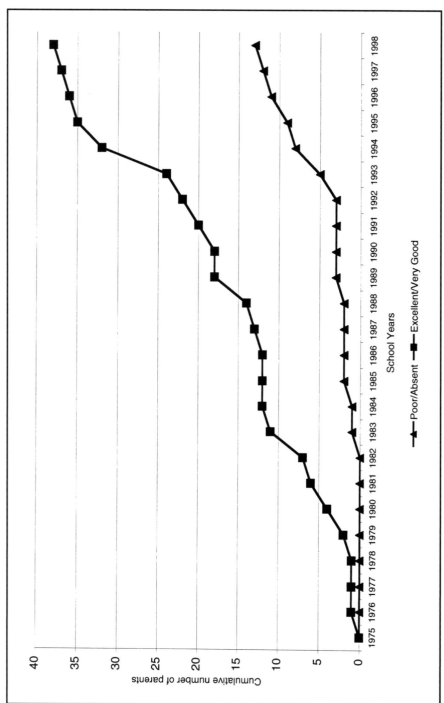

Figure 4.4. Trends in degree of parent participation.

absence of having direct contact with parents to provide them with education in the techniques of behavior management (i.e., didactic instruction, modeling, supervision of program implementation) presents professional and ethical issues. The dilemma of refraining from providing parents with assistance in managing problem behaviors while providing low-risk intervention strategies is demonstrated by the following example. As highlighted in the example, the goal is to demonstrate the positive impact of home programming on child behavior in an effort to motivate increased parent involvement.

The presenting problem was identified as a child's refusal to bathe. The consequence of the problem was that the child began to look unkempt and have an odor. Consultation with direct teaching staff indicated that the child was responding positively to a token reinforcement program and had demonstrated the ability to delay gratification at the Unit. Thus, the plan was to initially reinforce cleanliness in the Unit based on child appearance and home reports of child cooperation during the bathing routine. Following receipt of baseline data, development of an age-appropriate task analysis, parent distribution of points for completing the steps in the task analysis during the bathing routine, and reinforcement in the Unit contingent on meeting the performance criteria (i.e., number of points earned), the child's cooperation during bathing improved dramatically. External validity of program effectiveness came from teacher reports of significantly improved physical appearance and decrease in offensive body odor. Another positive outcome that resulted from program implementation was increased communication with parents and increased parental interest in working with Unit staff on the development of subsequent home programs.

Outcome

Critical to the discussion of outcome measures is discharge criteria. Our focus is on effecting change significant enough to allow the child to enter a community or school district setting. Therefore, the criteria for each individual child varies with respect to (a) the severity of the presenting problems, (b) the presence of appropriate intervention strategies that can be transitioned to other programs while still maintaining the child's current level of social development, and (c) the availability of a program that can meet current needs. Thus, a child who is transitioning from the Unit to a relatively small school district often will need more specific training and possibly more extended attendance at the Unit prior to entering such a district program than would a child from a larger district with more options.

Within this context, 29% of children with autism exit our program against our recommendation. The types of placement that the children transition to are difficult to categorize precisely given the geographic variation. As a guide, approximately 15% enter typical classrooms in their home school district, 60% enter special education classrooms in their home school district, 22% enter center-based special classroom settings, and 3% enter residential placement.

Because language and development is our primary focus, we assessed language progress using a simple, crude scale to evaluate magnitude of change:

1 = nonverbal	5 = words
2 = vocalizations	6 = phrases
3 = gestures	7 = sentences
4 = signs	8 = conversational speech

Children receive scores based on the proportion of their language or communication attempts that fall into each of the eight categories. Figure 4.5 presents the pre- and posttreatment scale rankings for children in two different groups: those who made good to excellent progress and those with poor to fair progress. The bubbles on the graph represent the admission language development (dark color) and discharge language development (light color). Each child has two balloons oriented vertically along the x-axis. The location of the balloon on the y-axis indicates the lowest value obtained on the scale and the size represents the range of values obtained on the scale. For example, a small balloon, low on the y-axis indicates poor language development that is restricted to one or two scale items. Conversely, a large balloon higher on the y-axis indicates a higher minimum skill level, as well as language development across a number of scale items. When only one balloon is displayed, it indicates that pre- and posttreatment scores completely overlap so that one balloon is obscured. The two groups, as would be expected, show very different degrees of progress. However, the figure is illustrative of the significant degree of change obtained for many children with autism and the clear differences between the two groups.

Systematic Assessment Data

Each child's progress is tracked molecularly on a daily basis as described in the curriculum section of this chapter. Overall assessment is compiled into an annual report which provides the following data: the current classroom behavior management needs and the current instruction management

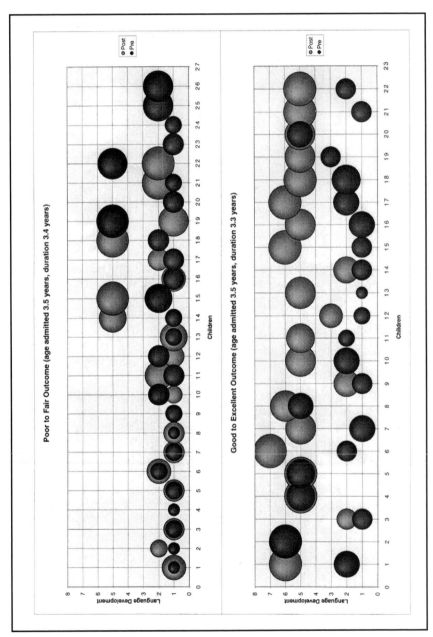

Figure 4.5. Comparison of language achievement by overall outcome evaluation.

requirements, as well as the child's current educational needs, including 10- or 12-month services and the current staff-to-child ratio that is appropriate for this child. Current standardized test results are reported, typically including scores from the *Peabody Picture Vocabulary Test–Revised* (Dunn & Dunn, 1981), the *Vineland Adaptive Behavior Scales–Classroom Edition* (Harrison, 1985), the *Slosson Intelligence Test* (Armstrong & Jensen, 1981), and additional tests that are appropriate for any individual child. A current overall grade level performance is assessed on reading, writing, and arithmetic readiness skills. Current status of classes of problem behavior and the typical antecedents of problem behaviors are reported, as is an assessment on the current level of communication development for each child.

A checklist indicating the degree of annual progress in the areas of the child's social and emotional development is completed, as is a summary of the child's characteristics of learning rate and pattern. Continuing assessment of the specific IGP goals targeted for a given child in an area is reflected in a table completed for each child, wherein each curriculum area is assessed for the factors that continue to limit progress in that area. Finally, an absolute ability level within the area is provided by comparing a child's current status to that of age-appropriate norms.

In addition to these types of assessments, a narrative description is included covering child progress; behavioral, social, and emotional development; and anticipated goals, objectives, concerns, and progress for the coming year. This section also includes a description of the level of parent involvement and the programs available to families.

In combination, these checklists, psychometric tests, behavioral observations, reports, and other information, such as rate of current progress, characteristics of learning rate and style, and current impediments to maintaining or accelerating progress, are compared annually to the intake level of functioning. The contrasts or similarities provide another means of assessing child progress, and assist in determining the appropriateness of the child's continuing in the program.

Future Effort

The knowledge base and practical experience acquired by the field of applied behavior analysis have resulted in an effective and replicable intervention for autism (Autism/Pervasive Developmental Disorders Guideline Panel, 1999; Romanczyk, Weiner, Ekdahl, & Lockshin, 1999). The outcomes are substantial and clinically significant. However, problems in service delivery remain a challenge. Perhaps one of the greatest impediments to progress is that the solid, proven methods of intervention are costly and require highly trained individuals. It is therefore difficult to maintain the public's attention and to assist parents to focus on effective intervention methods while there is a seemingly constant bombardment of "new breakthroughs" (often hyped by the media), which typically, with time, investigation, and reflection, are borne out to be simply a passing fad or gross misstatement of actual efficacy. It is easy to construct a long list of such cures and breakthroughs, and it is a sad commentary that the list will continue to grow (Romanczyk, 1994). This strikes to the heart of the issue confronting many parents: They are in great distress and there is a lack of consistent responses to their needs. Therefore, it is understandable that a parent would seek a "new" treatment, even if it is still unproven.

One weakness of many programs is how they are funded. Some operate on "soft" research money and thus must focus on relatively short-term and narrow issues; some rely heavily on parental help to seek continuing donations; and others, such as the Unit, are funded through the normal, but restrictive, state educational funding mechanisms and thus are limited in the range of services provided and the number of families served. For instance, although early intervention is extremely beneficial, funding for early detection programs is often minimal. Likewise, although parents of children with autism often undergo high levels of stress, it is difficult for a state-funded program in New York to acquire consistent funding to provide counseling, respite, and the broad range of services so important to the individuals experiencing chronic stress. Our data on parent participation and premature withdrawal from our program illustrate the difficulties encountered when attempting to provide services to families with diverse characteristics. Caution must be exercised in generalizing outcome reports that include highly motivated and cooperative families to the general population of families of children with autism. In this regard, our efforts continue to focus and emphasize the critical dimension of parental involvement. After several decades of intensive research efforts, we indeed possess most of the information and procedures necessary to significantly impact the lives of children with autism. Unfortunately, at this time of significant social and economic change, the willingness or ability to appropriately fund such programs that use effective interventions is the exception rather than the rule.

References

Achenbach, T. M. (1995) *Child Behavior Checklist for Ages 4–18*. Burlington: University of Vermont Department of Psychiatry.

American Psychiatric Association. (1994). *Diagnostic and statistical manual of mental disorders* (4th ed.). Washington, DC: Author.

Armstrong, R. J., & Jensen, J. A. (1981). *Slosson Intelligence Test for Children and Adults*. East Aurora, NY: Slosson Educational.

Autism/Pervasive Developmental Disorders Guideline Panel. (1999). *Clinical Practice Guideline: Autism / PDD, assessment and intervention in young children.* (Clinical Practice Guideline, No. 1). Albany: New York State Department of Health, Early Intervention Program.

Bayley, N. (1993). *Bayley Scales of Infant Development* (2nd ed.). San Antonio: Psychological Corp.

Carrow, E. (1973). *Screening Test for Auditory Comprehension of Language.* Boston: Teaching Resources Corp.

Dunn, L. M., & Dunn, L. M. (1981). *Peabody Picture Vocabulary Test–Revised.* Circle Pines, MN: American Guidance Service.

Estaban, S., Cochran, M., & Romanczyk, R. (1998). *Diagnostic and assessment instruments for autism: a review of recent journal publications.* Paper presented at the 24th Annual Convention of the Association for Behavior Analysis, Orlando, FL.

Harrison, P. L. (1985). *Vineland Adaptive Behavior Scales–Classroom Edition.* Circle Pines, MN: American Guidance Service.

Krug, D. A., Arick, J. R., & Almond, P. J. (1993). *Autism Screening Instrument for Educational Planning* (2nd ed.). Austin, TX: PRO-ED.

Lockshin, S. L. (1985). *Parent information series.* Unpublished manuscript.

Lockshin, S. L. (1998). *Parent information series.* Unpublished manuscript.

Lockshin, S., & Romanczyk, R. G. (1982). *The I.G.S. curriculum: Developing, implementing and evaluating a comprehensive individualized goal selection curriculum.* Paper presented at the Association of Behavior Analysis, Milwaukee, WI.

Mills, R. (1998). Least restrictive environment implementation policy paper. (Policy 98-02). Albany: New York State Education Department.

Romanczyk, R. G. (1984). A case study of microcomputer utilization and staff efficiency: A five year analysis. *Journal of Organizational Behavior Management, 6,* 141–154.

Romanczyk, R. G. (1986). *Clinical utilization of microcomputer technology.* New York: Pergamon Press.

Romanczyk, R. G. (1991). Monitoring and evaluating clinical service delivery: Issues of effectiveness of computer data base management. In A. Ager (Ed.), *Microcomputers in clinical psychology* (pp. 155–173). Wiley Press.

Romanczyk, R. G. (1994). Autism. In V. S. Ramachandran (Ed.), *The encyclopedia of human behavior* (Vol. 1, pp. 327–336). San Diego: Academic Press.

Romanczyk, R. G. (1996). Behavioral analysis and assessment: The cornerstone to effectiveness. In C. Maurice, S. Luce, & G. Green, (Eds.), *Behavioral intervention for young children with autism.* (pp. 115–217) Austin, TX: PRO-ED.

Romanczyk, R. G., Colletti, G., & Brutvan, L. (1982). *The data based staff meeting: Structure and procedures.* Paper presented at the Association of Behavior Analysis, Milwaukee, WI.

Romanczyk, R. G., & Lockshin, S. (1982). *The I.G.S. Curriculum.* Vestal, NY: CBTA.

Romanczyk, R. G., & Lockshin, S. (1984). Short term, intensive services: The deficit oriented, focused model. In W. Christian, G. Hannah, & T. Glahn (Eds.), *Programming effective human services* (pp. 433–456). NY: Plenum.

Romanczyk, R. G., Lockshin, S., & Matey, L. (1998). *The I.G.S. Curriculum–version 9.* Vestal, NY: CBTA.

Romanczyk, R. G., Matey, L., & Lockshin, S. B. (1994). The Children's Unit for Treatment and Evaluation. In S. L. Harris and J. S. Handleman (Eds.), *Preschool Education Programs for Children with Autism* (pp. 181–223). Austin, TX: PRO-ED.

Romanczyk, R. G., & Matthews, A. L. (1998). Physiological state as antecedent: Utilization in functional analysis. In J. K. Luiselli & M. J. Cameron (Eds.), *Antecedent control procedures for the behavioral support of persons with developmental disabilities* (pp. 115–138). Baltimore: Brookes.

Romanczyk, R. G., Weiner, T., Ekdahl, M., & Lockshin, S. B. (1999). Research in autism: Myths, controversies, and perspective. In D. Berkell (Ed.), *Autism: Identification, education, and treatment* (2nd ed.). Hillsdale, NJ: Erlbaum.

Schopler, E., Reichler, R. J., Devellis, R. F., & Daly, K. (1998). *The Childhood Autism Rating Scale*. Los Angeles: Western Psychological Services.

Slosson, R. L., Nicholson, C. L., & Hibpshman, T. L. (1990). *Slosson Intelligence Test* (Rev. ed.). East Aurora, NY: Slosson Educational Publications.

Sparrow, S. S., Balla, D. A., & Cicchetti, D. V. (1984). *Vineland Adaptive Behavior Scales*. Circle Pines, MN: American Guidance Service.

Taylor, J., Ekdahl, M., Romanczyk, R. G., & Miller, M. (1994). Escape behavior in task situations: Task versus social antecedents. *Journal of Autism and Developmental Disorders, 24*, 331–344.

Taylor, J., & Romanczyk, R. G. (1994). Generating hypotheses about the function of student problem behavior by observing teacher behavior. *Journal of Applied Behavior Analysis, 27*, 251–265.

Thorndike, R. L., Hagen, E. R., & Sattler, J. M. (1986). *The Stanford–Binet Intelligence Scale* (4th ed.). Chicago: Riverside.

Touchette, P. E., MacDonald, R. F., & Langer, S. N. (1985). A scatter plot for identifying stimulus control of problem behavior. *Journal of Applied Behavior Analysis, 18*, 343–351.

Wechsler, D. (1991). *Wechsler Intelligence Scale for Children–Third Edition*. San Antonio: Psychological Corp.

Williams. K. T. (1997). *Expressive Vocabulary Test*. Circle Pines, MN: American Guidance Service.

The Denver Model: A Comprehensive, Integrated Educational Approach to Young Children with Autism and Their Families

5

Sally J. Rogers, Terry Hall, Diane Osaki, Judy Reaven, and Jean Herbison

The Denver Model of preschool intervention for young children with autism began in 1981, with a 3-year grant from the U.S. Department of Education, Handicapped Children's Early Education programs, to establish a demonstration preschool classroom. The project was one of the programs of the JFK Partners, the Colorado University Affiliated Program for Developmental Disabilities at the University of Colorado Health Sciences Center (UCHSC). The Denver Model has been developed in three main phases. The first involved the first 4 years of federal funding to establish and implement the model, including materials, procedures, database, and replication; the 3 years of demonstration funding and 1 year of outreach, also funded by the Department of Education (Grant No. G008401921), constituted the first phase of model development.

The second phase began when federal funding ended and the program moved administratively into the department of psychiatry and its related hospital at UCHSC as a third-party reimbursed clinical program for preschoolers with autism or other disorders of development and behavior. Clinical services expanded as the program became better known and demands for services increased. From 1986 to 1998, the program provided two kinds of services: (1) center-based 4.5-hour daily preschool services for 12 to 18 children,

Program Information: The Denver Model, JFK Partners, University of Colorado Health Sciences Center, 4200 East 9th Avenue/C234, Denver, CO 80262; 303/315-6909.

Partial support for the first author in preparing this chapter was funded by Maternal and Child Health Bureau Grant No. 2T73MC00011-04, by the Administration on Developmental Disabilities Grant No. 90DD0414, and by National Institutes of Child Health and Human Development Grant No. PO1 HD35468-03. The original funding for the Denver Model was provided by the Office of Special Education and Rehabilitation Grant Nos. G008100247 and G008401921.

including both group and individual (one-to-one) interventions, and (2) clinical diagnosis–evaluation and educational recommendations for other children in the greater Denver area. During this period, outcome data were gathered and published and additional intervention approaches were added to the core model.

The third phase began in 1994, when the Denver Model staff began to provide ongoing educational consultation to local school districts involved in inclusive preschool services for young children with autism, and this activity increased over the next 3 years. By 1997, we were serving many more children through our diagnostic–evaluation activities and our community-based interventions than we were serving in our center-based preschool program. Health reimbursement systems were moving to managed care, and third-party payments were becoming far more difficult to obtain, with fewer and fewer children and families able to access the center-based model due to reimbursement restrictions for day hospital programs. At the same time, the educational philosophy in the state of Colorado, and of the Autism Society of America–Colorado Chapter, became strongly committed to inclusive education for all children with disabilities. In 1998, the decision was made to shift from the center-based preschool located on the UCHSC campus to a community-based model. Service delivery now centers on three activities: a diagnostic–evaluation clinic at JFK Partners, ongoing consultation contracts with school districts, and intensive community-based interventions with children and families enrolled in Denver Model services. The system of service delivery both for the center-based preschool program and for the current inclusive, community-based model are described below.

The university base for the Denver Model has had a profound influence on the development of the model over the past 18 years. The university emphasis on training of professionals and on the importance of linking clinical work with empirical research has fostered continuous model development, at both the theoretical level and the level of direct intervention. Even though there has been tremendous stability of the primary professionals involved in the development and delivery of the Denver Model over the 18 years of its existence, there has been continual development and refinement of treatment approaches over the years. Although some aspects of the model have remained unchanged (e.g., the emphasis on play, relationships, and communication), intervention approaches that are now core aspects of the model were not present during the early years (e.g., inclusive preschools and use of behavioral teaching techniques).

We are committed to continued model development as new interventions and approaches for young children with autism demonstrate their effectiveness. Our goal is not to reify a particular set of intervention practices developed 18 years ago, but rather to deliver the most effective services possible for each child and family, based on the most current knowledge available concerning autism, development, and treatment efficacy.

Theoretical Basis for the Denver Model Approach

The knowledge base, or conceptualization of autism, at the core of the Denver Model, is drawn from a developmental model of autism first articulated in a theoretical paper published in 1991 by Rogers and Pennington. In that paper, the authors suggested a developmental model for autism based on the model of interpersonal development provided by Daniel Stern in his 1985 book *The Interpersonal World of the Human Infant*. In Stern's interpersonal model of normal development, the first developmental phase is built on the very early capacities of the infant and caretaker to synchronize and coordinate movements, and on the infant's ability to distinguish change and novelty, and to perceive the caretaker as a separate person. These capacities give rise to experiences of emotionally based, interpersonal connectedness. These early motor patterns of synchrony, and the caretaker's ability to regulate emotional states of the very young infant, lead to the second developmental phase, that of emotional coordination and exchange. In this period, roughly from 3 to 8 months of age, the infant experiences myriad periods of coordination with the caretaker that occur in the medium of emotion, conveyed through movement patterns and facial and vocal expressions. The ability of the dyad to establish a dialogue built on coordination and synchrony of movements and emotions conveys to the infant the sense that people coordinate both as physical bodies and in the deeper, felt realm of emotional states. The third stage, that of intersubjectivity, allows this level of both bodily sharing and the sharing of inner states to move to a higher level, the conscious, intentional sharing of states of mind: goals, foci of attention, and intentional communication of emotion. The joint attention behaviors, social referencing, and intentionally shared emotion develop in this stage and demonstrate the infant's awareness of self and other as separate people with their own inner states that are sharable through movements, facial expressions, and vocalizations. This awareness allows the infant to map meaning onto words and gestures, and the co-occurrence of intersubjective awareness, symbolic capacity, and motor skill (including oral–motor skill) allows human infants to move into the fourth stage, that of rapidly expanding symbolic communication including language development.

In the developmental model of autism suggested by Rogers and Pennington (1991), and further elaborated by Rogers, Bennetto, McEvoy, and Pennington (1996) and Rogers (1999), a hypothesized deficit in imitation ability, perhaps due to an underlying impairment in praxis, or the capacity for planned, skilled movements and movement sequences, may prevent the earliest establishment of bodily synchrony and coordination that begins the interpersonal cascade. This hypothesis is based on the many empirical studies documenting imitation deficits in autism (Charman et al., 1997; DeMeyer, 1972; Sigman &

Ungerer, 1984; Stone, Ousley, & Littleford, 1997). For children with autism, arriving at the next stage of development, that of emotional coordination and communication, is also hypothesized to be impaired by core deficits in feeling other people's emotions (emotional contagion and empathy), as well as by atypical expressions of emotion that prevent the parent from easily mirroring back affective states. All of these emotional deficits in autism have been well documented in empirical studies of both children and adults with autism (Baron-Cohen, 1991; Carter et al., 1998; Charman et al., 1997; Hobson, 1986; Hobson, Ouston, & Lee, 1988; Loveland et al., 1997; Loveland et al., 1994; Yirmiya, Kasari, Sigman, & Mundy, 1989). Thus, the second main building block toward intersubjectivity—that of the establishment of emotional communication (the ability to connect with another person's inner experiences)—is also impaired in the child with autism. Without these two capacities, the young child with autism does not have the raw material for developing intersubjectivity. The joint attention behaviors do not develop because the child with autism is unaware that people have inner lives that can be communicated and shared through movements and sounds. Until this awareness develops, the young child with autism cannot move into intentional communication, and thus lacks communicative gestures, joint attention behavior, and emotional signaling.

Thus far, the hypotheses are built on established empirical findings, although for the most part involving older children with autism. The rest of the developmental model of autism to be described here is built on hypotheses that are currently being tested in empirical studies. The child with autism may have a fairly intact symbolic capacity, depending on his or her cognitive abilities. This is seen in young children with autism who learn symbols, such as letters, numbers, colors, names of movie characters, and other objects of intense importance to them. If the child with autism has fairly good oral–motor praxis skills, he or she may develop speech; however, without a knowledge of intersubjective communication, speech becomes a symbol system associated with objects in the world, rather than for sharing information about self and others. Thus, the early spoken vocabulary consists of echoed language; of video scripts; of letters, Disney characters, numbers, shapes, and so forth—names of favored concrete objects learned through repetition. If the child has more severe oral–motor dyspraxia, speech may not develop at all. For the speaking child, experiences with speech and association learning (and, most important, good intervention) eventually help the child understand the power of speech to communicate with others. As the child's awareness of others grows, joint attention behaviors develop and speech becomes more communicative. If the child is nonspeaking, awareness of intentional communication between people may never develop, and intense intervention focused both on (a) interpersonal coordination and the development of shared meaning and (b) development of oral–motor capacity to imitate speech is needed to help the child learn to communicate and become verbal.

Much of the symptom presentation in early autism involves negative symptoms, specifically the absence of developmentally crucial behaviors: imitation, symbolic play, emotion sharing, and joint attention. We understand the positive symptoms in autism—repetitive behaviors and unusual ways of handling toys and objects—in several ways. First, we see repetitive, perseverative behavior as reflecting central nervous system impairment that is nonspecific to autism. Second, we see the growing focus on objects and actions on objects as "filling in the void." Whereas for most young children, the vast majority of their waking hours are spent in social engagement and interaction with others (parents, siblings, and peers), the child with autism is outside the social loop. However, that child still needs ongoing activity, sensory experience and stimulation, and so fills his or her time with activities that are stimulating and understandable—the world of sensory experiences with objects and actions on them and relations among them. The young child with autism is busy and occupied, but in a state of "social deprivation" outside of the world of social interaction and meaningful language. Thus, in addition to primary central nervous system (CNS) deficits in autism, secondary isolation and increasing deprivation of typical social learning experiences arise. Month by month the child with autism falls farther and farther behind because he or she does not have access to the ongoing, ever-present language and social learning environment in which typical infants, toddlers, and young children are immersed for all their waking hours.

From this conceptualization of early autism come the main foci of treatment: (a) bringing the child into coordinated, interactive social relations for most of his or her waking hours, so that imitation and both symbolic and interpersonal (nonverbal, affective, pragmatic) communication can be established and the transmission of social knowledge and social experience can occur, and (b) intensive teaching to "fill in" the learning deficits that have resulted from the child's past lack of access to the social world, due to the effects of autism. The main tools for accomplishing these two major treatment goals include teaching imitation, developing awareness of social interactions and reciprocity, teaching the power of communication, teaching a symbolic communication system, and making the social world as understandable as the world of objects, so that the child with autism comes into the rich learning environment of social exchange. Just as the typically developing toddler and preschooler spend virtually all their waking hours engaged in the social milieu and learning from it, the young child with autism needs to be drawn back into the social milieu—a carefully prepared and planned milieu that the child can understand, predict, and participate in—and this requires planning for most of the child's waking hours as well, across all caretaking environments.

In summary, the main practices of the Denver Model reflect a dynamic systems (Newtson, 1993) approach to autism: that the symptoms and life course for a child with autism flow not only from the original neurobiological impairment(s), but also from the changed environment that the young child with autism develops within, changed by the child's behavior, by the ongoing symptom and behavioral changes occurring over time, and by the ongoing adaptation of those around the child to his or her behavior. In the Denver Model of treatment, we seek to provide alternative, intensified learning opportunities fitted to the learning profile of young children with autism and to alter the social experiences of the child to prevent or ameliorate the secondary, experiential deficits which have cascading negative effects and result in increased delays year by year. This conceptualization assumes some plasticity in the development of young children with autism and the capacity for greatly improved rates of learning. We do not consider mental retardation to be a core deficit in most children with autism. Rather, the IQ deficits are seen to reflect, *at least in part,* the lack of access to social information by the child with autism and the ever-intensifying effects of this deprivation over time.

Description of the Denver Model

Our approach to young children with autism is based on a knowledge base, described above; a set of beliefs; and a set of practices.

Beliefs at the Core of the Denver Model

The main beliefs that guide our intervention can be summarized as follows:

- Families should be at the helm of their children's treatment.
- Because each child with autism and his or her family is unique, goals, interventions, and approaches must be individualized.
- Children with autism can be successful learners. Lack of progress generally signals problems with the design and implementation of the educational activity, rather than the inability of the child to learn.
- Because autism is at its core a social disorder, treatment for autism must focus on the social disability. This requires that relationships be at the core of treatment of children with autism and their families.
- Children are members of families and communities and need to have a role in family life and family and community activities.
- Children with autism have minds, opinions, preferences, choices, and feelings; they have a right to self-expression and some control of their world.
- Autism is a complex disorder affecting virtually all areas of functioning; interdisciplinary professional guidance is needed to address the wide range of challenges that autism presents.

- Children with autism are capable of becoming intentional, symbolic communicators, and the majority of children with autism can develop useful, communicative speech when provided with appropriate interventions of sufficient intensity during the preschool years.

- Various intervention approaches for children with autism have demonstrated their effectiveness using various instructional methodologies; a comprehensive, contemporary treatment approach must be able to draw from all the expertise available in the field.

- Play is one of the young child's most powerful cognitive and social learning tools. Building play skills in young children with autism will maximize their capacity for independent learning.

- Successful intervention for young children with autism requires that most of their waking hours be spent in socially oriented activities. Providing more than 20 hours per week of structured intervention is necessary for optimum progress.

Practices that Constitute the Denver Model Intervention

Population Served

The Denver Model was developed to serve children during the preschool years. The curriculum and teaching practices are targeted for children ages 2 through 5 with autism spectrum disorders. Although this is the target population, we also have had the opportunity to serve a number of young children over the years who have other kinds of developmental and behavioral disorders. We have found that this approach also benefited those children greatly, as reported by Rogers and DiLalla (1991). Since the inception of the Denver Model, more than 100 young children have received ongoing services through the center-based preschool, and many more have received services through our diagnostic–evaluation clinic and school consultation activities.

Screening and Assessment Procedures

Careful developmental assessment is crucial to the Denver Model, since each child's curriculum is individualized and based on his or her current developmental strengths and needs. Assessment is carried out in two ways: the annual or biennial standardized assessment, and a quarterly curricular assessment to determine progress on objectives. Diagnostic assessment occurs when children enter Denver Model intervention, at which time they receive an interdisciplinary evaluation to establish diagnosis and current performance levels on standardized developmental measures. Development is assessed in eight areas: communication (receptive, expressive, and pragmatics), visual–perceptual cognition and concepts, fine motor, gross motor, sensory functioning, activities of daily living, play, and social interactions–skills. Diagnoses are formulated based on the *Diagnostic and Statistical Manual of Mental Disorders–Fourth Edition* (American Psychiatric Association, 1994), and family needs are assessed. Disciplinary assessment tools for communication, psychological assessment, and motor assessment that have been found most useful for young children with autism are described in the following text.

Standardized Assessment

COMMUNICATION ASSESSMENT. The purpose of a comprehensive communication assessment is to determine developmental levels in all communication domains in order to target intervention objectives and strategies. The main areas of assessment include receptive and expressive language, pragmatics, auditory processing, and oral–motor speech and feeding skills. Because impairments in speech, language, and communication affect the social use of language (i.e., pragmatics) in children with autism, a combination of formal and informal measures of assessment is essential in order to determine a child's communication profile and to identify treatment needs and recommendations. In addition to the information obtained from a caregiver interview focusing on the child's communicative behaviors and language skills, the following are some suggested formal assessment tools.

Receptive language tools include the *Peabody Picture Vocabulary Test–Third Edition* (L. M. Dunn, & Dunn, 1997), which measures single-word receptive vocabulary skills; the *Preschool Language Scale–Third Edition* (Zimmerman, Steiner, & Pond, 1992); the *Clinical Evaluation of Language Fundamentals–Preschool* (receptive and expressive scales) (CELF–P; Wiig, Secord, & Semel, 1992); and, for older children, the *Test of Language Development–Primary: Third Edition* (receptive and expressive scales) (TOLD–P:3; Newcomer & Hammill, 1997) and the *Oral and Written Language Scales* (receptive and expressive scales) (OWLS; Carrow-Woolfolk, 1996). This list is by no means conclusive, but can provide a fairly good measure of a child's comprehension of language.

Useful expressive language tools include the *Expressive One Word Picture Vocabulary Test–Revised* (Gardner, 1990) and the *Expressive Vocabulary Test* (Williams, 1997). Both tests evaluate single-word expressive vocabulary skills, as well as provide some preliminary means of testing word finding difficulty. The CELF–P, TOLD–P:3, and OWLS also contain expressive language scales, as does the *Mullen Scales of Early Learning* (Mullen, 1989).

Other expressive communication areas to informally evaluate include voice quality, fluency, and articulation skills. Articulation skills may be evaluated effectively by the *Goldman–Fristoe Test of Articulation* (Goldman & Fristoe,

1986), along with the *Kahn–Lewis Phonological Analysis* (Kahn & Lewis, 1986) to assess phonological patterns of sound production. Informal language and communication samples also provide further expressive language information. For some children with autism, executing oral–motor movements necessary to sequence sound combinations poses a major obstacle in speech and language acquisition. Thus, it may be necessary to evaluate oral–motor praxis skills. The *Test of Auditory–Perceptual Skills* (Gardner, 1985) or *The Token Test for Children* (DiSimoni, 1990) may be used to assess auditory processing and auditory memory skills.

For younger children, an assessment of pragmatic (social communication) skills should assess what a child intends to communicate and how that child actually communicates in a functional, successful manner. Young children with autism are impaired in communicative functions (Wetherby & Prutting, 1984), including ability to regulate another's behavior, to engage in and initiate social interactions with others, and to reference joint attention.

PSYCHOLOGICAL ASSESSMENT. There are several components to the psychological assessment of young children with autism: a comprehensive parent interview, cognitive or developmental assessment, adaptive behavior assessment, and structured play interaction. A typical parent interview gathers information about medical and developmental history, presenting problems and concerns, social and family history, and a review of interventions and current therapies. The *Autism Diagnostic Interview–Revised* (ADI–R; Lord, Rutter, & LeCouteur, 1994) is used by staff, faculty, and trainees who have been trained in the administration of the ADI–R.

The *Mullen Scales of Early Learning* (Mullen, 1989) is the standardized test used most frequently to assess the developmental functioning of young children, because of its separate verbal and nonverbal subdomains. Additional tools are also used to obtain information regarding cognitive abilities, including the *Leiter International Performance Scale–Revised* (Roid & Miller, 1997), the *Stanford–Binet Intelligence Scale: Fourth Edition* (Thorndike, Hagen, & Sattler, 1986), and the *Bayley Scales of Infant Development–Second Edition* (Bayley, 1993).

Adaptive behavior is assessed with one of the two following measures: *Scales of Independent Behavior–Revised* (Bruininks, Woodcock, Weatherman, & Hill, 1996) and *Vineland Adaptive Behavior Scales* (Sparrow, Balla, & Cicchetti, 1984).

Assessments of children's play and social interactions are used for several purposes. The level of play development is important for planning interventions, since development of increasingly sophisticated play, including symbolic play, is an important intervention goal in the Denver Model. Assessing social interaction skills in situations involving low levels of adult structure is similarly important for planning social interventions and targeting social skills to teach. It also allows for assessment of parent–child interaction skills and helps target the parents' own goals for increasing social interactions and fostering development with their children at home. Finally, autism-specific diagnostic instruments are administered during a semistructured play assessment. *The Childhood Autism Rating Scale* (Schopler, Reichler, & Renner, 1988) and the *Autism Diagnostic Observation Schedule–Generic* (Lord, Rutter, & DiLavore, 1998) are used by staff, faculty, and trainees who have been trained in the administration of these semistructured play interviews.

MOTOR ASSESSMENT. Because child functioning and performance is always expressed through the motor system, integrity of the motor system underlies all performance. Thus, assessment of the motor system is a necessary part of comprehensive assessment and intervention. The purpose of the motor assessment, carried out by an occupational therapist, is to identify the individual's abilities and limitations and then develop intervention objectives in two areas: adaptive behavior and motor performance. The following adaptive areas of performance are assessed and targeted for interventions: daily living skills, involvement in the tasks of family life, and independent play–leisure skills. Motor performance components evaluated include sensory integration, neuromuscular function, gross motor coordination, fine motor coordination–dexterity, visual–motor integration, and oral–motor control.

Both clinical and standardized motor assessment techniques are used. Clinical assessment includes gathering qualitative and quantitative data about the child's performance as he or she performs a series of tests that evaluate neuromuscular function. A sensory interview is also given to help evaluate sensory processing. Standardized assessments include the three motor scales of the *Mullen* (1989), the *Bruininks–Oseretsky Test of Motor Proficiency* (Bruininks, 1978), the *Peabody Developmental Motor Scales* (Folio & Fewell, 1983), and the *Miller Assessment for Preschoolers* (Miller, 1988). Other instruments used include *The Sensory Profile* (W. Dunn, 1991).

EDUCATIONAL ASSESSMENT. Early childhood special education professionals use detailed, criterion-referenced curricular tools to establish the child's current skill repertoire and the next developmental steps. Quarterly objectives are developed from these data in conjunction with information from informal classroom observations, parent concerns, and input from the rest of the multidisciplinary team members. This curricular assessment is carried out every 6 months for the center-based preschool and every quarter for the current community-based model. Tools for planning quarterly classroom objectives include the *Early Intervention Developmental Profile* (Rogers et al., 1979) and the *Preschool Developmental Profile* (Brown et al., 1981). The *Psychoeducational Profile–Revised* (Schopler, Reichler, Bashford, Lansing, & Marcus, 1990) is also used. Currently, a specific curricular tool, the Denver Model Curriculum (Osaki, Rogers, & Hall, 1997), is being developed and is replacing these other tools. Data from the overall assessment are used to formulate quarterly comprehensive educational objectives form the core of the child's interventions across all settings and people.

Quarterly Curricular Assessments. Quarterly curricular assessments examine the child's mastery of his or her quarterly objectives. A set of quarterly objectives, covering all seven areas assessed—communication (receptive, expressive, and pragmatics), visual–perceptual cognition and concepts, fine and gross motor, activities of daily living, play, and social interactions–skills—is written for each child, to be mastered in the following 12 weeks. At the end of the quarter, the child's performance on his or her individualized objectives is assessed, and a new set of objectives is established for the next 12 weeks. Curricular tools are used as needed to build the child's curriculum for each 12-week period. Data from the diagnostic assessments are used to guide the overall program as well.

Teaching and Administrative Staff

The Treatment Team. The Denver Model is an interdisciplinary model in which early childhood special education, child psychology, speech–language pathology, and occupational therapy are core disciplines for every child. The program has been directed by Sally J. Rogers since its inception. In both the center-based and the community-based delivery systems, a treatment team is responsible for an individual child's intervention plan and implementation. The treatment team is headed by the parents and one professional from the core disciplines who becomes the coordinator of a child's care. After the child has received an interdisciplinary assessment, the coordinator develops the child's quarterly objectives, teaching activities and programs, and data collection systems, and sets these up in a curricular notebook. The coordinator works directly with the family, the child, and the home and classroom staff to implement the objectives; provides whatever training is needed (home teaching assistants, inservices in community preschools, classroom assistants in community preschools); and monitors the child's progress through biweekly or monthly team meetings or "clinics" with all intervention providers. The clinic model was modeled from the UCLA Young Autism Project (Smith, Donahoe, & Davis, Chapter 3 in this volume). The coordinator observes and fine-tunes the intervention and reviews data at the clinic or team meetings, helps problem-solve, and ensures that the intervention is proceeding appropriately and the child is progressing as rapidly as possible.

Other team members support the head of a team with their disciplinary expertise. These professionals have varying roles on a child's team. They may act as consultants, therapists, or evaluators. Their roles may well change over time, as the child's needs change. They help the team leader update treatment objectives and plan and evaluate the course of treatment. In the Denver Model, the head of the team functions as a generalist, attending to all aspects of the child's development, seeking disciplinary help as needed, but carrying responsibility for the child's treatment and progress and orchestrating the various aspects of the child's treatment. Parents and the head of the team share responsibilities for all aspects of the team functioning.

Staff Training. In our center-based preschool, the head teacher trained all new staff members, and a series of inservice meetings were provided by each of the professional staff each year in each aspect of the model. Main coordinators observed ongoing treatment and fine-tuned with the head teacher as needed. The entire intervention team—teacher, assistants, speech therapist, occupational therapist, and psychology staff met for brief weekly staff progress meetings, at which the child's progress was reviewed, new plans were put into place, and any problems were reviewed. The team also held biweekly clinics in which the child worked with various staff members and child progress was assessed.

In the community-based model, the training approach is modeled after the UCLA Young Autism Project (Smith et al., Chapter 3 in this volume). Parents, home teaching assistants, and school staff are trained in teaching techniques and in delivery of the quarterly objectives by the main coordinator, who combines didactic teaching, role playing, and actual work with the child, by modeling and by practice and correction of the trainees. The training team is observed at regular intervals by the main coordinator, who meets with the whole team every 2 to 4 weeks for a 1½- to 2-hour clinic. In the clinic, each person takes a turn teaching the child, and the main coordinator provides feedback and training to refine the teaching skills of each team member, as well as the delivery of the curriculum. Teaching skills checklists are used to assess skill levels of the one-to-one teaching team. In community preschools, the main coordinator provides ongoing consultation to the teaching team, including inservice training and ongoing consultation (every 2 to 4 weeks). Through ongoing contacts, various aspects of the Denver Model are incorporated into the established classroom routine (see Appendix 5.B for the Denver Model Classroom Checklist). The objectives to be focused on in the class are developed mutually by the parents, the classroom staff, and the consultant, and the consultant provides ongoing help to the team on curriculum delivery, specialized teaching techniques, data collection, and updating of objectives.

Treatment Settings

The Center-Based Model. The core components of the Denver Model were built from the original center-based model, called The Playschool, a day treatment program that operated from 1981 to 1998 4.5 hours per day, 5 days per week (for the first two years, there was one morning and one afternoon 3-hour class).

There were six children per classroom, staffed by an early childhood special education teacher and two paraprofessionals. Each classroom was designed for children with autism. A strong interdisciplinary model prevailed, with each child's team consisting of a psychologist, speech–language therapist, and occupational therapist. Weekly team meetings were an important part of the child's treatment and were used to discuss progress, make changes, and add programs. The child's individualized program began from a careful assessment of his or her strengths and needs across developmental areas, from which annual goals and short-term objectives were written with specific teaching plans in place. Ongoing review in staff meetings and clinics was done weekly or biweekly to ensure progress.

Each classroom had daily classroom lesson plans with each child's individualized goals and objectives carefully woven into the planned activities. Transitions from one activity to the next were carefully orchestrated with specific plans to facilitate smooth transitions. Highly structured, routine-oriented small groups were used to teach and facilitate social interaction, group participation, and speech–language, and to practice and generalize specific developmental skills.

Speech–language and occupational therapy services were provided dependent on the child's individual needs. Although the original model sought to deliver all such services in the classroom milieu, after 2 years it became clear that many of the children made faster progress by receiving individual, one-to-one intervention in addition to ongoing classroom interventions. Daily one-to-one teaching sessions with the classroom teaching staff were added to the preschool day, as well as twice weekly one-to-one speech–language therapy and occupational therapy for those children who needed it. Most children received individual twice weekly therapy from both disciplines, as well as ongoing consultation to the team, parents, and child, whereas others may have received individual weekly therapy.

The Inclusive, Community-Based Model. Currently, interventions through the Denver Model involve three teaching settings: teaching within daily family routines, daily inclusive group preschool instruction, and one-to-one teaching. The amount of instruction delivered in each setting depends on the child's learning needs and learning style. Children with autism appear to need a significant number of hours per week of structured teaching in order to progress well. Instructional objectives are systematically taught in each setting. The empirical literature and our own experiences have convinced us that children need to receive more than 20 hours per week of planned, systematic instruction focused on a concrete set of short-term objectives. Children with autism need high levels of structure, organization, and predictability in their teaching environments. Adding these elements to teaching settings helps to reduce the difficulties that many children with autism have in organization, attention, task completion, and managing transitions and change.

Delivery of Teaching Within Settings

Teaching Within Family Routines. Each individual family determines how a child's current treatment objectives will be incorporated into family routines. Activities like meals, bathing, playtime, chores, and family outings are core learning experiences; children with autism need to become active members with valued roles in their families' routines.

Teaching Within Inclusive Preschool Settings. Inclusive group preschools provide important learning situations that cannot be duplicated elsewhere. Young children with typical development have social abilities that can scaffold interactions involving peers with autism. Daily preschool is a crucial part of children's treatment once they are 3 years old. However, children with autism need very carefully orchestrated teaching experiences and routines in order to benefit from group preschool and to be able to generalize what they have learned at home and through direct instruction. Careful planning and coordination across all treatment givers and family members is necessary to realize the benefits of preschool. Progress in preschool is reflected through systematic implementation of short-term objectives and ongoing evaluation through performance data.

Intensive One-to-One Teaching. Children with autism generally progress more rapidly when they receive carefully designed, regular, one-to-one teaching from adults. The kind of individual treatment may vary widely for different children or for the same child at different points in development. Several hours daily of intensive, highly structured, one-to-one instruction is necessary for some children to develop to their fullest capacity. For children whose development is less severely affected, however, the use of other kinds of teaching settings may be the best supplement to daily preschool: speech–language therapy, regular play groups with typical peers, music, dance, art, gym, or science classes for preschoolers. By embedding carefully designed learning objectives and direct instruction into these typical activities, such normalized community-based group activities become additional focused sources of intervention for the child with autism. Some children can learn effectively in carefully structured small group situations but need individual instruction for motor problems, speech dyspraxia, or play development. Although the type and amount of individual teaching will vary from child to child and for the same child at different developmental points, the intervention goal is to fill the day for each young child with autism with carefully planned and delivered interventions that promote social and communicative development and address the individualized needs of each child.

Main Aspects of the Intervention Approach

Design and Implementation of the Intervention Plan. The intervention plan and curriculum for each child with autism need to be individually constructed.

Children receiving Denver Model treatment have quarterly objectives that are very specific; cover all affected areas of development, including play, social relationships, and family routines; and drive the child's treatment across all settings. The team leader and the parents formulate this plan, with input from the interdisciplinary team that supports the child's care. Quarterly objectives are written, and teaching plans and activities are developed for each of the teaching settings. This constitutes the child's curriculum. The child's curriculum is packaged in a notebook that contains goals and objectives, instructional plans and activities, and data collection systems. Various objectives and teaching activities are assigned to each treatment setting (i.e., preschool class, intensive teaching, home teaching). The curriculum is then implemented across settings and monitored frequently, with progress data gathered and analyzed throughout the teaching quarter. Progress is reviewed at biweekly clinics or team meetings and adjustments made as needed to assure progress. The objectives and teaching plan drive all of the child's instruction in all of the settings, allowing for maximum generalization and practice. Some key skills that children with autism particularly need to master have been outlined and appear as *The Denver Model Curriculum* (Osaki et al., 1997); it is considered a guideline, not a comprehensive curriculum.

Emphasis on Relationships, Shared Control, and Positive Emotion. Children learn from people with whom they have positive emotional relationships. Autism particularly affects children's ability to engage in social relationships. In the Denver Model, teaching is embedded in positive social relationships between adults and children with autism. Fostering warm, affectionate, playful relationships is part of day-to-day, moment-to-moment treatment. Development and maintenance of positive affect during teaching is a core part of the model. Although it may seem as if playful interactions would naturally occur in a preschool classroom, these must be a focus of attention when the classroom involves young children with autism. First, the core deficits in social initiation result in a lack of bids from the child for the teacher's attention. Second, because children with autism tend to become engaged in materials rather than in the social milieu, opportunities to facilitate the child's active participation in the interaction may be missed without conscious planning. The child's emotional state, including his or her affect, attention, and arousal, are monitored continuously, and the adult uses specific techniques to optimize the child's affect, attention, and availability for learning. Sensory–social routines are primary regulators of affect, attention, and arousal, and given the social reciprocity embedded in them, sensory–social routines maintain the child and adult "in relationship" throughout the teaching periods.

In satisfying dyadic relationships, partners share control of interactions. One exerts control in a relationship through a variety of communicative means. Opportunities to exert control are opportunities to communicate. In the Denver Model, children learn to exert control in interactions by making choices, by requesting that activities be finished, through turn taking in songs, and by participating in other joint activity routines. Therapists monitor the active–passive balance of their interactions with children, to assure that children have the opportunities to initiate interactions and activities throughout their teaching sessions. Teaching activities that place the child in a relatively more passive learner stance alternate with sensory–social or other social activities in which the child takes a more active role in directing the interaction.

Content Areas. Seven content areas are addressed in each child's individualized curriculum: communication, social interactions, play skills, fine and gross motor development, cognition, and personal independence and participation in family life routines. A developmental orientation dominates the initial approach to choosing appropriate objectives and learning activities. However, because children are in inclusive settings, they need to have the skills that their age-mates have to gain the most from peer encounters. Thus, chronologically important skills are also stressed, and task analysis is used to break down skills into small, easily mastered components, with shaping and chaining used to develop complex skill sequences. Using chronologically appropriate materials is stressed. Teaching techniques vary with the individual child. Structured teaching, modeling, observational learning from peers, learning through play and manipulation—all the processes through which young children learn—are used in the Denver Model, with interventionists selecting from whatever teaching techniques are most effective for the individual child at his or her current developmental level and optimum learning style. Children with autism vary widely in their learning styles, rates, and characteristics. Denver Model interventionists must be quite familiar with a very wide range of intervention techniques, ranging across theoretical orientations and educational practices, in order to maximize the learning rate and repertoire of each child.

COMMUNICATION. Communication and imitation are the means by which people carry out social relationships and pass on their culture and accumulated social knowledge to the next generation (Bruner, 1972, 1975; Tomasello, Kruger, & Ratner, 1993). Nothing is more important for a young child with autism than the development of intentional, spontaneous communication. All children need a useful communication system, and this need dominates the treatment. The Denver Model uses a multifaceted approach to development of communication that includes four separate teaching strands, each with its own sequential curriculum, that begins in the first treatment session and permeates all of the child's treatment.

1. *Teaching the child to use nonverbal intentional communicative gestures.* We develop the foundations of nonverbal communication through elicitation and shaping, first of natural gestures ("talking bodies"), then of conventional gestures, to serve a variety of communicative functions. These are

taught in natural communicative situations built from the child's existing communicative and behavioral repertoire and built on the child's own preferences and desires.

2. *Teaching motor imitation.* Children are taught to imitate an adult's movements. Motor imitation begins with a variety of actions on objects, then proceeds to imitation of a variety of body movements. Next, for nonverbal children, we teach imitation of a variety of oral–facial movements, and, when those are learned, vocal and speech sounds. Although communicative speech depends on many abilities in addition to imitation, one cannot learn to speak if one cannot imitate other people's speech. We conceptualize the difficulties with imitation as at least partially due to dyspraxia, and we understand imitation training as a direct intervention for dyspraxia. Once children can imitate speech sounds and consonant–vowel combinations, (a) the child's speech approximations are paired with the child's nonverbal intentional communicative acts (gestures, pictures, etc.) in all communicative exchanges, beginning with a very limited vocabulary and slowly expanding it as children learn to use speech meaningfully and spontaneously, and (b) imitation of speech shifts entirely to natural communicative situations in order to help children understand speech as a means to an end, rather than understanding speech as an imitative act.

3. *Teaching the meaning and importance of speech.* Young children with autism are taught to respond to simple verbal instructions from the very first session. Direct teaching of motor responses to spoken directions assists children with auditory discrimination of speech sounds and association of speech sounds with meaning. Receptive language is taught at increasingly complex levels as children master earlier levels. For the few children who have great difficulty learning to discriminate speech, additional supports, such as print, pictures, or manual signs, are used initially to accompany adult speech. These supports are withdrawn as the child demonstrates increasing capacity to discriminate speech sounds but may be used initially to teach each receptive skill.

4. *Teaching symbolic representations.* Children with autism may not understand that one object can be used to represent another, as in a picture communication system. In the cognitive curriculum, children are taught various relationships among objects and object representations through matching and sorting activities on a large number of dimensions. They are taught that objects and characteristics of objects (color, size, texture, categories, etc.) can be represented through pictures, visual symbols, written words, manual signs, and so on. Many characteristics of people can also be taught in this way, and these programs involve social stimuli as well.

Thus, manual and visual systems are used to provide a first communication system, for nonspeaking children, to support and assist children's learning of the meaning of speech, and to provide an effective nonverbal communication system. A combination of communication systems encourages the children to be more flexible, successful communicators. One such visual system is *The Picture Exchange Communication System* (PECS; Bondy & Frost, 1994), which has proven to be an effective means of supporting a child's current expressive communication skills, as well as to encourage the verbal production of a larger number of words to comment, request, or respond. The PECS has also been an effective means of increasing a child's ability to initiate appropriate social interactions with others.

PLAY. The Denver Model began with a focus on developing play skills. Play of all kinds—social, physical, constructive, symbolic, and independent—is built into the child's curriculum because of the crucial role it plays in normal development. Children with autism cannot benefit maximally from interactions with other children if they cannot engage in the core social and learning play activities that preschoolers use. Age-appropriate play skills are directly taught in individual teaching and directly guided in inclusive preschool experiences. Besides the inherent developmental value of play skills, the ability to engage in age-appropriate play helps the child with autism fit in to the group and reduces the risk of social isolation.

SENSORY ACTIVITIES. In the Denver Model, the child's sensory system is viewed as a crucial regulator of affect, attention, and arousal. Sensory activities are primary means to optimize attention and positive affect in order to facilitate learning. Sensory-based activities are included through (a) sensory–social dyadic routines and (b) planned group sensory activities. *Sensory–social routines* are dyadic interactions involving simple, repeated social routines that engage the child at both sensory and affective levels. Sensory–social routines engage the child as an active, communicating participant, who initiates, maintains, and responds to the ritualized interaction. Sensory–social routines alternate with structured teaching activities in one-to-one teaching sessions to maintain positive relationships and to maintain optimum levels of arousal and attention for learning. In addition, these pleasurable activities provide a break for the child from the demands of more taxing learning tasks. *Planned group sensory activities* occur several times throughout the preschool classroom day: during periods of messy art, water table activities, and playground time, during which children participate in movement activities (swinging), aerobic activity (walking, jogging, bike riding), and "heavy" work (pulling and pushing loaded wagons and wheelbarrows for proprioceptive input). While these activities are delivered to the group, each child's participation and response is individually planned in line with his or her sensory profile.

PERSONAL INDEPENDENCE AND PARTICIPATION IN FAMILY ROUTINES. In the Denver Model, child independence is highly valued. Skill development in the area of personal independence and participation in family routines is developed by carrying out routines of daily living, independent play, and independent, goal-directed tasks and chores that contribute to family life. This is often a potential area of strength for persons with autism, and developing these skills as fully as possible allows persons with autism to demonstrate their competence. Visual strategies are used as needed to scaffold these activities and maximize independent functioning. These objectives are primary targets for structured interventions carried out in home routines, but they are actively taught in all three treatment settings.

SOCIAL SKILLS. The ability to initiate, maintain, and appropriately terminate social interactions and to engage in a wide range of social activities is crucial for the interpersonal and communicative development of young children with autism. Social skills to be taught are specified in quarterly objectives and woven into all three teaching settings. Social skills are taught through naturalistic procedures, carefully embedded in natural social exchanges like sensory– social activities, group activities with family and at preschool, and dyadic interactions that occur in all settings.

The entire communication curriculum is by nature a social curriculum as well. Other main teaching areas also tap core social behaviors: imitation skills, play skills, and participation in family routines. Across teaching settings, specific activities that will support social development are set up. Mealtime is a good example. Both at preschool and at home, mealtimes occur in groups and certain social behaviors are targeted: requesting desired foods with eye contact and symbolic communication, passing objects to others when they request, capturing adult attention and eye contact in order to make a request, and handing out napkins and other items to each person at the table.

Inclusive preschool provides several activity periods that lend themselves to dyadic interactions. Sensory activities like water table hold a group of children closely together, providing maximum opportunity to imitate peers. Adults' careful manipulation of the objects in the water creates a strong motivation for the child with autism to request, share, and pass objects, and to watch others. Careful adult prompts and teaching strategies can support skill learning without taking the child's attention away from his or her peers.

Similarly, children with autism who have learned (through one-to-one instruction if needed) to imitate actions on objects and sequences of actions, like making simple art projects, have the core skills needed to follow a peer's lead. Seating the child with autism across from a friendly, familiar peer and encouraging that peer to show the child with autism how to do the project allows for peer modeling to occur with minor "invisible" prompts (e.g., adults behind children, not interrupting their attention to the peer). Likewise, teaching the child with autism to complete a number of art projects from set materials allows one to direct peers to model the child with autism as well.

Thus, teaching social skills occurs across all three teaching settings and is carefully planned and carried out in naturalistic social routines, allowing the child's own needs and interests to motivate behavior and for the effects of the social act to lead to natural rewards for the child.

MOTOR SKILLS. The Denver Model staff understand that deficits in motor development, motor sequencing, and motor planning (dyspraxia) may be present in autism and can interfere greatly with social exchanges, play, independence in daily living skills, and preschool participation. Interventions in this area are aimed at functional skill development for play and learning. Motor skill development is taught through one-to-one instruction and carefully planned classroom activities, via systematic instruction with a variety of typical preschool activities and toys, adapted as needed. Gross motor play is taught as part of play and leisure skills activities, involving ball play including catching and throwing, riding a tricycle using playground equipment independently, and preschool movement games.

Hand development is a particular focus of intervention across the preschool years, because later problems with dressing skills, handwriting, and other fine motor tasks are seen as resulting from both poor muscle tone and dyspraxia, as well as the accumulating effects of lack of practice and challenge over the years. Initially, cause-and-effect and one-step action toys are used to build hand and finger manipulation, hand strength, bilateral coordination, and purposeful play. As the hands are developing through a developmental motor sequence, tool use is incorporated into toy play and eventually into writing, art activities, home activities, dressing skills, and other preschool activities.

CLASSROOM ROUTINES. In both the center-based classrooms and integrated classroom settings, the day is structured into specific activity periods, each of which focuses on specific objectives for the individual child. (See Table 5.1 for a list of classroom activities and the relevant developmental skills that can be embedded in each activity.) The preschool class schedule is carefully marked by concrete transition cues, careful use of physical space and visual–spatial cues, and personal schedules fitted to each of the children (similar to and influenced by the work of the TEACCH program; Mesibov, Schopler, & Hearsey, 1994). While in group activities, children have some choices about materials, actions, and length of engagement with materials; each activity period is carefully structured, with set places to sit, specific concrete activities that occur in the same place and time each day, and careful planning, to assure that each of the child's quarterly objectives are actively taught inside the group program. Opportunities for social engagement with peers are highlighted and orchestrated by the design of group activities. Child seating, arrangement of materials, and teaching strategies are planned to foster peer interaction. The amount of adult assistance for each child is individually determined by the child's needs during each activity. In some teaching programs (e.g., learning to tap an adult on the arm to get his or her visual attention), two adults may work with one child. For other activities (e.g., snack time) some children may need only verbal guides from an adult at the table, whereas another child may need complete one-to-one assistance. Thus, the teacher–child ratios are determined by the learning needs and skill levels of each child. However, because

Table 5.1

Main Classroom Activities and Related Developmental Skills

Activity	Related Skills
Opening and closing circle	• Independent transitions • Following adult instructions in a group • Active participation (and imitations) in peer group games, songs, and routines • Taking and giving objects to peers • Communication and literacy skills
Meals	• Independent transitions • Self-care skills: toileting, washing, eating, food preparation, cleanup • Giving objects to others • Communication and literacy skills
Table-top activities	• Independent transitions • Fine motor skills • Independent work skills • Cognitive skills • Parallel play (imitation) with peers • Following a work schedule • Sensorimotor play skills • Communication and literacy skills
Thematic play	• Sensorimotor play skills • Symbolic play skills • Imitation of peers and adults • Communication with peers • Interactive play with peers • Independent transitions
Open-ended sensory activities (e.g., sand and water table, messy art activities	• Sensory objectives • Parallel play, peer imitation • Interactive play • Communication skills • Self-care (hand washing or cleanup)
Playground time	• Gross motor objectives • Communication objectives • Parallel play • Interactive play

a primary goal is that each of the child's activities are immediately understandable and appealing to the child, careful planning of individual children's materials and learning activities within the group activity period reduces the need for constant one-to-one physical guidance. Child independence in personal care skills, play, and transitions is highly valued, and the environment, staff usage, and activities are carefully planned to promote personal independence for each child. Appendix 5.A provides a checklist of key features of the Denver Model in an inclusive classroom.

TYPICAL DAILY SCHEDULES OF INTERVENTION. For a child in a center-based classroom, a typical schedule might be the following:

7:30–8:30 a.m.	Home dressing and mealtime programs, including communication systems
9:00–3:00	Preschool interventions
3:00–5:00	Play at home, outings and errands with family; for some children, one-to-one home teaching
5:00–7:00	Chores, mealtime programs, self-care routines around bath and toileting, communication systems
7:00–8:00	Play objectives at home, or structured teaching programs delivered by parents
8:00 p.m.	Book routines and bedtime

Total number of hours involved across the entire week includes 30 hours of classroom intervention and 1 to 2 hours of daily home teaching for 7 days, for a total of 37 to 44 hours per week of structured and preplanned intervention activities.

For a child in a community-based program, a typical schedule might be as follows:

7:30–8:30 a.m.	Home dressing and mealtime programs, including communication systems
9:00–12:00	Inclusive preschool intervention
12:00–1:30	Mealtime programs, hygiene programs
1:30–4:30	One-to-one structured teaching programs
4:30–5:30	Play indoors and outdoors (gross motor objectives, independent play objectives), outings, errands
5:30–7:00	Chores, mealtime programs, self-care routines, communication systems
7:00–8:00	Play, dressing, bath and toileting programs
8:00 p.m.	Book routines and bedtime

Weekly intervention hours across the entire week include 12 hours of pre-school, 15 hours of structured one-to-one teaching in addition to school, and 7 to 14 hours of structured home routines, for a total of 34 to 41 hours per week of structured and preplanned teaching.

Behavior Management

The Denver Model seeks to optimize relationships in the family and teach new, adaptive skills that allow children greater control, autonomy, competence, and personal satisfaction within their social experiences. The tools to accomplish these goals include functional analysis; communication training; structured teaching of alternative, more conventional behaviors; redirection; and adding structure and visual cues to the physical environment

Young children with autism can present a variety of challenging behaviors that occur across settings and may be very frustrating for parents, caregivers, educators, and therapists. These challenging behaviors are not viewed as intentional acts of opposition or defiance, but rather represent the most efficient and effective ways that a child has found for expressing a particular set of wants and needs, given the child's limited repertoire of skills. The pervasive deficits of autism make it difficult for the child to understand and easily participate in social interaction, communicate with others, develop new skills, and accommodate to the environment, thus providing ideal conditions for the development of challenging behaviors. Two key questions to ask when evaluating unwanted behaviors and planning interventions are (1) What is the child's goal? and (2) What do we wish the child woud do instead?

We agree with Barkley (1987) that an important beginning point in behavioral interventions is in "improving the general relations between parent and child" through the use of child-centered play periods (p. 76). Although Barkley's work is focused on oppositional children, we have found that parents of young children with autism, especially those who face great behavioral challenges from their children, often find that they spend little time with their children in positive, enjoyable interactions in which they can provide noncontingent positive regard and affection. Such periods provide important positive experiences for parents and children, and they can provide needed emotional energy for parents to carry out structured teaching and behavioral intervention programs. Thus, building in daily, brief play periods that both parents and children find enjoyable is crucial first intervention.

The next step in our efforts to reduce the frequency and intensity of inappropriate behaviors that occur in children with autism is to teach specific adaptive skills intensively across all areas of functioning, emphasizing skills that will provide children with the most control across settings, such as functional communication, play, and appropriate involvement with life routines and materials. Structured and systematic one-to-one instructional approaches are used to teach new skills. The specific teaching of new skills is a proactive and preventative approach to thwarting the development of negative behavior across settings, as the child learns to generalize the new skills in a variety of environments.

In addition to using structured and systematic one-to-one teaching approaches for new skills, we make environmental accommodations (see Lord, Marcus, & Schopler, Chapter 9 in this volume), taking into consideration each child's individual strengths and needs, in continued efforts to prevent challenging behaviors from developing. The physical layout of preschool settings (integrated or segregated), with an emphasis on clear physical and visual boundaries, in combination with visual structure (daily schedule, individualized work systems), is helpful in facilitating smooth transitions between activities, and in delineating the beginning and ending of various work tasks and activities.

Even though proactive approaches in the form of structured teaching and environmental accommodations have been put in place, difficult behaviors will continue to be present on many occasions. In these cases, functional assessments (e.g., *Functional Analysis Screening Tool,* Iwata, 1995) are performed to identify specific areas for intervention. Functional assessments often include comprehensive interviews with the parents or other caregivers, as well as teachers and other therapists. Direct observations of the difficult behaviors, coupled with user-friendly data collection systems, lead to initial hypotheses about the functions of the behaviors.

Based on the results of the functional assessment, intervention strategies are implemented. The strategies are varied and focus on building and supporting positive behavior, including reinforcement-based teaching of replacement behaviors based on the functional equivalency of the challenging behavior, environmental adaptations, and instructional adaptations (antecedent manipulations) with minimal use of negative consequence-based interventions. Positive behavioral supports (Koegel & Koegel, 1995) provide a framework for our treatment interventions, and we are careful to include interventions that address current behavioral concerns in the short term, including crisis management as well as long-term prevention.

Role of Families

Families are at the helm of their child's treatment; their styles, values, preferences, goals, and dreams guide their child's treatment plan. Parents are the primary teachers of all young children; parental teaching for young children with autism is crucial to the child's progress. However, autism is a complex disorder and parents may need guidance, support, and help in various aspects of designing and carrying out treatment for young children with autism.

Parent and family involvement is an essential component of Denver Model intervention. Beginning with the diagnostic evaluation, parents are encouraged to observe and actively participate in the assessment process, both to share historical and developmental information with team members and to work directly with the assessment team to provide accurate information about their child's developmental abilities. Home visits are scheduled as needed, and have been found to be quite helpful in providing additional information that is useful diagnostically as well as in planning treatment interventions. Additionally, the assessment period represents the beginning of intervention. Focused teaching techniques are typically demonstrated in our first contacts (i.e., use of a visual schedule, one-to-one teaching strategies, positive behavioral supports). In this way, parents have the opportunity to see the efficacy of these approaches and the learning capacity of their child from their very first contacts.

The initial parent–professional sessions lay the groundwork for intervention. In these sessions, parents gain information about their child's diagnosis, his or her individual strengths and needs, and educational needs. They also gather information about service delivery systems: accessing school services, applying for Medicaid waivers, and other potential funding. A review of various treatment options is provided, as well as references for written material that will be helpful in making decisions about treatment direction and strategy. Parents are often given information on local parent support and advocacy groups at this time. Also, if parents are interested, the therapist can serve as a go-between in connecting parents of newly diagnosed children and autism and veteran families.

Parents may also use these initial sessions to discuss their reactions to the diagnostic information that has been shared with them. They are encouraged to bring other family members (grandparents, siblings, etc.) as desired for support or to hear the information from the professional staff directly. Because parents may later decide to include grandparents, siblings, or other caregivers in the treatment protocol, these initial contacts can be very helpful in laying the foundation for later participation.

Preparation for Individualized Family Service Plan (IFSP) and Individualized Education Plan (IEP) meetings is given careful attention. Because these meetings are crucial for accessing educational services across the child's entire educational future, parents need to be familiar and comfortable with the structure of the meetings and with their role as primary advocates for their children. We help parents prepare for these meetings in several ways: (a) by having them generate lists of their child's strengths and needs, as well as their goals for their child's progress over the coming year; (b) by walking them through the entire IFSP or IEP format; (c) by giving them assessment information ahead of the meeting so that they have an opportunity to ask questions and digest the meaning of the assessment data; and (d) by encouraging them to invite to the meeting several other people who know the child and his or her needs and strengths and who will be potentially strong advocates. We join the parents at the meeting and help structure the meeting so that the parents have a very active and direct role in describing their child and generating strengths, needs, and annual objectives.

Once the child enters Denver Model intervention, a shared definition of the working relationship is formulated between the main coordinator and the parent–family, taking into consideration the needs and desires of each family member. The extent to which parents and other family members are involved varies considerably and can range from many hours of direct teaching, where parents teach many of the structured one-to-one programs on a daily basis, to carrying out structured interventions within the daily life routines of the family for 1 to 2 hours per day, such as during mealtimes, dressing, toileting, bathing, and bedtime. Parents are active in formulating priorities for intervention. Parents are asked about their wishes, hopes, and dreams for their children in the short term and in the future; a treatment plan is then put together based on the parents' concerns and priorities (i.e., specific communication objectives, social–interaction objectives, and goals for independent living). As specific teaching plans are developed for each objective, parents participate either by learning to implement the teaching plan themselves, by facilitating communication of the new teaching plan to other "home teachers," or by identifying routines or opportunities throughout the day to implement (generalize) these new skills, once new skills are mastered in a structured teaching session. When targeting challenging behaviors, parents are enlisted as co-therapists to complete functional assessments of behavior, collect data, and assist in generating a plan for teaching alternative behaviors. Parents actively implement these plans throughout the child's waking hours at home.

Outcome Measures

Four papers describing the effectiveness of the Denver Model have been published in peer-reviewed journals. In the first paper, Rogers, Herbison, Lewis, Pantone, and Reis (1986) described the effects of the original demonstration grant, involving a developmentally oriented, center-based model that emphasized play, language, cognition, and social relations. The outcomes of 18 children with diagnoses of autistic disorder or pervasive developmental disorder not otherwise specified (PDDNOS) who participated over a 2.5-year period were assessed. Mean chronological age of the group was 44.81 months ($SD = 11.40$) and mean nonverbal IQ was 67.68 ($SD = 18.75$). Mean verbal IQ can be estimated at 34 from the language data presented in the paper. Initial severity of autism symptoms was assessed using the CARS (Schopler et al., 1988), with a mean score of 36.63 ($SD = 6.84$). Socioeconomic status (SES) varied widely, with a mean of 3.17 ($SD = 1.31$) on the Hollingshead Four Factor Index (Hollingshead, 1975). Ethnicity was broadly representative of the

Denver metropolitan area. Functioning was assessed before and after 6 months of treatment delivery using a curriculum tool, the Early Intervention Profile and Preschool Profile (Schafer & Moersch, 1979), which assessed development in the areas of cognition, language, perceptual–fine motor, gross motor, social–emotional, and self-care. Play skills were assessed using the Play Observation Scale (Rogers et al., 1986), a time sampling procedure used to score symbolic play abilities in a semistructured lab setting. Social skills were assessed with the experimenter in the symbolic play paradigm. Additionally, for 13 children, time sampling procedures were used to rate social behaviors in a 10-minute, lab-based, mother–child dyadic play session.

Pre- and posttreatment assessment was carried out on the profiles by comparing outcome scores to projected scores that estimated what the second set of scores would have been based only on children's initial developmental rates. This projected score was used to estimate the child's progress without any intervention. Actual posttreatment scores were significantly higher than projected scores in four areas: cognition, language, perceptual–fine motor, and social–emotional, with t scores (one-tailed) ranging from 1.95 to 2.91, and ps ranging from .03 to .007. Posttreatment gains on fine motor skills approached significance ($p = .06$), and the means on the other two scales also surpassed the estimated scores. The data demonstrated that the treated children had made 6 to 7 months of progress in the initial 6 months of treatment, thus achieving a normal developmental rate (a rate of 1.0) , a marked acceleration over their initial learning rates (which ranged from .27 in communication to .36 in motor skills). Statistically significant gains in symbolic play development were also found for use of symbolic agents, complexity of symbolic play, and overall level of symbolic functioning. Several markers of improved social functioning were found, including statistically significant improvements in the social–communicative play levels with the experimenter, and several areas of statistically significant improvement in the mother–child play interaction, including increases in child positive affect and social initiations and decreased negative responses to mother's initiations. Maternal behavior was quite stable across the two samples; thus, changes in child behavior did not appear due to maternal elicitations of the behavior. The improvement in social interactions was demonstrated across three separate measures and with various partners, adding convergent validity to the impact of this model on social development in young children with autism.

The second paper, by Rogers and Lewis (1989), elaborated the outcome analyses on a larger group. Data were analyzed for 31 children (including the 18 reported above). Their ages, IQs, CARS scores, and SES were very similar to those reported for the previous study. Changes on the developmental profiles (Schafer & Moersch, 1979) and the CARS scores represented the outcome variables. Children's gains over the estimated scores demonstrated more growth than the gains reported in the first paper. $T(30)$ scores ranged from 2.52 to 3.69, and p values ranged from .001 to .009 (one-tailed), with the children demonstrating highly significant gains in five of the six areas, and gains approaching significance in self-care ($t = 1.38$, $p = .09$). The children continued to demonstrate a learning rate of approximately 1.0 during the 6 months after their enrollments, gaining approximately 1 month of skill for each month of treatment in each developmental area. A subgroup of 15 children was followed across 12 months of treatment; their rate of development in each of the six areas continued either to accelerate or to remain at normal levels (1 month of developmental progress for each month of treatment). Examination of the acquisition of useful, communicative, multiword speech in this group revealed that whereas 53% of children had useful speech at the beginning of treatment, 73% had acquired useful speech by the end of treatment. Thus, 47% of initially nonverbal children had useful speech by the end of treatment. Symbolic play gains and social–communicative gains were highly significant, as in the first paper. Finally, CARS scores rated blindly from videotapes before and after treatment revealed a significant decrease over 6 months of treatment, dropping from a mean of 35.12 (moderate symptoms of autism) to 28.96 (not autistic) [$t(27) = 6.23$, $p < .001$]. When progress of children diagnosed with PDDNOS was compared to that of children diagnosed with autistic disorder (who were more severely impaired in all areas than the PDDNOS group), we found *greater* relative improvement in the group with autistic disorder, thus demonstrating the effectiveness of this model for both higher functioning and lower functioning children, and supporting our ideas about the relative plasticity of development early in autism.

A third study (Rogers & DiLalla, 1991) compared the effects of the Denver Model on the progress of (a) a group of 49 children with autism and PDDNOS and (b) a group of 27 children with other kinds of behavioral and/or developmental disorders but without any of the symptoms of autism. The characteristics of the group with autism were virtually identical to those reported in the earlier studies in terms of age, IQ, CARS scores, and SES. The outcome data on the developmental profiles (Schafer & Moersch, 1979) and the CARS were quite similar to the earlier studies, with the autism spectrum group demonstrating significantly greater posttreatment gains than were expected from the predicted scores, in five of the six areas. The developmental rates of this group were even higher than in past papers, with the children gaining 7.2 months of progress in each area, on the average, in a 6-month period of treatment, a rate of 1.12. The group with autism spectrum disorders made relatively greater gains in a variety of areas, including cognition and language, than the group without autism. Furthermore, when matched on initial age and developmental level with the comparison group, the group with autism achieved the same rate of progress on various measures of development during intervention as the nonautistic comparison group, even in the area of language development. This study again reinforced the idea that there is considerable learning potential in young children with autism, and that the autism per se does not lead to slower learning rates or slower language acquisition rates than for children with other kinds of developmental disorders. This study also examined a group of 13 children with autism who had received 19 months of intervention in the model. In that period, this group had achieved 17 months of language progress, although one would have expected only 7 months of progress based on the initial data. Thus, it appears that the initial developmental acceleration achieved in the model is not simply an initial reaction to a new learning environment, but rather represents an ongoing acceleration of development that is sustained as long as the treatment is sustained. These data suggested to us that developmental deviations associated with autism were not fully set early in development, and that appropriate, intensive early intervention could change the developmental course of the disorder.

The fourth study is perhaps the most important of the four reported here in demonstrating the effectiveness of the Denver Model. This study (Rogers, Lewis, & Reis, 1987) involved replication of the Denver Model by four independent agencies in four rural communities and one urban community in Colorado. This study examined both the treatment fidelity of the replication site and the pre- and posttreatment gains made by the 11 children with autism in those sites in areas of cognition, language, motor skills, social–emotional, and self-care skills. The children in these sites were older than the children in the previous papers (mean age = 56 months), with more severe cognitive delays (mean cognitive levels of 14.65 months; all children had mental retardation as well as autism), and most important, had already been receiving interventions in these sites for 1 or more years. No increases in staff ratios, treatment hours, or other services were provided. The only change made in these classrooms was the use of the Denver Model approach, rather than the more typical developmental approach that had been delivered to these children. The staff were trained in the Denver Model through on-site workshops, spending time in the model classrooms in Denver, and sharing of videotapes every 6 weeks. Denver Model staff reviewed the tapes and sent back suggestions. Two follow-up site visits focused on model implementation, one at 2 months and one at 6 months. Data collected after 6 months of implementation revealed that the outreach site personnel had learned significant information that was useful in the classroom, documented through objective measures of knowledge about education of children with autism. Each site implemented each of the five components of the Denver Model with high degrees of model fidelity, as documented by blind video ratings. The target children demonstrated statistically significant treatment gains over estimated levels in five of the six areas, and the sixth (self-care) approached significance. Furthermore, the children gained 3.71 months of development over the first 4 months of model implementation, which represents more than triple their initial rate of development.

Thus, the model has been examined with large groups of children with consistent evidence of developmental acceleration in all areas. Furthermore, the model has been replicated at five independent sites, with intervention outcomes as strong as in the model programs and considerable acceleration of development even for older and lower functioning children who had been receiving other kinds of intervention for a period of years. The within-group pre- and posttreatment designs used to evaluate the effectiveness of the Denver Model for early treatment of young children with autism have been considered an acceptable approach to program evaluation in the field of early childhood special education (Fewell & Sandall, 1986). However, without using control groups and without providing higher degrees of methodological control, these methodologies do not demonstrate unequivocally that this intervention causes these changes. In early intervention models, preliminary positive data from pre- and posttreatment designs need to lead to the application of methodologically rigorous controlled designs. We are seeking to apply methodologies involving control groups of matched children, random assignment, blind raters, numerous outcome measures, and long-term follow-up, in order to test the causal effects of the Denver Model (Rogers, 1998).

Major Issues for the Present and Near Future

Four main issues stand out at the present time. These involve model definition, funding, training, and outcome studies. The first involves defining the Denver Model in terms of its current practices, its deliverers, and its recipients. The change from a center-based to a community-based model has meant that responsibility and control of model delivery have shifted from the professional staff to the hands of family and home staff. As preschool models in general become widely disseminated and delivered by staff members who have not been trained by the model originators, important aspects of the model may become diluted, as local professionals add their own practices and beliefs to existing models. When evaluating model efficacy, it is crucial that the model be tightly defined and the degree of model fidelity be measurable. Our group is currently working to define the Denver Model quite tightly, so that outcome studies can reflect the degree of model fidelity implemented for individual children. An example of this kind of work is the Denver Model Classroom Checklist presented in Appendix 5.B, which allows an inclusive preschool setting to be rated according to the presence of elements considered core to the Denver Model.

Funding is the second main issue. The current community-based model has been developed as a funding alternative to the center-based model that was operated at the UCHSC for many years. Using existing preschool classrooms and school staff supported by the school districts, while providing most of the additional teaching hours through the use of persons with bachelor's level education and parents, saves tremendously in professional fees, as does the use of the generalist model. Once a team is trained, the coordinator's time averages 1 hour to 2 hours per week of professional fees (reimbursable by third-party payments, either Medicaid or insurance), with another 15 hours per week provided by bachelor's level people being paid $10 to $15 per hour, generally from a combination of family funds and educational or community funding. Consultations from other professionals on the team are likewise reimbursable by third-party sources. The initial costs of setting up and training a team are challenging to many families, and not usually reimbursable by third-party payors. At this point, the funding for each child's program is individually determined, because Medicaid funds are generally not available in Colorado for home teachers at this time. Helping families locate funding and working with community resources to make more funds available for this kind of intensive approach to early autism are crucial activities for our team.

Locating and training a sufficient supply of home teaching assistants is the third issue that we currently face. The shift to a community base has allowed us to support many more than the 12 to 18 children that made up the center-based preschool. However, providing intensive intervention in the community-based model is built on locating and training home teaching assistants. We are working to identify university resources that can supply a continuous flow of students for training, practicum hours, and assignment to families. Until that is achieved, much of the effort expended to locate home teaching assistants falls to parents, and it is a difficult load to undertake. Funding for training a home team similarly falls to parents and whatever community resources each family can obtain. Colorado needs to implement the support for home teams that other states have implemented through state Medicaid funds.

The final challenge to our model, and to many others, involves documentation of treatment efficacy. Our existing outcome data, described above, are based on the center-based model. We are currently working on outcome assessment of children in the community-based model, as well as on designing outcome studies that involve control groups of children receiving other types of intervention. Assessing treatment efficacy for young children with autism, receiving thousands of hours of intervention over a period of years, is difficult work. Yet it is crucial work, for we must provide parents with the information they need to make informed decisions about their children's care.

The final issue, for present and future, is to continue to evolve the model and incorporate new practices as we and others define new, successful intervention approaches and as more is learned about the core nature of autism. We need to continue to evolve the Denver Model, rather than reify it, through new research and new learning, and continual work with children and families, in order to maximize outcomes for children and families.

Appendix 5.A
The Denver Model Classroom Checklist

Name: _____   Date: _____

Area of Rating	±	Notes
Classroom Environment		
Work and other areas are clearly and visually marked off.		
The child's work, seating, and standing areas are labeled and are part of the whole group.		
Distractions are minimized in work area.		
The child is positioned to maximize focus on task or person.		
Schedule		
There is a consistent daily schedule for the class as a whole.		
The target student has an individualized schedule that includes every major transition.		
The individualized schedule is appropriate for the child's functioning level.		
The child's schedule supports independent transitions.		
More preferred activities follow less preferred activities.		
Transitions		
The child's destination point is visually marked.		
The child's destination path is clear and easy to navigate.		
Endings of activities are consistently marked.		

Area of Rating	±	Notes
No major distractions occur along the transition route.		
Teacher is prepared to begin next activity when the child is at destination point.		
Curriculum/Instruction		
The child has well-written set of short-term objectives in place.		
Data collection systems are in active use.		
Instructional programs are clearly defined and carried out consistently across teachers.		
Every minute of the child's day is considered in the classroom plan.		
The majority of the teaching occurs within the ongoing activities of the class rather than alone and separately.		
The main classroom teacher is actively teaching the target child during group activities.		
Direct instruction and frequent practice trials are used for new skill acquisition.		
Generalization of already learned skills is carried out in group activities.		
Teaching materials are well organized so that there is little down time during instruction.		
The child's notebook, including individual data sheets, graphs, and instructional programs, are well organized and up to date.		

Area of Rating	±	Notes
The child is appropriately engaged in goal-directed or social activities during the majority of free time.		
In large group activities the child is actively engaged by the teacher at least every 2 minutes.		
The child is engaged in constructive play, thematic play activities, and social play with peers at some point during each day.		
Student motivation is kept high through frequent task changes.		
Some reinforcement plan is in place for all teaching activities.		
The child is motivated by the current reinforcement system.		
The child is actively engaged in educational or social activities at least 75% of the time.		
Imitation is emphasized.		
The child is engaged in at least part of each classroom activity, using the same materials as other students and carrying out individualized objectives that are embedded "invisibly" in the ongoing activity.		
Personal Independence and Competence		
The child sets up, completes, and puts away activities.		
The child's strengths are capitalized on during group activities.		
The child moves independently through transitions.		

Area of Rating	±	Notes
The child is responding independently and successfully for the majority of instructions rather than hand-over-hand prompting.		
Social Interactions		
All adults in the room engage the child in unconditional and friendly interactions, marked by positive affect and reciprocal engagement.		
All adults in the room interact with the child and are implementing the goals and objectives.		
Adults prompt peers to engage the child.		
Regular classroom staff and other students rather than one particular person provide much of the support for the child.		
Some activities are set up to foster social interaction among peers.		
Adults do not distract the child from focussing on the teacher.		
Social skills are both directly and incidentally taught and practiced throughout the day.		
Communication		
Each child uses an expressive system to initiate, make choices, state needs, protest, and make requests.		
Expressive system is conventional so that peers comprehend the child.		
The environment is structured so that the child needs to communicate frequently.		
All adults handle communication similarly.		

Area of Rating	±	Notes
Child-initiated communication is acted upon immediately without correction.		
The communication system is used across the school day in all settings.		
Behavior		
More attention is paid to desirable behaviors than undesirable behaviors.		
Minimal social engagement occurs around unwanted behavior.		
Unwanted behavior is handled by redirection to more appropriate activities.		
Everyone is kept safe.		
Intervention occurs early in a chain of negative behavior.		
Tasks are not removed in the face of negative behavior.		
The child is supplied with conventional communication to express negative feelings.		
There is minimal physical management of the child.		
Behavior plans are based on functional analysis.		
The child has frequent access to preferred people, activities, and reinforcers.		
Behavior is being managed by positive approaches and antecedent control rather than negative consequences.		

References

American Psychiatric Association (1994). *Diagnostic and statistical manual of mental disorders* (4th ed.). Washington, DC: Author.

Barkley, R. A. (1987). *Defiant children: A clinician's manual for parent training*. New York: Guilford Press.

Baron-Cohen, S. (1991). Do people with autism understand what causes emotion? *Child Development, 62,* 385–395.

Bayley, N. (1993). *Bayley Scales of Infant Development* (2nd ed.). San Antonio: Psychological Corp.

Bondy, A. S., & Frost, L. A. (1994). The picture exchange communication system. *Focus on Autistic Behavior, 9,* 1–19.

Brown, S. L., D'Eugenio, D. B., Drews, J. E., Haskin, B. S., Lynch, E. W., & Rogers, S. J. (1981). Preschool Developmental Profile: Volume 5. In D. S. Schafer & M. S. Moersch (Eds.), *Developmental programming for infants and young children.* Ann Arbor: University of Michigan Press.

Bruininks, R. (1978). *Bruininks-Oseretsky Test of Motor Proficiency.* Circle Pines, MN: American Guidance Service.

Bruininks, R., Woodcock, R., Weatherman, R., & Hill, B. (1996). *Scales of Independent Behavior–Revised.* Chicago: Riverside.

Bruner, J. S. (1972). Nature and uses of immaturity. *American Psychologist, 27,* 687–708.

Bruner, J. S. (1975). The ontogenesis of speech acts. *Journal of Child Language, 2,* 1–19.

Carrow-Woolfolk, E. (1996). *Oral and Written Language Scales.* Circle Pines, MN: American Guidance Service.

Carter, A. S., Volkmar, F. R., Sparrow, S. S., Wang, J., Lord, C., Dawson, G., Fombonne, E., Loveland, K., Mesibov, G., & Schopler, E. (1998). The Vineland Adaptive Behavior Scales: Supplementary norms for individuals with autism. *Journal of Autism and Developmental Disorders, 28,* 287–302.

Charman, T., Swettenham, J., Baron-Cohen, S., Cox, A., Baird, G., & Drew, A. (1997). Infants with autism: An investigation of empathy, pretend play, joint attention, and imitation. *Developmental Psychology, 33,* 781–789.

DeMyer, M. K., Alpern, G. D., Barton, S., DeMyer, W. E., Churchill, D. W., Hingtgen, J. N., Bryson, C. Q., Pontius, W., & Kimberlin, C. (1972). Imitation in autistic, early schizophrenic, and nonpsychotic subnormal children. *Journal of Autism and Childhood Schizophrenia, 2,* 264–287.

DiSimoni, F. (1990). *The Token Test for Children.* Allen, TX: DLM Teaching Resources.

Dunn, L. M., & Dunn, L. M. (1997). *Peabody Picture Vocabulary Test* (3rd ed.). Circle Pines, MN: American Guidance Service.

Dunn, W. (1991). The sensorimotor systems: A framework for assessment and intervention. In F. Orelove & D. Sobsy (Eds.), *Educating children with multiple disabilities: A transdisciplinary approach* (2nd ed.) (pp. 33–78). Baltimore: Brookes.

Fewell, R. R., & Sandall, S. R. (1986). Developmental testing of handicapped infants. *Topics in Early Childhood Special Education, 6*(3), 86–100.

Folio, M. R., & Fewell, R. R. (1983). *Peabody Developmental Motor Scales.* Allen, TX: DLM Teaching Resources.

Gardner, M. F. (1985). *Test of Auditory–Perceptual Skills.* Burlington, CA: Psychological and Educational Publications.

Gardner, M. F. (1990). *Expressive One-Word Picture Vocabulary Test–Revised.* Novato, CA: Academic Therapy.

Goldman, R., & Fristoe, M. (1986). *Goldman–Fristoe Test of Articulation.* Circle Pines, MN: American Guidance Service.

Hobson, R. P. (1986). The autistic child's appraisal of expressions of emotion: A further study. *Journal of Child Psychology and Psychiatry, 27,* 671–680.

Hobson, R. P., Ouston, J., & Lee, A. (1988). Emotion recognition in autism: Coordinating faces and voices. *Psychological Medicine, 18,* 911–923.

Hollingshead, A. B. (1975). *Four factor index of social status.* Unpublished manuscript.

Iwata, B. (1995). *Functional Analysis Screening Tool.* Gainesville: The Florida Center on Self-Injury.

Kahn, L., & Lewis, N. (1986). *Kahn–Lewis Phonological Analysis.* Circle Pines, MN: American Guidance Service.

Koegel, R. L., & Koegel, L. K. (1995). *Teaching children with autism: strategies for initiating positive interactions and improving learning opportunities.* Baltimore: Brookes.

Lord, C., Rutter, M., Risi, S. DiLavore, P. (1998). *Autism Diagnostic Observation Schedule.* Lord, C., Rutter, M., & Le Couteur, A. (1994). Autism Diagnostic Interview–Revised: A revised version of a diagnostic interview for caregivers of individuals with possible pervasive developmental disorders. *Journal of Autism and Developmental Disorders, 24,* 659–685.

Loveland, K., Tunali, B., Chen, Y. R., Ortegon, J., Pearson, D., Brelsford, K., & Gibbs, M. C. (1997). Emotion recognition in autism: Verbal and nonverbal information. *Development and Psychopathology, 9*(3), 579–593.

Loveland, K., Tunali-Kotoski, B., Pearson, D., Brelsford, K., Ortegon, J., & Chen, R. (1994). Imitation and expression of facial affect in autism. *Development and Psychopathology, 6,* 433–444.

Mesibov, G. B., Schopler, E., & Hearsey, K. A. (1994). Structured teaching. In E. Schopler & G. B. Mesibov (Eds.), *Behavioral issues in autism* (pp. 195–207). New York: Plenum Press.

Miller, L. J. (1988). *Miller Assessment for Preschoolers.* San Antonio: Psychological Corp.

Mullen, E. (1989). *Mullen Scales of Early Learning.* Cranston, RI: T.O.T.A.L. Child.

Newcomer, P. L., & Hammill, D. D. (1997). *Test of Language Development–Primary* (3rd ed.). Austin, TX: PRO-ED.

Newtson, D. (1993). The dynamics of action and interaction. In L. B. Smith & E. Thelen (Eds.), *A dynamics systems approach to development: Applications* (pp. 241–264). Cambridge, MA: MIT Press.

Osaki, D., Rogers, S. J., & Hall, T. (1997). *The Denver Model Curriculum.* Unpublished manuscript.

Rogers, S. J. (1998). Empirically supported comprehensive treatments for young children with autism. *Journal of Clinical Child Psychology, 27,* 168–179.

Rogers, S. J. (1999). An examination of the imitation deficit in autism. In J. Nadel & G. Butterworth (Eds.), *Imitation in infancy* (pp. 254–283). Cambridge, England: University of Cambridge Press.

Rogers, S. J., Bennetto, L., McEvoy, R., & Pennington, B. F. (1996). Imitation and pantomime in high functioning adolescents with autism spectrum disorders. *Child Development, 67*(5), 2060–2073.

Rogers, S. J., & DiLalla, D. (1991). A comparative study of a developmentally based preschool curriculum of young children with autism and young children with other disorders of behavior and development. *Topics in Early Childhood Special Education, 11,* 29–48.

Rogers, S. J., Donovan, C. M., D'Eugenio, D. B., Brown, S. L., Lynch, E. W., Moersch, M. S., & Schafer, D. S. (1979). Early Intervention Developmental Profile: Volume 2. In D. S. Schafer & M. S. Moersch (Eds.), *Developmental programming for infants and young children*. Ann Arbor: University of Michigan Press.

Rogers, S. J., Herbison, J., Lewis, H., Pantone, J., & Reis, K. (1986). An approach for enhancing the symbolic, communicative, and interpersonal functioning of young children with autism and severe emotional handicaps. *Journal of the Division of Early Childhood, 10,* 135–148.

Rogers, S. J., & Lewis, H. (1989). An effective day treatment model for young children with pervasive developmental disorders. *Journal of the American Academy of Child and Adolescent Psychiatry, 28,* 207–214.

Rogers, S. J., Lewis, H. C., & Reis, K. (1987). An effective procedure for training early special education teams to implement a model program. *Journal of the Division of Early Childhood, 11*(2), 180–188.

Rogers, S. J., & Pennington, B. F. (1991). A theoretical approach to the deficits in infantile autism. *Development and Psychopathology, 3,* 137–162.

Roid, G. H., & Miller, L. J. (1997). *Leiter International Performance Scale–Revised.* Wood Dale, IL: Stoelting.

Schafer, D. S., & Moersch, M. S. (1979). *Developmental programming for infants and young children.* Ann Arbor: University of Michigan Press.

Schopler, E., Reichler, R. J., Bashford, A., Lansing, M., & Marcus, L. M. (1990). *Psychoeducational Profile–Revised.* Austin, TX: PRO-ED.

Schopler, E., Reichler, R. J., & Renner, B. R. (1988). *The Childhood Autism Rating Scale.* Los Angeles: Western Psychological Services.

Sigman, M., & Ungerer, J. (1984). Cognitive and language skills in autistic, mentally retarded, and normal children. *Developmental Psychology, 20,* 293–302.

Sparrow, S. S., Balla, D. A., & Cicchetti, D. (1984). *Vineland Adaptive Behavior Scales.* Circle Pines, MN: American Guidance Service.

Stern, D. N. (1985). *The interpersonal world of the human infant.* New York: Basic Books.

Stone, W. L., Ousley, O. Y., & Littleford, C. D. (1997). Motor imitation in young children with autism: What's the object? *Journal of Abnormal Child Psychology, 25*(6), 475–485.

Thorndike, R. L., Hagen, E. P., & Sattler, J. M. (1986). *Stanford–Binet Intelligence Scale–Fourth Edition.* Chicago: Riverside.

Tomasello, M., Kruger, A. C., & Ratner, H. H. (1993). Cultural learning. *Behavioral and Brain Sciences, 16,* 495–552.

Wetherby, A. M., & Prutting, C. A. (1984). Profiles of communicative and cognitive– social abilities in autistic children. *Journal of Speech and Hearing Research, 27,* 364–377.

Wiig, E. H., Secord, W. A., & Semel, E. (1992). *Clinical Evaluation of Language Fundamentals–Preschool.* San Antonio: wPsychological Corp.

Williams, K. T. (1997). *Expressive Vocabulary Test.* Circle Pines, MN: American Guidance Service.

Yirmiya, N., Kasari, C., Sigman, M., & Mundy, P. (1989). Facial expressions of affect in autistic, mentally retarded and normal children. *Journal of Child Psychology and Psychiatry, 30,* 725–735.

Zimmerman, I. L., Steiner, V. G., & Pond, R. E. (1992). *Preschool Language Scale–3.* San Antonio: Psychological Corp.

Alpine Learning Group 6

Linda S. Meyer, Bridget A. Taylor, Len Levin, and Julia R. Fisher

Population Served

The Alpine Learning Group (ALG) serves individuals diagnosed with autism and pervasive developmental disorders (American Psychiatric Association, 1994). For a child to be considered for admission, a diagnosis of pervasive developmental disorder or autistic disorder must be obtained by an independent clinician. Learners demonstrating a wide range of skill levels are admitted to the education and outreach programs.

All children enrolled in ALG's center-based program are classified as eligible for special education and related services according to New Jersey's state education classification system. As of July 1998, the New Jersey Administrative Code (6A:14-4-4.7) defines special class programs as serving students who have similar educational needs in accordance with their Individualized Education Programs (IEPs). ALG's special class programs are named Autistic (for learners 5 years of age and older) and Preschool Disabled (for learners less than 5 years old).

ALG's goal is to provide programming for approximately 25 to 30 learners, ages 3 to 21. The majority of referrals for admissions are from parents, although Child Study Teams and Special Services Departments (i.e., school districts' IEP committees) also request information regarding placement. An

The authors thank the instructional staff, learners, and parents of Alpine Learning Group for their collaboration leading toward the continuing evolution and refinement of Alpine Learning Group. Special appreciation is given to Linda Moran for making key contributions to the development of the manuscript.

Program Information: Alpine Learning Group, Inc., 777 Paramus Road, Paramus, NJ 07652; 201/612-7800

interested parent or professional is required to visit ALG's program during a regularly scheduled visiting day and fill out a Request for Intake Form to be considered for admission.

Since July 1989, 33 children have been enrolled in ALG's program for more than 2 years. The average age of all children at the time of enrollment is 4 years 5 months. The age range at the time of enrollment is 3 years 1 month through 7 years 9 months. Six (approximately 18%) have been female.

Assessments

When a preschooler or toddler begins ALG's outreach or education program, three standardized tests are usually administered: the *Vineland Adaptive Behavior Scales* (Sparrow, Balla, & Cicchetti, 1984), the *Stanford–Binet Intelligence Scale–Fourth Edition* (Thorndike, Hagen, & Sattler, 1986), and the *Peabody Picture Vocabulary Test–Third Edition* (Dunn & Dunn, 1997). Informal skill assessments are conducted annually to determine deficit areas. Formal skill assessments (e.g., academic achievement tests) are administered and standardized tests are readministered triannually, when appropriate.

Instructional and Administrative Staff

Two instructional positions are available at ALG: classroom teacher and classroom instructor. A teacher must be a certified special education teacher. In New Jersey, the mandated certificate is called "Teacher of the Handicapped." An instructor holds a bachelor's degree in a related field, usually psychology, sociology, or education. ALG's preschool classrooms maintain a one-to-one teacher–student ratio. Typically, a classroom of four preschoolers has two full-time teachers and two instructors.

Administrative staff include three nonteaching directors and one head teacher. All administrative staff are actively involved in the day-to-day programming with learners through supervision, educational clinics, teacher and instructor trainings, and home visitations.

ALG does not currently employ related service personnel such as speech–language pathologists, occupational therapists, or physical therapists. ALG's curriculum comprises teaching programs to facilitate the development of both language skills and fine and gross motor skills. ALG instructional personnel implement these programs in the classrooms throughout the school day. Consequently, separate, pull-out related services are not needed. Appropriate referrals or consultations are arranged if deemed necessary by ALG administration.

Instructional staff receive ongoing training and supervision in all teaching and intervention procedures. A 40-hour staff training consisting of didactic and hands-on training is conducted every August. Teachers and newly hired instructors are required to attend. Some of the topics covered include reinforcement, shaping, discrete-trial teaching, incidental teaching, functional analysis, managing challenging behavior, problem solving, programming for generalization, and professionalism. During this training week, learners are brought to the center and instructional staff participate in hands-on training sessions to practice the skills learned in the didactic lecture. Continued training and supervision occur over the course of the year through staff meetings and classroom supervision.

Regularly scheduled inservices and research meetings are held to continually enhance the teaching skills of the staff. Current and seminal research articles, pertinent to the education and treatment of individuals with autism, are reviewed at staff meetings. Research meetings are held biweekly with a core group of administrative and instructional staff interested in developing research protocols to empirically assess novel interventions.

A comprehensive annual employee performance evaluation is conducted with all instructional staff (McClannahan & Krantz, 1993). Data are collected on the performance of pivotal teaching skills. Objective measures include the frequency of behavior-specific praise, the systematic use of prompts (e.g., most to least), the number of learning opportunities presented, the percentage of on-task behavior of learners, the ability to implement a written teaching protocol, and the ability to use and understand behavior terminology. In addition, staff are rated by colleagues (i.e., fellow ALG staff) in the areas of helpfulness, professionalism, and effectiveness with learners. Annual performance and colleague evaluations serve as tools to assess ALG's ongoing training programs and to determine the need for additional training for any instructional personnel.

Curriculum

ALG is committed to meeting the needs of each learner. Its curriculum comprises individualized skill acquisition programs that have clearly defined behavioral objectives, specific teaching procedures, measurement procedures to determine the effectiveness of the interventions, and teaching steps to ensure generalization across stimuli (e.g., settings, relevant caregivers).

During the first few days of school, a skills assessment is administered to each learner to determine baseline rates of the learner's responses across a variety of skill areas (e.g., leisure, academic, daily living, fine motor). When a skill deficit is identified, an individualized skill acquisition program to target the deficit is either obtained from ALG's database of skill acquisition programs or, if necessary, written by an instructor, teacher, or director. To guarantee that the target objective and teaching strategies are appropriate for the learner, parent and director approval are required prior to implementation of the skill acquisition programs. Subsequently, the teaching program is added to the learner's daily schedule and is implemented by the learner's teacher or instructor. Currently ALG has approximately 600 individualized skill acquisition programs across a broad range of curriculum areas. ALG's preschool curriculum areas and examples of specific skill acquisition programs are listed in Table 6.1.

Initial teaching objectives typically focus on increasing a learner's instructional attending, imitative repertoire, receptive language, expressive language, and play skills. Special emphasis is placed on reducing nonfunctional responses (e.g., finger movements, hand flapping) by interrupting the behavior and teaching alternative, more appropriate responses (e.g., keeping hands in lap).

Children are enrolled in classes of two to four learners and are typically matched with peers who demonstrate comparable skill levels. Learners receive instruction in an individually designed teaching area containing all necessary teaching stimuli. Teaching periods are 30 or 45 minutes in length. During each teaching period, an instructor or teacher is assigned to a learner and is responsible for teaching specific skill acquisition programs to that learner. On average, three programs are taught per teaching period. Preschoolers commonly receive instruction related to one target objective (e.g., verbal imitation) several times during the school day to allow for repeated practice of an emerging skill. Most skill acquisition programs are taught during one-to-one teaching sessions. Small group and paired instruction sessions are scheduled throughout the day and provide opportunities to teach socially relevant behavior with peers, such as turn taking, responding in a group, and attending to peers. Figure 6.1 is a sample preschool schedule for one of ALG's 3-year-old learners.

Learner independence is promoted through the use of photographic or textual daily activity schedules (McClannahan & Krantz, 1999). For each learner, skill acquisition programs and daily activities are represented photographically in three-ring binders, along with Language Master cards containing scripted, audiotaped initiations related to each activity. Learners are prompted to attend to photographic stimuli representing scheduled teaching programs (e.g., a picture of a box of objects to indicate a labeling task), to run a Language Master card through a Language Master machine which provides a scripted statement related to the task for the learner to imitate (e.g., "Let's look at some toys"), to listen to the audiotaped model, and to repeat the verbal initiation to the teacher. The teacher then responds to the initiation (e.g., "Okay, let's look at some toys"), the learner independently gets the teaching materials, and the teaching interaction proceeds. During subsequent teaching days, supplementary prompts (e.g., audiotaped models) are systematically faded.

Table 6.1
Preschool Curricula

Curriculum Area	General Skill Promotion	Examples of Specific Skill Acquisition Programs
Attending	Orientation to visual and auditory stimuli	• Establishes eye contact in response to name • Sustains eye contact during a story or description of an event • Sustains eye contact during a lesson
Community	Uses and participates appropriately in municipal resources and activities	• Stays with an adult while walking • Uses playground equipment appropriately • Tolerates a haircut
Expressive Language	Nonverbal or verbal communication with others	• Requests preferred items • Labels objects • Uses "yes" and "no"
Fine Motor	Small muscle coordination	• Cuts using scissors • Colors within a boundary • Operates a mouse on the computer
Gross Motor	Large muscle coordination	• Rides a bicycle • Swings on a swing • In-line skates
Handwriting	Graphomotor skills	• Imitates graphomotor movements • Writes name • Circles and prints words corresponding to pictures
Imitation	Nonverbal imitative ability	• Imitates gross motor movements • Imitates actions with objects • Imitates a video model

(continues)

Table 6.1 *Continued*

Curriculum Area	General Skill Promotion	Examples of Specific Skill Acquisition Programs
Leisure	Recreation skills: independent or group spectator or participant	• Completes play sequence • Uses pictorial cues to build a structure • Sits appropriately while watching television
Preacademic	Acquisition of skills leading to academic tasks	• Matches identical pictures • Identifies letters • Identifies colors
Reading	Decoding and reading sight words; comprehension of written material	• Matches words to objects • Provides sound for written letters and/or letter combinations • Reads words
Receptive Language	Understanding of oral language	• Follows one-step instructions • Identifies pictures and objects • Identifies familiar people
Science	Knowledge about self and environment	• Identifies weather • Identifies animals • Names seasons
Self-Care	Independent personal hygiene	• Urinates in the toilet • Puts on clothing • Washes hands
Socialization	Social interaction skills	• Reciprocates social comments • Initiates greetings • Makes play initiation statements
Social Studies	Knowledge of family, community, and country	• Answers general knowledge questions

(*continues*)

Table 6.1 *Continued*

Curriculum Area	General Skill Promotion	Examples of Specific Skill Acquisition Programs
		• Identifies community helpers
		• Identifies days of the week
Work Studies	School-related work skills	• Raises hand to seek assistance
		• Completes tasks independently
		• Completes worksheets

Data collected at ALG on the use of these schedules throughout the school day revealed that learners with daily activity schedules with programmed initiations performed a higher rate of initiations toward adults and peers than did learners without daily schedules. In addition, adults were observed to prompt a greater number of initiations from learners whose programs were in daily schedules. Subsequently, daily schedules were implemented with all learners at ALG, including preschoolers. Figure 6.2 shows the rates of prompted and unprompted initiations toward adults and peers for learners who had daily schedules with programmed initiations and for learners who did not have daily schedules.

Some published curricula have been adapted by ALG instructional personnel for use with ALG learners. Examples of published reading curricula include the *Edmark Reading Program* for word recognition and beginning comprehension, *Explode the Code* (1994) for phonics, and *Starting Comprehension* (Staman, 1998) for beginning comprehension . Expressive language and general knowledge skills have been taught using *Manual of Exercises for Expressive Reasoning* (Lingui Systems, 1993). Numeration skills have been addressed using the Continental Press mathematics curricula (Gallivan, Greenburg, & Moss, 1980). Computer programs such as Reader Rabbit's Toddler (1997) have been used to teach mouse skills (i.e., pointing and clicking) and Words and Concepts II (Wilson & Fox, 1993) software has been used to teach receptive language concepts.

To assess learner progress, data are collected during the implementation of all skill acquisition programs and behavior reduction procedures. Pretest and posttest measures assess performance of target responses in the absence of prompts and reinforcement. Interobserver agreement data are collected on all

MARY L.

Programs	Time	Instructor	Mon	Tue	Wed	Thu	Fri
Identifies Familiar People (Photographs)	9:00–9:45	Margie	x	x	x	x	x
Imitates Audiotaped Models			x	x	x	x	x
Imitates Vocal Models			x	x	x	x	x
Spontaneously Requests Preferred Items (Incidental Teaching)			x	x	x	x	x
Independently Uses Mouse in Reader Rabbit	9:45–10:15	Jenn	x	x	x	x	x
Establishes Eye Contact in Response to Name			x	x	x	x	x
Follows Two-Step Instructions			x	x	x	x	x
Peer Initiations (Incidental Teaching)	10:15–10:45	Kirsten (M–T)	x	x	x	x	x
Imitates Block Constructions		Margie (W–F)	x	x	x	x	x
Matches Category Cards			x	x	x	x	x
Imitates Graphomotor Responses	10:45–11:15	Adrienne	x	x	x	x	x
Colors Within a Boundary			x	x	x	x	x
Imitates Audiotaped Models	11:15–11:45	Margie	x	x	x	x	x
Follows an Independent Activity Schedule			x	x	x	x	x
Imitates Completed Actions			x	x	x	x	x
Lunch	11:45–12:15	Jenn	x	x	x	x	x
Eats with a Fork			x	x	x	x	x
Rides a Tricycle	12:15–12:45	Adrienne	x	x	x	x	x
Imitates Vocal Models	12:45–1:15	Kirsten	x	x	x	x	x
Identifies Possession			x	x	x	x	x
Describes Pictures Using a Full Sentence			x	x	x	x	x
Identifies Familiar People (Photographs)	1:15–1:45	Adrienne	x	x	x	x	x
Identifies Numerals			x	x	x	x	x
Follows Two-Step Instructions			x	x	x	x	x
Gets Objects from a Distance	1:45–2:15	Jenn	x	x	x	x	x
Independently Uses a Mouse in Reader Rabbit			x	x	x	x	x
Imitates Completed Actions			x	x	x	x	x
Establishes Eye Contact	2:15–2:45	Kirsten	x	x	x	x	x
Identifies Possession			x	x	x	x	x
Spontaneously Requests Preferred Item (Incidental Teaching)			x	x	x	x	x

Figure 6.1. Sample preschool schedule for 3-year-old.

mastered objectives to ensure reliability of data collected. The data are reviewed daily by the classroom teachers, and modifications in teaching strategies are implemented if the data indicate that the learner is not acquiring the skill.

Learners, teachers, and parents participate in monthly educational clinics supervised by the director of educational programming. The clinics serve several functions: to assess the rate of acquisition of target objectives, to engage in collaborative problem solving when acquisition is slow or inconsistent, and to determine programming modifications or additions, if necessary.

Instructional strategies implemented at ALG are based on the principles of applied behavior analysis. Commonly used teaching interventions include time delay procedures (Taylor & Harris, 1995), discrete trial teaching, incidental teaching (Hart & Risley, 1975; McGee, Krantz, & McClannahan, 1985), video modeling (Charlop & Milstein, 1989; Taylor, Levin, & Jasper, 1999), photographic and textual activity schedules (Krantz, MacDuff, & McClannahan, 1993), use of audiotaped prompts via Language Master machines (McClannahan & Krantz, 1999), observational learning, peer modeling, small group and paired instruction, shaping, prompting, and systematic prompt fading (Cooper, Heron, & Heward, 1987). Novel interventions such as the implementation of a

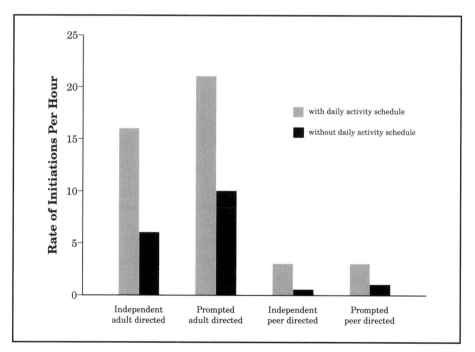

Figure 6.2. Rate of initiations per hour for students with and without daily activity schedules.

"tactile prompt" (Taylor & Levin, 1998) to promote initiations are evaluated empirically.

Challenging behavior (e.g., tantrums, self-injury, aggression) is addressed by (a) conducting a functional assessment (Carr et al., 1999) or an analogue functional analysis (Iwata, Dorsey, Slifer, Bauman, & Richman, 1982) to determine the controlling variables (i.e., antecedents, consequences, and setting events) and (b) developing an intervention based on the results of the assessment. For example, if it is determined that the target behavior is maintained by escape from aversive stimuli (e.g., difficult task demands), then instructional staff might be directed to teach the learner to use an alternative communicative response (e.g., to ask for a break), or to increase the density of positive reinforcement during the aversive situation (e.g., using primary reinforcers while implementing errorless teaching procedures), or to modify the antecedent stimuli (e.g., via curriculum modification) to decrease the learner's motivation to escape (Carr & Durand, 1985). Additional behavior reduction techniques that reflect current research findings in the behavioral literature are also used. Examples include extinction, differential reinforcement of low rates of behavior (DRL), response cost, and differential reinforcement of the nonoccurrence of behavior (DRO) (Cooper et al., 1987). Staff are carefully trained and supervised during the implementation of all behavior management techniques. Parents must provide written consent before instructional staff implement a procedure. A Human Rights Committee, consisting of a senior behavior analyst, parents of present and previous learners, and education and legal personnel, evaluates the effectiveness and social validity of all ALG intervention procedures.

Opportunities for Peer Interaction and Inclusion

Initially, learners participate in either ALG's intensive center-based education program or its home-based outreach program. When data indicate that a learner has developed effective receptive (e.g., is able to follow common one-step instructions) and expressive (e.g., is able to request tangible items) language skills and demonstrates minimal disruptive or stereotypic behavior, opportunities are provided for interaction with typical peers. These opportunities include peer modeling and participation in an educational setting with typically developing peers supported by a trained staff person.

Peer modeling is offered to preschoolers and consists of brief (1 to 2 hours), regularly scheduled teaching sessions with one or two typically developing, age-matched peers. Typical peers are usually relatives of other children enrolled in the program. During these sessions, specific objectives are identified for the learner with autism (e.g., responds to peer initiations) and peers are taught to engage in specific responses with the learner with autism (e.g., to prompt or reinforce the child with autism) (Strain & Odom, 1986; Taylor & Jasper, 1999). When acquisition of target objectives is achieved, additional opportunities for inclusion with typical peers in less restrictive educational settings may be pursued through ALG's supported inclusion program.

The supported inclusion program provides academic and social opportunities for a learner with autism in a less restrictive setting, usually the setting (i.e., public or private) the learner would attend if he or she did not have autism (Johnson, Meyer, & Taylor, 1996). A referral for participation in supported inclusion may be made by a parent, director, teacher, or child study team member. The decision for a learner to participate in an inclusion program is made collaboratively by assessing whether or not the learner has prerequisite skills necessary to succeed (i.e., learn) in the more typical environment.

A trained support person accompanies the learner to the inclusion site to facilitate the acquisition of skills that will subsequently enable the learner to function independently, without support, in as many areas as possible. To achieve this goal, the support person is trained to implement systematic prompting and fading procedures at the inclusion site, implement formal motivational systems, provide supplemental instruction, and record objective data to evaluate progress (Levin, Meyer, Dragwo, & Romano, 1998). In addition, ALG's director of support services provides ongoing training and supervision for support personnel and for classroom teachers throughout the school year. If the learner meets programmed objectives, the time in the regular education setting is gradually increased in preparation for a full transition.

Once an ALG learner makes a full transition to a less restrictive setting, follow-up services may be provided. Specifically, ALG senior clinical staff may provide ongoing consultation related to school, home, or community issues. In addition, the learners may attend ALG's extended year program (i.e., 6-week summer session) for more direct instruction on target objectives such as social, academic, or work study skills.

Family Involvement

ALG serves families, not only the learners with autism. Parent participation is an integral part of ALG's preschool program. Parents are required to implement teaching procedures in their homes, observe their children in programming, and attend monthly parent meetings. Consequently, comprehensive services are available to support collaboration between parents and ALG clinical staff.

ALG offers family consultation services to the families of learners enrolled in the education program. Family consultation has two primary goals: (1) for the learner to display stimulus generalization across settings (i.e., from school to home) and (2) for the learner to learn new functional skills in the home and community. When a learner enters ALG, the family receives weekly visits (more if necessary) for the first 6 months of enrollment from one of the clinical, doctoral level directors. Also within the first 6 months of enrollment, the family participates in a didactic parent training course that covers the basic principles and common techniques associated with applied behavior analysis. During the second 6-month interval, the family receives visits every other week from the same ALG director. During the second year of enrollment, the family receives visits twice per month from a designated family consultant (i.e., usually the learner's certified special education teacher) under the supervision of the director of support services, who accompanies the family consultant on approximately half of the home visits. If extra visits (e.g., daily) are required to address crises or to implement interventions any time during a learner's enrollment, then provisions are made for these extra visits to occur.

At the time of enrollment, a comprehensive assessment of home-based and community skills is conducted by the director of support services via parent interview and direct observation. Domains assessed include self-care, leisure, receptive and expressive language, community, and problem behavior. Deficits and behavioral challenges are identified via the implementation of the assessment. Subsequently, target objectives are discussed and prioritized collaboratively with the family. Decisions are made with respect to the original location of the intervention (i.e., school or home), the intervention agents (i.e., school personnel or home caregivers), the components of the intervention (e.g., DRO or functional communication training, primary or secondary reinforcement systems) and the type of data collection system that will be employed.

Through the implementation of individualized teaching programs, learners acquire a variety of skills in the home. Skills include, but are not limited to, following independent activity schedules, participating in cooperative leisure activities with other family members, and performing age-appropriate self-care skills. Learners also acquire skills to participate in community activities, such as shopping, going for haircuts, and going to the library. Eating, sleeping, and toileting issues are also addressed.

Hypothesis-driven interventions (i.e., with respect to potential maintaining variables) to address severe problem behavior in the home, such as aggression or tantrums, are developed by the ALG clinical staff (Repp, Felce, & Barton, 1988). Subsequently, with extensive support from ALG staff (e.g., three or four consecutive, daily home visits), an intervention is implemented and data are collected by the family to determine the efficacy of the treatment.

ALG offers a variety of services to immediate and extended family members. For example, a lecture series is offered to grandparents, aunts, uncles, significant family friends, older siblings, and cousins so these caregivers can respond to a variety of situations encountered in the home and community in an effective manner. Siblings of our learners are provided with opportunities to participate in ALG's sibling education and support groups and special sibling events (e.g., tie-dye shirt day). Participation in these groups is at the discretion of the family and is voluntary. Families' estimated needs for support and education are continually assessed.

ALG has an open door policy. Parents may observe their children during programming hours at any time, unannounced, and may stay as long as they like. A minimum of 3 hours of classroom observation is required each month. This time can include participation at monthly clinics, specially arranged training time, or general class observations.

During observations parents must adhere to observation policies and procedures to ensure that continuity of programming is maintained. Specifically, parents must report to the office upon arrival and obtain a clipboard that contains a simple form with questions about their visit (e.g., "Did you achieve the goals of your visit?"). Parents are also asked to refrain from speaking to instructional staff during these visits and to interact minimally with the learners. Specific parent training sessions are scheduled separately from these observation hours.

Parents, directors, and teachers attend mandatory, monthly meetings. Topics include a review of ALG policies and procedures (e.g., how to provide feedback to teaching personnel), agency issues (e.g., expansion or move to a new site), current topics and issues (e.g., new state regulations or the latest "miracle cure" documented on a tabloid television show), and programming issues (e.g., how to promote generalization to home or community).

On an annual basis, parents are required to evaluate the effectiveness of ALG's intervention services by responding to a written questionnaire about ALG's education and family consultation programs. The results are summarized and contribute to ongoing program development.

Description of ALG Outreach

The Alpine Learning Group Outreach Program currently serves 14 families throughout New Jersey and New York. Outreach is the newest program within the agency and was established as a means of extending ALG's services to toddlers newly diagnosed with autism or pervasive developmental disorders. We believe that it is important to teach toddlers with autism in environments that are comparable to those in which typically developing peers learn. The most appropriate and typical learning environment for a toddler is at his or her home, with parents and family members serving as primary "teachers." Therefore ALG Outreach develops and supervises intervention programs within the home in which parents and family members (as well as tutors hired by the families) receive the training and guidance required to successfully teach and interact with their children.

Parents establishing a home-based intervention program through ALG Outreach are responsible for providing their child with a minimum of 20 hours of treatment per week. On average, families receiving Outreach services provide their children with 30 hours of direct instruction per week. Home tutors are hired by families to implement teaching programs. Because of the nature of a home program, parents or caregivers must assume the role of team coordinator (i.e., communicating changes in curriculum or teaching strategies to hired tutors, scheduling sessions, supervising data collection and data summaries). Consequently, parents or caregivers are required to provide direct teaching to their children for several sessions per week so they are familiar with the programs and techniques that they oversee.

When a family enters the Outreach program, the Outreach team conducts an individualized educational assessment develops a program plan for each learner and, during a 10-hour didactic training, teaches all team members, parents, and family members about the principles of applied behavior analysis and related instructional strategies. Teaching procedures used in Outreach programs are consistent with procedures implemented in the day education program (e.g., incidental teaching, photographic schedules). In-home supervision begins at 10 hours per week and gradually decreases to 3 to 6 hours per week, where it remains until the learner reaches age 5 or is no longer in need of services. The presence of team and family members is required during weekly clinics in which interobserver-agreement data are collected, new programs are introduced, teaching procedures are modified to address poor acquisition of target objectives, teaching is critiqued, and instructional strategies are modeled.

All families and learners in the Outreach program have access to ALG's broad-based curriculum, precise data collection systems, and comprehensive training model. The program also offers support to siblings (through the sibling support program) and transition planning when a learner is ready to move into a school setting. When learners acquire basic prerequisite skills, ALG may support a learner in a regular education setting, in a manner that is consistent with ALG's education program's supported inclusion model.

Program Evaluation

Annually, ALG conducts a comprehensive program evaluation consisting of internal and external evaluations. Once per year, a program evaluation rating scale is sent to all instructional and administrative staff, school district personnel, and parents. Consumers are asked to rate ALG on its ability to provide effective intervention to learners with autism, as well as the staff and administration's cooperativeness, availability, and communication skills. In addition, since 1992, ALG has been conducting annual external evaluations. Specifically, annual program evaluations on program effectiveness for each learner have been conducted by an outside, independent consultant with expertise in the area of autism intervention. During the 1997–1998 school year, the independent external evaluator rated 99% of ALG's individualized skill acquisition programs as demonstrating behavior change in the desired direction and 100% as being appropriate and functional (i.e., social validity measure). Figure 6.3 shows the percentage of programs rated as appropriate and effective (i.e., behavior change in the desired direction) on external evaluations since 1992.

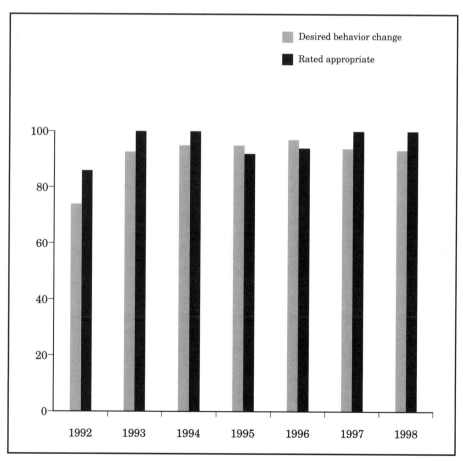

Figure 6.3. The percentage of Alpine Learning Group educational programs rated as appropriate and as having desired behavior change.

Transition Outcomes

Since July 1989, 26 preschool learners have enrolled in ALG's center-based program and remained for at least 24 months. The average age at time of enrollment was 3 years 11 months (3-11). ALG's youngest learner at time of enrollment was 3-1 and the oldest preschool learner at time of enrollment was 5-0. As of February 1999, seven (27%) of ALG's total preschool enrollment made the transition from ALG's center-based program into public school settings. Table 6.2 provides details regarding each learner's transition and current placement.

Table 6.2
Alpine Learning Group (ALG) Transition Statistics for Students Enrolled at 5 Years of Age and Younger as of February 1999

Age at Grad-uation	Gender	Tenure at ALG	Graduate Placement	Support	Current Placement	Support
5.8	F	23 months	Public School/ Kindergarten	Self-contained/ mainstreaming opportunities	Public School/ 7th grade	Resource room
5.5	M	22 months	Public School/ Kindergarten	None	Public School/ 5th grade	None
10	M	61 months	Public School/ 3rd grade	Classroom aide	Public School/ Self-contained 7th grade	In-class support for student with autism
7.3	F	49 months	Public School/ 1st grade	In-class support for student with autism; resource room	Public School/ 5th grade	In-class support for student with autism; resource room
8	M	47 months	Public School/ 2nd grade	In-class support for student with autism	Public School/ 5th grade	In-class support for student with autism
5.9	M	22 months	Public School/ Kindergarten	None	Public School/ 2nd grade	In-class support for student with autism
9.6	M	72 months	Public School/ 3rd grade	In-class support for student with autism	Public School/ 4th grade	In-class support for student with autism

ALG's Outreach program has served 30 learners since the fall of 1995. The average age at which a learner began to receive services was 2-8. The youngest learner was 2-0, the oldest 3-9. Aging out of the Outreach program, 19 learners made the transition to a variety of settings: 13 (68%) enrolled in private or public, center-based programs serving individuals with autism; 1 (5%) enrolled in a private school serving individuals with communication impairments; 2 (11%) received services from their school districts' special education departments; and 3 (16%) enrolled in their local public school kindergarten classes.

Issues for Future Efforts

As ALG provides intensive behavioral intervention services for preschoolers with autism, it is essential to continually question and test empirically the efficacy of the various components of the program model. Efforts must increase in two additional areas as well: (1) providing equal access to effective intervention to all children and their families and (2) routinely providing outcome measures that document effectiveness and acquisition of a wide variety of skills.

With respect to programming for young children with autism, one issue that divides behavior analysts is the type of environment in which the children should receive intervention services. Specifically, whereas ALG's center-based program provides intensive behavioral intervention in a segregated setting, others advocate placement in inclusive preschool settings (e.g., McGee, Daly, & Jacobs, 1994). To date, however, no empirical demonstrations (i.e., objective, direct comparisons of the two models) have elucidated the advantages or disadvantages of the different strategies. Rather than advocating for the model in which one is invested, professionals should work collaboratively, across program models, to collect objective measures documenting the effectiveness and shortcomings of program models. For example, learners receiving services in an integrated preschool may learn to emit appropriate social behaviors with peers (e.g., responding, initiating), but they may not learn to perform as many self-care or academic skills as learners receiving intervention in a more controlled, segregated setting. Several outcomes resulting from this line of inquiry are possible: Perhaps a model intervention program combining the most effective components of each existing program would emerge. Or perhaps a combination of specific learner characteristics (i.e., the behavioral manifestation of autism in that each learner) would lead to a better outcome in one program, whereas a different set of behavioral characteristics would be more amenable to the other intervention model. As responsible scientist and practitioners, we must continually assess the effectiveness of our intervention models and address challenges not only from outside of our discipline (i.e., applied behavior analysis) but also from within the discipline.

Behavioral intervention models vary with respect to specific program components; however, several variables block many families from gaining access to any type of intensive behavioral services. For example, families are frequently not reimbursed by early intervention agencies and public school districts. The variability from town to town, county to county, and state to state is huge. Some families receive full reimbursement, whereas others receive partial coverage. Many families receive nothing except generic speech–language and occupational therapies for 2 hours per week. One of ALG's goals is to offer a sliding fee scale to families through the use of scholarships and grant monies. The long-term solution, however, has to be more equitable funding to all families from traditional funding sources.

When funding is not an issue, parents still have difficulty gaining access to adequate training and support in their homes. The paucity of professionals able to teach parents to use instructional strategies to promote language and to use effective behavior management strategies in the home is evident by the sizable waiting list for admission to programs such as ALG. Expanding specialized special education graduate school programs to train professionals in this field and specialized certification (e.g., in applied behavior analysis) may address this concern. In addition, center-based programs must offer training and the necessary supports in the home to help families implement interventions and address challenging situations.

One challenge that caregivers and professionals continue to address is the development of social behavior in children with autism. Perhaps a productive way to address this challenge would be to focus on new outcome measures that reflect the overall sociability of the learner, specifically outcome measures that assess a student's desire for social interaction. The effectiveness of behavioral interventions to facilitate the occurrence of specific topographies of social behavior, such as frequency of reciprocal interactions (McGee, Almeida, Sulzer-Azeroff, & Feldman, 1992), frequency of initiations to peers (Krantz & McClannahan, 1993), and length of social interactions (Kamps, Barbetta, Leonard, and Delquadri, 1994), is commonly accepted. However, the essence of the social deficits typically displayed by learners with autism—that is, the lack of desire for social interaction—is usually not addressed. Yet professionals refer to this characteristic all of the time when describing children as being more or less "social." If a specific measure to assess desire for social interaction was used, then the answer to the fundamental question plaguing clinicians and researchers might be evident: Under what conditions does this critical characteristic, desire for social interaction, develop?

A more general point is that the effectiveness of broad-based (i.e., across all skill areas) intensive behavioral interventions cannot be measured by a single outcome measure at one point in time. Comprehensive measures that are objective and clinically and socially meaningful should be routinely implemented. While a transition to a public school is one positive outcome, it is usually more dependent upon the climate and philosophy of a particular school district than the actual effectiveness of the intervention or the skill level of the learner. Consequently, multiple measures that would provide some kind of convergent validity with respect to the efficacy of the intervention need to be analyzed. For example, data that reflect improvements in a family's quality of life (Carr et al., 1999) should be collected. Is the family able to participate in significantly more community activities (e.g., eating at restaurants, attending family functions, going to the movies) than before the child's enrollment in the program? Do these improvements maintain over time? Data that reflect the learner's ability to choose and participate in appropriate leisure activities, his or her ability to eat a healthy variety of food items, a desire for social interaction with peers, and the learner's level of compliance in the home should all be part of a multicomponent outcome measure used to assess the efficacy of an intervention model.

References

American Psychiatric Association. (1994). *Diagnostic and statistical manual* (4th ed.). Washington, DC: Author.

Carr, E. G., & Durand, V. M. (1985). The social-communicative basis of severe behavior problems in children. In S. Reiss & R. R. Bootzin (Eds.), *Theoretical issues in behavior therapy* (pp. 219–254). New York: Academic Press.

Carr, E. G., Levin, L., McConnachie, G., Carlson, J. I., Kemp, D. C., Smith, C. E., & Magito McLaughlin, D. (1999). Comprehensive multi situational intervention for problem behavior in the community: Long-term maintenance and social validation. *Journal of Positive Behavior Interventions, 1*, 5–25.

Charlop, M. H., & Milstein, J. P. (1989). Teaching autistic children conversational speech using video modeling. *Journal of Applied Behavior Analysis, 22*, 275–285.

Cooper, J. O., Heron, T. E., & Heward, W. L. (1987). *Applied behavior analysis.* New York: Macmillan.

Dunn, L. M., & Dunn, L. M. (1997). *Peabody Picture Vocabulary Test* (3rd. ed.). Circle Pines, MN: American Guidance Service.

Edmark Reading Program, Level One. (1977). Bellevue, WA: Edmark.

Explode the Code. (1994). Cambridge, MA: Educators Publishing Service.

Gallivan, C., Greenburg, I. H., & Moss, A. R. (1980). *Numbers.* Elizabeth, PA: Continental Press.

Hart, B. M., & Risley, T. R. (1975). Incidental teaching of language in the preschool. *Journal of Applied Behavior Analysis, 8*, 411–420.

Iwata, B. A., Dorsey, M. F., Slifer, K. J., Bauman, K. E., & Richman, G. S. (1983). Toward a functional analysis of self-injury. *Analysis and Intervention in Developmental Disabilities, 2*, 3–20.

Johnson, S. C., Meyer, L., & Taylor, B. A. (1996). Supported inclusion. In C. Maurice, G. Green, & S. Luce (Eds.), *Behavioral interventions for young children with autism: A manual for parents and professionals.* Austin, TX: PRO-ED.

Kamps, D. M., Barbetta, P. M., Leonard, B. R., & Delquadri, J. (1994). Classwide peer tutoring: An integration strategy to improve reading skills and promote peer interactions among students with autism and general education peers. *Journal of Applied Behavior Analysis, 27,* 49–61.

Krantz, P. J., MacDuff, M. T., & McClannahan, L. E. (1993). Programming participation in family activities for children with autism: Parents' use of photographic schedules. *Journal of Applied Behavior Analysis, 26,* 137–138.

Krantz, P. J., & McClannahan, L. E. (1993). Teaching children with autism to initiate to peers: Effects of a script-fading procedure. *Journal of Applied Behavior Analysis, 26,* 121–132.

Levin, L., Meyer, L., Dragwo, D., & Romano, J. (1998). *Integrating children with autism: Strategies for regular education teachers and inclusion personnel.* Invited workshop presented at the 15th annual Center for Outreach and Services for the Autism Community conference, Long Branch, NJ.

LinguiSystems. (1993). *Manual of Exercises for Expressive Reasoning, I and II.* Moline, IL: Author.

McClannahan, L. E., & Krantz, P. J. (1993). On systems analysis in autism intervention programs. *Journal of Applied Behavior Analysis, 26*(4), 589–596.

McClannahan, L. E., & Krantz, P. (1999). *Activity schedules for children with autism: Teaching independent behavior.* Bethesda, MD: Woodbine House.

McGee, G. G., Almeida, M. C., Sulzer-Azaroff, B., & Feldman, R. S. (1992). Promoting reciprocal interactions via peer incidental teaching. *Journal of Applied Behavior Analysis, 25,* 515–524.

McGee, G. G., Daly, T., & Jacobs, H. A. (1994). The Walden preschool. In S. L. Harris & J. S. Handleman (Eds.), *Preschool education programs for children with autism* (pp. 127–162). Austin, TX: PRO-ED.

McGee, G. G., Krantz, P. J., & McClannahan, L. E. (1985). The facilitated effects of incidental teaching on preposition use by autistic children. *Journal of Applied Behavior Analysis, 18,* 17–31.

New Jersey Administrative Code, 6A:14-4-4.7. (1998).

Reader Rabbit's Toddler [Computer Software]. (1997). Cambridge, MA: The Learning Company.

Repp, A., Felce, D., & Barton, L. (1988). Basing the treatment of stereotypic and self-injurious behavior on the hypotheses of their causes. *Journal of Applied Behavior Analysis, 21,* 281–290.

Sparrow, S. S., Balla, D. A., & Cicchetti, D. V. (1984). *Vineland Adaptive Behavior Scales.* Circle Pines, MN: American Guidance Service.

Staman, A. L. (1998). *Starting comprehension: Stories to advance reading and thinking.* Cambridge, MA: Educators Publishing Service.

Strain, P. S., & Odom, S. L. (1986). Peer social initiations: Effective intervention for social skills development of exceptional children. *Exceptional Children, 52,* 543–552.

Taylor, B. A., & Harris, S. L. (1995). Teaching children with autism to seek information: Acquisition of novel information and generalization of responding. *Journal of Applied Behavior Analysis, 28,* 3–14.

Taylor, B. A., & Jasper, S. (1999). *Incorporating peers in the treatment of children with autism.* Manuscript submitted for publication.

Taylor, B. A., & Levin, L. (1998). Teaching a student with autism to make verbal initiations: Effects of a tactile prompt. *Journal of Applied Behavior Analysis, 31,* 651–654.

Taylor, B. A., Levin, L., & Jasper, S. (1999). Increasing play-related statements in children with autism toward their siblings: Effects of video modeling. *Journal of Developmental and Physical Disabilities.*

Thorndike, R. L., Hagen, E. P., & Sattler, J. M. (1986). *The Stanford–Binet Intelligence Scale* (4th ed.). Chicago: Riverside.

Wilson, M. S., & Fox, B. J. (1993). *Words & Concepts II* [Computer Software]. Winooski, VT: Laureate Learning Systems.

The Walden Early Childhood Programs

7

Gail G. McGee, Michael J. Morrier, and Teresa Daly

The Walden Early Childhood Programs take a comprehensive incidental teaching approach to providing a continuum of early education to toddlers, preschoolers, and pre-kindergarten–aged children, including children with autism and their typical peers. The name Walden reflects a blend of Skinner's (1948) utopian education with a natural developmental approach symbolized by Thoreau (1847). The curriculum is grounded in the assumption that early childhood education for all young children should appropriately concentrate on language and social development, and that incidental teaching procedures offer an ideal medium for accomplishing the goals of inclusion. The promotion of engagement is emphasized through environmental engineering that highlights children's most highly preferred materials and activities. Finally, active family collaboration is a priority.

The original Preschool program, established in 1985 as the Walden Learning Center, was affiliated with the Department of Psychology at the University of Massachusetts at Amherst. In the fall of 1991, the Walden project relocated to the Department of Psychiatry and Behavioral Sciences at the Emory University School of Medicine in Atlanta, Georgia, where it is a component of the Emory Autism Resource Center. A Toddler Center was added to the original Preschool program in 1993. In 1994, a Pre-Kindergarten classroom was opened to complete the early childhood continuum.

This chapter is dedicated to the memory of Ellen P. Reese, who encouraged our early efforts and who provided an elegant model of professional dedication. Special tribute is also due to Grandma Ceil, who danced inspiration and joy into the hearts of Walden children and staff, and to her daughter Beth Sulzer-Azaroff, who made Walden a possibility.

Program Information: Walden Early Childhood Programs, Emory University School of Medicine, Emory Autism Resource Center, 718 Gatewood Road, Atlanta, GA 30322; 404/727-8350.

The Toddler program begins active early intervention in the natural environments of children's homes and a child care center. The original Preschool continues to operate as a university-based lab school, which permits the study of what is possible under nearly ideal conditions. The Pre-Kindergarten prepares children for continuing school inclusion and full community participation. Although the Preschool began and continues as a lab school, the Toddler Center is being fully or partially replicated outside of academic settings elsewhere in Georgia, as well as in Alabama, California, and Maryland.

Walden originated as a systematic replication of the Toddler Center model for typical children's day care (O'Brien, Porterfield, Herbert-Jackson, & Risley, 1979). Of key importance was the model's organization of staff and setting to maximize naturally occurring teaching opportunities (Allen & Hart, 1984; Twardosz, Cataldo, & Risley, 1974). Hallmarks of the model are an overlapping activity schedule and designated teaching zones (LeLaurin & Risley, 1972; Risley & Favell, 1979). However, substantial adaptations have been needed to meet the needs of children with autism, to serve an inclusive group spanning a broad age range, and to incorporate new findings on incidental teaching and peer interactions.

Vigorous efforts have been invested in obtaining community input, both in the original (Sulzer-Azaroff, Jones, & McGee, 1986) and new program sites. Community advisory boards have played key roles in ensuring program responsiveness to both rural (Western Massachusetts) and urban (Atlanta) concerns. Relocation also required adaptation to vastly different political and philosophical orientations in the Northeast and the South. For example, a regional difference that influenced program development pertained to ideology regarding the appropriateness of academic preparation in preschool programs. In Georgia, parents demanded rigorous attention to educational outcomes, whereas in Western Massachusetts a more laissez-faire developmental approach was the community norm. Walden responded by blending systematic academic preparation into a developmentally appropriate early childhood curriculum.

From the outset, the resources of an applied laboratory have made it feasible to obtain empirical answers to clinical challenges, and Walden has provided a setting to conduct practical field tests of research findings. The original Preschool program was developed in the absence of specific start-up funds, but graduate students and collateral research funding were critical assets. Development and evaluation of the Toddler Center was supported by a "3 + 2" demonstration model grant from the U.S. Department of Education. Start-up of the Pre-Kindergarten classroom was accomplished with seed funding from various state and foundation grants.

In 1999, the overall Walden program cost per child with autism was approximately $22,000 per year. However, this figure does not fully account for the resources available to research programs in university settings (e.g., low-cost student labor, data analysis resources, equipment). There have been significant differences in mechanisms for funding operating costs across program locations and across ages. In Massachusetts, state law mandating "maximum feasible benefits" required local school districts to support full tuition and travel costs for children with autism, but at the time it was more difficult to obtain funding for intensive treatment of children below 3 years of age.

In Georgia there has been an advantage of core support that reduces program tuition, because Walden is now part of a larger state- and foundation-funded autism center. There is public early intervention funding for the Toddler Center, in which the tuition for children with autism is $15,000 per year. However, the situation is more challenging after children turn 3 years old. Some school systems have paid full or partial costs ($14,400 per year for the Preschool and $12,000 per year for the Pre-Kindergarten), but public funding has often required parental threats of litigation along with legal representation. In a few cases, insurance reimbursements have assisted families in covering tuition costs. There has also been block grant day care funding to partially cover costs for both children with autism and typical children who meet qualifying guidelines. For many families, however, the high cost of even the subsidized tuition poses a tremendous hardship, and accessibility for all children is dependent on vigorous program fund-raising and generosity of the local philanthropic community.

Healthy to the goals of inclusion, the primary regulatory standards in both Massachusetts and Georgia have been monitored by the day care licensing agencies. The center-based program components are classified as private preschools, and day care regulations for typical children have been applied to all children. Although quality programs for children with special needs require that such standards be exceeded in many areas (e.g., adult–child ratios), environmental normalization has been encouraged, and accepted special education practices have been challenged (e.g., teachers are prohibited from using a "disapproving tone" to correct toilet accidents). Extramural grant funding has also been accompanied by program review, with formal site visits conducted by representatives of the U.S. Department of Education, the Georgia Department of Human Resources, and the Georgia Childcare Council.

Participating Children

Walden enrolls both children with autism and typical children, beginning as young as 15 months of age and continuing up until the age of kindergarten entry. Initially the program enrolled approximately one typical child for every child with special needs, but the current program aims to include each child with autism with at least two typical peers. The program evaluation data presented at the end of this chapter will report the progress of children with autism who have graduated following participation in a substantial portion of the curriculum, although not necessarily the entire current continuum of Toddler to Preschool to Pre-Kindergarten.

Thirty-four children with autism have graduated following at least 18 months of intensive early treatment at Walden. Excluded from this report are children enrolled during or after 1999, children who participated less than 18 months or left prior to the age for entry to kindergarten, and children who attended only the Toddler or Pre-Kindergarten program but not the Preschool program. The primary reasons for attrition have been financial considerations and family or program relocation.

Walden graduates with autism included 29 males and 5 females. Their average age at entry to Walden was 3 years 6 months (3-6) (range 2-0 to 5-6), and their average age at graduation was 6-0 (range 4-11 to 7-4). Of these children, 18% were from economically disadvantaged families, and 21% represented minority groups. The majority of the children did not participate in entry testing in a manner that made it possible to derive a valid score of intellectual ability. The average IQ was 74 (range < 29 to 91) for the 11 children who did obtain full composite scores during entry testing.

Three of the children in the sample of Walden graduates with autism had hearing loss, vision impairment, or both. Nine of the graduates with autism had documented evidence of neurological impairment, including cleft palates and other midline damage requiring surgery, seizures, chronic toxic lead levels, and an undeveloped myelin sheath. One child had additional diagnoses of cytomegalovirus and cerebral palsy, and one child subsequently received an additional diagnosis of Tourette's syndrome. Four children with autism were from homes in which English was a second language.

Initial Screening and Assessment

Currently, most children enter Walden as toddlers and stay until they go to kindergarten. Referrals of toddlers with autism come primarily from autism diagnostic clinics, from developmental pediatricians and pediatric neurologists, and from early intervention specialists with Georgia's Part C (Babies Can't Wait) program. Children are accepted at older ages when a rare opening exists, and accommodations are made to provide the families of these children with components of the treatment package that are more intensive during the toddler year (i.e., toilet training, family program).

Prior to opening the Toddler Center, entry to Walden required that children with autism have an independent diagnosis of autism spectrum disorder, which was confirmed in an in-house screening. Currently, admission requires that each child with autism meet preestablished diagnostic criteria based on standardized assessment instruments and clinical information. Certified examiners administer the *Autism Diagnostic Interview–Revised* (ADI–R; Lord, Rutter, & LeCouteur, 1994), which is a semistructured parent interview, and the *Autism Diagnostic Observation Schedule* (ADOS; Lord, Rutter, DiLavore, & Risi, 1999), which is administered in an interactive session with the child, whose social and communicative behaviors are sampled with familiar (parents) and unfamiliar adults. In addition, the early childhood coordinator and the toddler classroom coordinator independently complete *The Childhood Autism Rating Scale* (CARS; Schopler, Reichler, & Renner, 1988) based on observations of the child's behavior among peers and teachers in the Toddler classroom. Cumulative information is then compiled and reviewed for documentation of the presence of the behavioral characteristics of autism, based on criteria in the *Diagnostic and Statistical Manual of Mental Disorders–Fourth Edition* (DSM–IV; American Psychiatric Association, 1994).

Due to the lack of diagnostic certitude for children under the age of 36 months, there is a two-stage screening for young children when their initial assessment results are ambiguous. Entry to the Toddler classroom requires documentation of the presence of autism on either the Social or Language scale of the ADI–R and ADOS–G, and the other domains must fall at least in the range of pervasive developmental disorder. If the diagnosis of autism was not conclusive on all assessments at the time of the initial screening, a child is assessed again at the time of exit from the Toddler Center. Entry to the Preschool requires that the presence of autism be documented by all three instruments and according to DSM–IV criteria.

Additional entry criteria require that children be ambulatory for reasons of safety. Children have never been denied entry to Walden based on level of functioning, performance on tests of intellectual ability, or other indicators of severity of impairment. Parents are asked to sign a preadmission agreement that children may not be maintained on psychotropic or other behavior control medications. Also prohibited is participation in other alternative or potentially conflicting therapeutic interventions for autism, in order to preclude confounds with Walden's ongoing research on treatment outcomes. However, many of the Walden graduates have participated concurrently in private speech or occupational therapy sessions at some point during their enrollment.

Prospective typical children are observed during an informal classroom visit to determine whether they present the age-appropriate language and social skills that permit them to serve as peer models. Children with English as a second language have been accepted throughout the program's history, with experience indicating that young typical children rapidly become English fluent. Participation by gifted "typical" students is also common in university-based settings.

For purposes of describing participants in collateral research projects, all children are tested within 6 months of admission (or when age eligible) with the following standardized instruments: *The Stanford–Binet Intelligence Scale–Fourth Edition* (Thorndike, Hagen, & Sattler, 1986) or the *Bayley Scales of Infant Development–Second Edition* (Bayley, 1993), the *Psychoeducational Profile–Revised* (Schopler, Reichler, Bashford, Lansing, & Marcus, 1990), the *Peabody Picture Vocabulary Test–Revised* (Dunn & Dunn, 1981), and *The Expressive One-Word Picture Vocabulary Test* (Gardner, 1990). To expedite educational planning, all children are also assessed on the age-appropriate version of the *Learning Accomplishment Profile* (Sanford & Zelman, 1981), and parents of children with autism serve as respondents on the *Vineland Adaptive Behavior Scales* (Sparrow, Balla, & Cicchetti, 1984).

An important luxury afforded by Walden's lab-school status is the availability of objective behavioral measures taken from a quarterly videotaped database, which provides critical data for documenting entry and exit levels of functioning. Each child is videotaped daily for 5 minutes across a 10-day block, and a systematic sampling procedure is arranged to track children across different activities, times of day, and days of the week. The unique feature of the videotaped database is that there are no contrived observational conditions. Children are videotaped at preset times wherever they happen to be, doing whatever they happen to be doing. Videotapes are scored by a highly trained research team, who obtain objective, reliable measures of more than two dozen language, social, and engagement variables.

Preschool Personnel

The program director, who originated the Walden programs, is a licensed clinical psychologist; she has a background in behavior analysis and 18 years of experience in treatment of children with autism. Among the roles served by the director are program and research design, participation in clinical decision making and parent negotiations, immediate review of child safety issues, and fiscal and administrative support. The director supervises an early childhood coordinator, who is a certified teacher and has 10 years experience on the Walden team. The early childhood coordinator is responsible for the planning of individualized clinical treatment plans, oversight of classroom operation, enrollment and assessment, program evaluation, and supervision of the classroom coordinators.

Each classroom is staffed by a classroom coordinator (who serves online as lead teacher for part of each day), backup lead teachers, and teachers. The classroom coordinators are responsible for day-to-day management of the program. These positions require astute clinical judgment, effective training skills, efficient administration abilities, and a superb sense of parent and public relations. The coordinators must be experienced in both behavior analysis and the Walden approach, and lead teachers must be proficient in all Walden teaching and training routines. In the Toddler classroom, family liaisons must be qualified lead teachers in the child's classroom.

In the Toddler and Preschool classes, a one-to-three adult–child ratio is maintained throughout the day, so that at any given time, a lead teacher and three to five teachers are working with the children. Due to the intensity of the teaching demands, "on the floor" time is limited to 4 hours per day for each staff member. The adult–child ratio is reduced to one-to-six in the Pre-Kindergarten class in order to begin preparing children for conditions in public school kindergartens.

Backgrounds of the Walden staff have varied across program years, and the result has been interdisciplinary enrichment. Staff have presented undergraduate to postdoctoral training in psychology, early childhood education, special education, communication disorders, occupational therapy, social work, and varied other disciplines. Psychiatry residents also contribute teaching time during their rotations. Selection is based on "Peace Corps" levels of enthusiasm, energy, patience, and professional motivation, which are qualities we have found easier to select for than to train. Specific credentials and experience are less important due to the availability of a rigorous and ongoing program of training and supervision. In fact, over the years, the specialized training opportunities available at Walden have yielded a largely overqualified staff.

The Emory Autism Resource Center offers Walden significant collateral program and staffing resources. For example, the diagnostic clinic staff assists with assessments, family program staff members contribute parent seminars, and research team personnel provide crucial data on child progress. Collateral projects permit full-time employment for part-time Walden teachers, as well as provide varied training and job advancement opportunities for personnel.

The Walden curriculum was developed with the assistance of an array of interdisciplinary consultants, including ongoing input from nationally recognized autism and early childhood experts. Technical assistance is usually secured in the form of program development advice, based on the premise that children need specialty input blended into their daily activities. For example, although children with autism do not participate in traditional speech therapy sessions at Walden, our intensive language curriculum was developed with substantial input from certified speech–language pathologists and leaders in the field of language development.

Staff Preparation and Supervision

Staff acquire and maintain new skills via intensive hands-on training and feedback, with consistency of performance ensured through ongoing performance appraisal. Classroom teachers are trained to mastery in every routine they will be assigned. For example, all teachers are trained in zone-based routines, such as managing free play, conducting small group activities, and serving snack or lunch. Based on assignments, some are trained for specialized zones, such as dramatic play, peer incidental teaching, or social games. All teachers are prepared in procedural proficiency, such as teaching independence, prevention of challenging behaviors, and safety and emergency procedures, as well as in incidental teaching. Lead teachers are trained and supervised similarly, through use of a checklist that assesses both their training and classroom management skills.

Initial staff training takes place over a period of 1 month. An apprenticeship training system includes opportunities to observe and model an experienced teacher (while reviewing the designated zone checklist), along with opportunities for direct practice with immediate feedback. As the trainees gain familiarity with the routines, providing opportunities for positive feedback, their performance begins to be evaluated with a zone-based checklist. (An example of the performance checklist for the Snack Server routine is shown in Figure 7.1). The specificity of the checklist components prompts the trainers (the lead teacher or experienced teachers) to comment on relevant aspects of the trainee's performance, immediately after observing for a 5-minute period. Training continues on zone-based checklists until the trainee demonstrates mastery by achieving all components on two consecutive checklists for each routine.

Procedural checklists are also introduced during the first weeks, using a similar training format. Based on in-house research and experience in the preschool setting, training of incidental teaching has been broken into two phases. First, teachers are given checklist-based training in the easiest case scenario, a one-to-one session with preselected materials and clearly designated written instructions for teaching a specific skill. Next, training is provided on more sophisticated incidental teaching skills, including how to adjust the timing of prompts to children's differing initiation skills. Specifically, the teacher learns to approach and wait for a child's initiation, then to comment on the child's activity, and, if necessary, to gently control access to the child's preferred materials or activities.

Maintenance of proficiency is ensured by at least monthly performance appraisals with a more general classroom checklist. If there is slippage on the general checklist or any concerns regarding teacher performance, there is a return to mastery training on specific zone- or procedure-based checklists. The checklists serve as a mechanism for providing frequent, specific praise to teachers, which keeps staff morale and performance quality at high levels.

Didactic training and written materials are also provided, although the assumption is that skills are acquired in-vivo, and that workshops and readings provide knowledge and rationales for the procedures teachers have learned. During orientation, weekly staff meetings, and periodic curriculum days, training presentations are offered in areas such as incidental teaching

SNACK SERVER

Criterion: +, 0, NA

	Trainer			
	Date			
1. Get ready to work with children, maintain high standards of cleanliness (wash hands, put on rubber gloves, pull back hair)?				
2. Get children settled and begin serving quickly?				
3. Prompt requests following the Requesting Skills chart?				
4. Talk up to all children at appropriate contact and developmental levels?				
5. Allow children room for independence?				
6. Stay in zone until activity ends?				
7. Mark on the Snack record what the children ate?				
8. Correctly handle disruptions or dawdling? Signal the lead teacher if the zone becomes disorganized?				
9. Finish serving each child within 10 minutes and end snack within 30 minutes of start of snack?				
10. Confine adult conversation to teaching and essential zone coordination?				
11. Clean up snack area?				
Feedback received?				

Figure 7.1. Snack Server's training checklist.

research, promoting peer interactions, or arranging environments to support engagement. In recent years, there has been increased attention to direct instruction in applied behavior analysis and general principles of learning, because staff members become better trainers when they understand the terminology and rationales for the procedures they have been prepared to implement.

All management level staff members participate in weekly clinical meetings, which have a goal of training clinical problem-solving skills in the context of addressing child-specific issues. All staff must also complete state-required training for child care professionals, including first aid, disease and injury prevention, cardiopulmonary resuscitation, prevention and detection of child abuse and neglect, nutrition, and 10 additional hours of approved professional education sessions each year. Additionally, Walden teachers are given access to visiting experts, and the program covers the expenses of management personnel who make presentations at regional and national conferences.

An Incidental Teaching Curriculum That Promotes the Development of Social Communication

An interface of skillful teachers and an environment rich with children's choices permits children to enjoy their early childhood years while receiving intensive instruction. Effective participation in society is the overriding goal. Incidental teaching combined with social inclusion and early intervention offers a powerful mix of educational technologies. However, the complexities of this approach have required development of a curriculum that specifies what children need to learn, what teachers need to do to individualize for children at wide-ranging developmental levels, and what classroom organization will foster children's and teachers' best performances.

Intensity of Intervention

At least 30 hours per week of planned instruction is provided to children in all Walden programs, which operate continuously throughout the year. In the Toddler program, treatment is provided in half-day sessions at the center, with additional hours provided in children's homes. The Preschool and Pre-Kindergarten operate for 6 hours per day, 5 days per week. In addition, early care and after-care time ensures that children are kept productively engaged, which makes it possible to attract typical children who need child care, and which adds up to 17.5 additional hours per week of engaged time for the children with autism.

Benefits and Challenges of Social Inclusion

Typical children are wonderful intervention agents for children with autism—they are active and interesting and they provide invaluable social learning opportunities. Walden makes an assumption that learning how to learn from peers is best accomplished when children are as young as possible. Another advantage of inclusion in early childhood programs is that daily observation of typical children assists in the selection and pursuit of functional, normalized intervention goals for children with autism.

Social inclusion affords typical children the benefits of enriched classrooms, including high teacher–child ratios, well-prepared and closely supervised teachers, and individualized instruction. There is evidence that helping other children can contribute to improved self-esteem (Devin-Sheehan, Feldman, & Allen, 1976), and typical children enrolled in day care centers that include children with disabilities have been found to have advanced peer interaction skills (Daly, 1991). Although more difficult to validate, early social inclusion may give children a lasting appreciation of differences among people.

There are some free effects of keeping children with autism in close proximity to typical peers. Specifically, levels of self-stimulatory and other autistic behaviors are lower when children with autism are close to typical peers, in contrast to when they are near other children with autism or alone (McGee, Paradis, & Feldman, 1993). However, mere exposure to typical peers is not sufficient for remediation of the severe developmental delays associated with autism. True social inclusion does not occur without directly teaching both typical children and children with autism how to interact with one another. Careful planning and scheduling of activities are essential to promoting inclusion. There is no reason to expect benefits from including a young child with autism in a regular classroom without support, because it is likely that the child will end up alone while typical peers interact with one another.

Therefore, teachers must "market" and arrange various activities in a way that keeps children with autism constantly surrounded by the momentum of normal child behavior. To succeed in achieving inclusion and benefit for all children, socially inclusive preschools must incorporate the intensive and systematic treatment needed by children with autism into an environment that is stimulating and fun for typical children.

Most important, social skills do not come naturally to children with autism; they must be taught directly.

Incidental Teaching in an Inclusive Preschool

Teaching in the course of children's ongoing play activities is a traditional early childhood strategy for ensuring that children enjoy and cooperate with instruction. However, teaching in the course of ongoing activities in typical environmental settings is a marked departure from traditional methods of educating children with autism. Rather, traditional education for children with autism has usually consisted of highly structured, discrete trial lessons that are provided to children seated in distraction-free settings. Incidental teaching procedures provide an alternative, which meets the needs of both typical children and children with autism, and which blends well with normalized preschool activities.

Incidental teaching procedures were first developed to facilitate typical (and disadvantaged) children's use of complex language forms (Hart & Risley, 1968, 1974, 1975, 1982). This history is relevant because the ultimate success of social inclusion requires concurrent attention to the needs of typical children as well as those of children with special needs. The most significant findings from incidental teaching research are reports of enhanced generalization, for both typical children (Hart & Risley, 1980) and children with autism (McGee, Krantz, Mason, & McClannahan, 1983; McGee, Krantz, & McClannahan, 1985, 1986). In a nutshell, research suggests that incidental teaching procedures will maximize learning by all children.

Walden maintains a classical definition of incidental teaching as a systematic protocol of teaching interactions. Components of the procedure include (a) *natural environment is arranged to attract children* to desired materials and activities (e.g., preferred toys are displayed in activity areas, and teachers circulate continuously among children to promote high levels of engagement); (b) *the child "initiates" the teaching process* by indicating an interest in an item or topic, either by gesturing or verbalizing (e.g., the child points to a block, or says "I want the block"); (c) *the teacher uses the child's initiation as an opportunity to prompt an elaboration* related to the child's topic of interest (e.g., the teacher asks "What shape block?"); and (d) *the child's correct response to the teacher's prompt results in a confirming response, then contingent access* to the item or topic of interest (e.g., the child says "I want a square block," and the teacher immediately provides it, saying "Terrific, here's a square block; let's build a tower with it").

Incidental teaching requires teachers to maintain high levels of enthusiasm as they make a rapid series of complex teaching judgments. Thus, in addition to performing the normally demanding duties of providing child care and enriching early childhood activities, incidental teachers must constantly track children's interests to identify the perfect timing of the "teachable moment." Because children with autism are impaired in the ability to initiate interactions, their indications of interest must be primed through careful attention to the selection, display, and delivery of reinforcing materials. Environmental engineering is also crucial to maintaining high levels of child engagement.

Curriculum Topics for Inclusive Early Childhood Programs

A comprehensive incidental teaching curriculum was developed to ensure that each child receives intensive, individualized instruction during the course of his or her preferred play activities. In incidental teaching classrooms, the child determines when instruction will occur (by initiating or overtly indicating an interest in an item or topic); the teacher responds by engaging the child in a teaching interaction. An incidental teaching curriculum must specify the teacher's agenda, or the content and extent of the elaboration that will be requested. A comprehensive curriculum must ensure that *what* is taught is a systematic representation of the competencies children need to learn.

Because normalization of social communication is the goal for children with autism, it is necessary to attempt fundamental change in the core language and social disabilities associated with autism. An incidental teaching approach is aimed at achieving broad, generalized improvements beyond those that have been specifically programmed into the curriculum. Children learn to respond in moderately high arousal conditions that represent the multiple cues and distractions inherent in everyday environments. The Walden emphasis on language and social development supports the effort to meet the needs of an inclusive group of children, because language and social growth are the primary agenda for all young children. The relative distribution of curriculum goals in language, social, and behavioral domains shifts across the developmental continuum of the Toddler, Preschool, and Pre-Kindergarten programs, as shown in Figure 7.2.

In the Toddler classroom and home-based programs, the initial focus is on the children's social responsivity to adults and engagement with classroom materials and activities. In an incidental teaching environment, children with autism must be prepared to accept and enjoy teachers' approaches. Concurrently, early emphasis on maintaining high levels of engagement is essential to setting the stage for teachable moments. For young children with autism to be normally engaged, it is necessary to directly teach play skills. Initial functional verbalizations, or at least verbal approximations, are vigorously promoted from the outset of treatment. Another goal is for children to develop a tolerance of being in close proximity to other children, and some children move on to beginning social imitation and synchrony of play (i.e., doing the same thing as other children). Additionally, independence in daily living skills, including dressing and toileting, is actively taught to all children enrolled in the Toddler program. Parent involvement is critical to teaching the core abilities noted above, as well as to addressing the individualized goals established by families (e.g., a mother who visits the park with neighbors may want her child to learn to ride a tricycle).

Verbal, expressive language, or learning how to talk, is the major priority for children with autism in the Walden Preschool. An incidental teaching environment provides frequent opportunities to make choices and to experience the natural consequences of language. Acquisition of correct grammar and syntax, development of the pragmatics of communication, and elaboration of conversational skills are major priorities throughout the preschool day. Children also begin regular daily practice in peer interaction skills, and

	Toddler Year 1	**Preschool** Year 2	**Pre-Kindergarten** Year 3
Communication	Initial Verbalizations Verbal Requests Vocabulary	Pragmatics of Conversation Amount of Talking Complexity of Language Correct Syntax Elaborated Vocabulary	Vocabulary and Corrections
Social	Adult Responsivity Tolerance of Peer Proximity Play Skills	Focus on Peers Synchrony of Play Response to Peer Interactions	Conversation with Peers Peer Negotiation Attraction of Peer Bids Initiation of Interactions Sustained Interactions Community Participation
Behavior	Engagement Independent Daily Living Cooperative Home Behaviors	Decreased Behavior Problems	Conventional School Behavior Academic Readiness

Figure 7.2. Sequence of goals across Walden treatment continuum.

active teaching of social imitation and play synchrony continues. Behavioral difficulties tend to be infrequent in incidental teaching environments that are filled with children's most highly preferred toys and activities, but individualized behavioral goals are targeted as needed.

The overriding goal of the Pre-Kindergarten is to prepare children to learn how to learn from other children, so that the content of their interactions will shift appropriately with advancing years. Specifically, successful children have learned "when in doubt, do what other children are doing," a strategy that highlights the importance of continuing inclusion. To achieve the broader goal, it is necessary to directly teach age-appropriate skills in responding to and initiating interactions, taking turns, sharing, joking, and maintaining conversations with peers. The Pre-Kindergarten curriculum also aims at preparing children for the behavioral and academic expectations of regular kindergarten classrooms.

Classroom Organization that Supports Teachers' Use of the Curriculum

The environment and staff are arranged into teaching zones. Zones are designated by teaching activity rather than by space, per se. Clearly defined zones help teachers identify the children and teaching agendas they are responsible for at a given moment. Teaching occurs continuously throughout traditional early childhood activities, during play (free play, playground, games), during instructional sessions (morning circle, kindergarten readiness groups, art and science activities, story, one-to-one teaching sessions), and during care routines (snack, lunch, bathroom, naps).

In the Toddler and Preschool classrooms, children move through teaching zones as their interests draw them, increasing their opportunities for communication to make their choices known. They learn that verbal language permits them to select to engage with their most highly preferred toys and activities, which are the materials used for instruction. As shown in Table 7.1, a schedule of multiple and concurrent zones overlaps up to four activity options at any given time. Overlapping zones minimize group transitions, eliminate wasted waiting times, and permit children to begin and end activities at their preferred pace. By providing children with choices as to how to spend their time, occasions for incidental teaching are plentiful.

The lead teacher assists children with transitions across zones, capitalizing on children's desires to change activities as prime language instruction opportunities. The zone manager's focus remains constantly on the children. For example, rather than having the zone manager interrupt her teaching to find extra scissors for an art activity, the lead teacher is available to cover logistics. Physical and functional separation of teachers across zones also contributes to child focus.

Table 7.1

Daily Preschool Schedule (and Teaching Goals)

Time	Zone 1	Zone 2	Zone 3	Zone 4
9:00	Health Check (Body Part Labels)	Free Play (Engagement, Play Skills)	Arrivals (Greetings)	Toileting (Independent Self-Care)
9:15	Health Check (Body Part Labels)	Free Play (Engagement, Play Skills)	Special Activity (Language, Fine Motor, Art, Science)	One to One (Prepositions)
9:30	One to One (Conversation)	Free Play (Engagement, Play Skills)	Special Activity (Language, Fine Motor, Art, Science)	One to One (Non-echoic Verbalizations)
9:45	Snack (Verbal Requests)	Free Play (Engagement, Play Skills)	Hand Washing (Independent Self-Care)	One to One (Vocalizations)
10:00	Snack (Verbal Requests)	Free Play (Engagement, Play Skills)	Special Activity (Language, Fine Motor, Art, Science)	Toothbrushing (Independent Self-Care)
10:15	Teacher Break	Free Play (Engagement, Play Skills)	One to One (Pronouns)	Circle Time (Group Imitation)
10:30	Transition to Outside (Independent Dressing)	Toileting (Independent Self-Care)	Ready Table (Independent Play)	Outdoor Free Play (Language, Gross Motor)
10:45	Slide (Language, Gross Motor)	Swings (Language, Gross Motor)	Outdoor Free Play (Social Interaction, Gross Motor)	One to One (In Context, Verbal Imitation)
11:00	Cooperative Games (Social Interaction)	Outdoor Free Play (Safety)	One to One (Participation in Games)	Exercises (Imitation, Gross Motor)
11:15	Swings (Language, Gross Motor)	Slide (Language, Gross Motor)	Outdoor Free Play (Social Interaction)	One to One (Sentences)

(continues)

Table 7.1 Continued

Time	Zone 1	Zone 2	Zone 3	Zone 4
11:30	Transition Inside (Independent Dressing)	Free Play (Vocabulary)	Teacher Break	Work Jobs (Kindergarten Readiness, Math)
11:45	Dramatic Play (Peer Interaction)	Free Play (Vocabulary)	Lunch (Peer Conversation, Eating, Independence)	Peer Teaching (Peer Interaction)
12:00	Peer Teaching (Peer Interaction)	Free Play (Vocabulary)	Lunch (Peer Conversation, Eating, Independence)	One to One (Prepositions)
12:15	Peer Teaching (Peer Interaction)	Free Play (Vocabulary)	Lunch (Peer Conversation, Eating, Independence)	One to One (Play Skills)
12:30	Dramatic Play (Peer Interaction)	Free Play (Vocabulary)	Lunch (Peer Conversation, Eating, Independence)	Toothbrushing (Independence)
12:45	Pre-Kindergarten Group (Kindergarten Readiness)	Free Play (Vocabulary)	One to One (Eye Contact)	Teacher Break
1:00	Story (Group Attending)	Free Play (Vocabulary)	Table-Top Game (Turn Taking)	One to One (Turn Taking)
1:15–2:00	Nap (Rest)	Teacher Break	Computer (Reading)	Quiet Activity (Independent Play)
2:00	Social Games (Social Interaction)	Free Play (Peer Interaction)	One to One ("Yes," "No")	One to One (Attending Social Games)
2:15	Snack (Verbal Requests)	Free Play (Peer Interaction)	Social Games (Social Interaction)	One to One ("Yes," "No")
2:30	Snack (Verbal Requests)	Free Play (Peer Interaction)	Hand Washing (Independent Self-Care)	One to One (Pronouns)
2:45	Dramatic Play (Peer Interaction)	Free Play (Peer Interaction)	Toileting (Independent Self-Care)	Departures (Farewells, Independent Dressing)

Each zone is overlaid with teaching goals. Designation of which goal(s) will be the teaching agenda in each zone has permitted preplanning of environmental arrangements, preferred instructional materials, activities, and teaching procedures. In many zones, the curriculum is presented in levels to help teachers adjust to children's wide-ranging abilities, so that all children can be kept happily challenged. Cue cards posted in the classroom remind teachers what the desired responses are for children at differing levels, and ongoing performance appraisals promote teachers' use of classroom prompts.

For example, requests are targeted at two daily snacks. When a child with no language reaches for a snack, the child may be prompted to vocalize a sound. A child with new language will be prompted for requests of one word, then for two-word phrases, and eventually for complete sentences. At the highest level, children are encouraged to request more abstract information from one another ("Where does milk come from?").

Similarly, new vocabulary is taught in a midday free-play zone. Words targeted each week correspond to play materials in the classroom, with words and toys rotating weekly. Words are leveled so that there are some for all to learn, and some for more advanced children. Body parts are taught within a morning health check activity, and child culture conversational language (e.g., "Wow," "Awesome") is promoted during lunch (McGee & Daly, 1999a).

Activities interspersed throughout the day offer direct instruction and practice in peer interactions. During peer incidental teaching, a typical child learns to use requests about preferred toys to get a response from a peer with autism (McGee, Almeida, Sulzer-Azaroff, & Feldman, 1992). Dramatic play sessions take place in centers with thematic materials that support pretend activities, such as visits to McDonald's or a beauty parlor, and interactions are directly prompted among two typical children and one child with autism (Odom & Strain, 1986). Cooperative games are played by the Preschool and Pre-Kindergarten children at recess, followed by an outdoor exercise session to promote gross motor imitation of peers (Carr & Darcy, 1990). Each afternoon, three social games are selected from a rotating pool designed to attract children with autism via a salient sensory component (e.g., taking turns spinning in a chair or painting to opera music). Afternoon free play also targets a leveled social skill each week (e.g., during a week in which peer greetings are targeted, the teachers may prompt nonverbal children to wave to their peers and encourage higher level children to use each other's names in conversation).

Some individualized incidental teaching sessions are provided daily to each child with autism, usually in areas that require massed teaching opportunities (e.g., use of pronouns eye contact). However, sessions that preclude the availability of typical peers are kept at a minimum, with no more than four 15-minute sessions per child per day. Where possible, one-to-one instruction is scheduled to occur within other group activities.

Daily living skills are taught as opportunities arise naturally in the classroom routine (e.g., toothbrushing after lunch). Some teaching opportunities are subtly contrived and blended into classroom routines. For example, Walden children do not wear shoes in the classroom, so that they get daily repeated practice in independently getting shoes on and off at arrivals, recess, and departure.

Unlike the Toddler and Preschool classrooms, the Pre-Kindergarten classroom program requires children to move as a group during most of the classroom day. Thus, multiple overlapping zones that were needed to create maximum language teaching opportunities are replaced with a series of small group and whole class activities. In short, children are weaned from a free-choice environment because group transitions are characteristic of most kindergartens, and children must learn self-control of their behavior in less accommodating situations. There are, however, several periods during which children can select to play in an array of centers (i.e., art, computer, free play, housekeeping, listening, dramatic play), and transition across these areas requires verbal negotiation with peers.

Academics are targeted at various table-top activities, and through the use of commercially available computerized instruction. A literacy curriculum blends instruction in various prereading and reading skills into the classroom environment and activities. Independent work habits are practiced during a period in which children complete projects or Work Jobs adapted from the *Mathematics Their Way* curriculum (Baratta-Lorton, 1976). Finally, in the Pre-Kindergarten, one-to-one sessions are replaced with planned peer interaction sessions, which includeone or one or two peers and a supervising teacher.

Assessment of Child and Curriculum Progress

In an incidental teaching environment, teachers cannot be burdened with routine data collection responsibilities. The solution has been to construct a series of assessment probes, which vary in frequency and format depending on the goal. Two-week blocks of daily videotapes are scored at quarterly intervals to assess goals pertaining to generalized improvements across the day. However, to avoid the delays that can accrue in scoring research data, similar measures of language, social, and behavioral progress have been blended into a weekly classroom observation assessment. Using a time-sampling procedure, a program evaluator independent of the classroom conducts observations of each child, including children with and without disabilities. Across a period of 10 weeks, enough assessment samples have been collected to track individual child progress on variables that take time to detect generalized behavioral gains.

For objectives that require more frequent tracking, practical teacher-collected probes have been built into daily routines. For example, during a midday free play session that targets vocabulary, the teachers record each child's first response of the day on a data sheet that is taped to a toy shelf with attached pen; probes are comprised of each child's first responses across 5 consecutive days. More traditional trial-by-trial assessment is conducted during one-to-one sessions. Critical to the success of instruction, comprehensive reinforcement assessments are administered to children with autism on a monthly basis.

A comprehensive program evaluation system is also conducted weekly. The system monitors areas such as teacher training, safety, and children's participation and apparent enjoyment of activities. The program evaluator completes a form that structures suggestions and comments resulting from classroom and chart observations. Also included in the weekly report is documentation on program operation (e.g., attendance charts) and child progress data. The report and accompanying data are presented to the early childhood coordinator, who in turn reviews the results with the classroom coordinator in an individual supervisory meeting. The edited report then serves as the agenda for weekly teacher staff meetings, and a monthly summary of the report is forwarded to the program director.

Prevention of Behavior Problems in Early Childhood Programs

The typical children in inclusive classrooms provide constant reminders that perfect behavior is not a normal goal for young children. Moreover, traditional strategies used to manage behavior problems in autism treatment programs are often unacceptable to parents of typical children. On the other hand, inclusion does impose some requirements that disruptive or bizarre behaviors are minimized. Future success in kindergarten requires that all children learn to control their environment through positive means. The philosophy at Walden is that increasing fun decreases problem behaviors (McGee & Daly, 1999b). More precisely, prevention of behavior problems buys time to teach long-term replacements for challenging behaviors.

The Walden curriculum vigorously targets adaptive communication skills, such as verbal expression of displeasure, needs, and desires; sharing and turn taking; and following conventional classroom rules. In addition, effective incidental teaching requires powerful fuel in the form of children's highly preferred play materials and activities, the presence of which helps to reduce or crowd out problem behaviors (Mason, McGee, Farmer-Dougan, & Risley, 1989). An incidental teaching curriculum also decreases problems because children are permitted to make choices of where they want to be and what they want to be doing. Zone-based classrooms with multiple, overlapping activity schedules minimize waiting or down times, which are prime opportunities for problem behaviors. At Walden, children learn to cope with the demands of traditional classrooms after they have developed language and graduated into the Pre-Kindergarten.

The promotion of engagement is the most important strategy for prevention of behavior problems, and Walden research has been invested in developing procedures that secure and maintain consistently high levels of engagement (McGee, Daly, Izeman, Mann, & Risley, 1991). For example, a plan for biweekly rotation of classroom toys has been shown to reduce problem behaviors such as name calling, tattling, and fighting, while simultaneously increasing positive social behaviors such as peer cooperation (McGee & Daly, 1999b). Frequent praise, tickles, hugs, and access to preferred activities are abundantly available for appropriate engagement.

The program is designed to avoid power struggles between children and teachers by limiting the number of classroom rules, and by preparing teachers in planned ignoring of insignificant problem behaviors (e.g., whining). When behavior problems do occur, analysis and teaching of natural consequences are the rule. Initial analysis focuses on whether preventive environmental arrangements are feasible (e.g., can toy shelves be relocated to break up a classroom racetrack?). If several children display problems in an activity, an informal assessment examines whether the activity is boring (e.g., children's behavior during storytime was improved by having the teacher bring story-related props and wear a Merlin hat with story wand). More challenging behavioral requirements are introduced gradually (e.g., the school year begins with a very brief circle activity, which increases in duration as children learn the songs and other skills needed for participation).

Individualized positive behavior support programs are necessary on rare occasions, but the number of such programs is kept as low as possible in the interest of ensuring precise teacher implementation. A functional analysis precedes the design of any behavioral support program, and there is a firm prohibition on presentation of aversive stimuli. For example, a child with limited language who tantrums to leave an activity may be allowed to bring a favorite toy to the activity, and taught to point and later to say "go" in order to exit. In sum, positive behavior support programs must be instructional in the interest of building skills that contribute to future prevention.

Given an incidental teaching approach, it is crucial to avoid the side effects of punishment, including social avoidance and emotional responding. Traditional compliance training is not used because it is counterproductive to efforts to get children to initiate interactions. Therefore, alternative orientation procedures had to be developed to increase a child's tolerance for teacher approach, by pairing the approach with the delivery of highly preferred stimuli.

Experience taught us that, although many behavioral irregularities resolve when a child develops functional communication skills, others do not. Thus, self-stimulatory behaviors are greatly reduced when children learn to play, yet subtle remnants can remain. It is likely that incidental teaching classrooms present an increased risk of inadvertent reinforcement of self-stimulatory behaviors, because teachers are prepared to move in quickly to reward a language production or social overture, and few behavioral issues are specifically targeted. Such risks can be reduced when teachers are trained in basic principles related to delivery and timing of reinforcement, and when supervisors provide ongoing monitoring and feedback. Similarly, the development of the Walden Pre-Kindergarten program represented an acknowledgment that certain nonreinforcing school behaviors (e.g., waiting in a line) must be directly taught.

In sum, a preventive classwide approach to positive behavioral support must be carefully planned, and effective implementation requires rigorous teacher training and supervision. By acknowledging that positive behavioral support is much more than the absence of punishment, it is possible to accomplish fundamental changes in language and social behaviors that will yield normalized behavior control in children's futures.

An Incidental Teaching Family Program

The goal of the Walden Family Program (McGee, Jacobs, & Regnier, 1993) is to enable parents to maximize their child's overall progress and to advocate for education and lifelong community inclusion. The family program continuum includes (a) a 1-year intensive home-based program when children are in the Toddler Center; (b) ongoing technical assistance throughout the preschool years; and (c) advocacy preparation and transition planning during the Pre-Kindergarten program. Consistent and effective communication between parents and professionals is a priority. In addition, parents of all children are encouraged to participate in parent information seminars, as well as to be actively involved in classroom activities and school social events.

Intensive Program

During their child's year in the Toddler Center, parents of children with autism are asked to commit to personally implementing a home teaching schedule for at least 10 hours each week. A family liaison, who is also an experienced teacher in the child's classroom, visits the family for up to 4 hours per week. The parents and family liaison form a true collaboration as they work together to select the goals to be addressed in the home teaching plan. The goals are then designated for specific teaching times that conveniently occur during the family's normal home routines.

Parents are encouraged to plan on teaching for approximately 2 hours each day, although 15-minute teaching blocks need not be consecutive. Thus, a parent may conduct some teaching, drive to pick up siblings at soccer practice, and later complete teaching in the evening at bath time. The family liaison initially demonstrates the teaching plan, and then coaches the parents as they develop the specialized teaching skills needed to implement their home program.

Consistent with an incidental teaching approach, participating families are given a broad array of program choices from which they determine the focus and format of their individualized program. The underlying assumption is that parents will be most effective in providing and advocating for children's treatments that are compatible with their self-identified needs (Dunst, Leet, & Trivette, 1988). Most parents opt for specialized training to take place during weekly home visits. However, individual preferences are respected, and some meetings occur at the center, clinic, or other day care programs.

The parents design their individualized family plan by selecting topics from a menu of approximately 50 packaged modules that address common treatment needs of toddlers with autism, or by creating home programs specific to their family and child. Accompanying each module are written materials, many of which have been edited by parents to be parent friendly. Reference materials and videotaped vignettes are available as appropriate. Modules are grouped into five categories: Incidental Teaching, Advocacy, General Information, Family Issues, and Other Instructional Packages. For example, the Incidental Teaching modules are designed to enable parents to teach language and social skills in the course of their daily routines at home. Some of the daily routines that parents have chosen to use for teaching are Meal times, Bath time, Outside play, Television viewing, and Dressing. Parents are strongly encouraged to work with center teachers to toilet train their child before transition to the Preschool, because the Toddler program has the best capability of sending support staff to the home.

Ongoing Technical Assistance in the Preschool

The emphasis in the Preschool Family Program is on keeping children talking at home, and on supporting parents' efforts to provide their child and family a normal lifestyle both at home and in the community. When a child moves up to the Preschool, parents have already learned the skills to develop and implement their own home programs. However, they still appreciate advice on finetuning their procedures, and the need continues to coordinate efforts between home and school. The frequency of individually scheduled parent meetings is reduced to monthly school contacts, unless difficulties arise. Because special requests and circumstances are also accommodated, we have helped parents learn to train sitters, siblings, and Sunday school teachers.

Preparation for Transition

When children are in the Pre-Kindergarten, the focus of the Family Program shifts to building social networks and planning for the kindergarten year. Parents are invited to learn how to promote peer interactions and encouraged to arrange regular visits of neighborhood children to provide additional social learning opportunities. It is also strongly recommended that parents enroll their children in extracurricular community activities. Parents are advised to try several activities until they identify one that matches their child's interests and skills, and they are assured that even failed attempts provide useful information regarding their child's readiness to function in unsupported conditions. When a child is successful on the YMCA swim team, ballet, or judo lessons, evidence is accumulated to support the child's readiness for inclusion in kindergarten.

From the beginning of their child's enrollment at Walden, parents are educated on the importance of proactive advocacy. This training intensifies when children enter the Pre-Kindergarten, with a goal of preparing parents with the information, knowledge, and skills that enable them to be effective lifelong advocates for their children. Specific advocacy modules, comprised of seminars and written resource materials, include the following: Inclusion, Knowing the Laws, Professional Jargon, Negotiating Individualized Educational Plans, Available Community Programs and Activities, State-of-the-Art Intervention Technology, and Evaluation of Future Classrooms.

Parents are assisted in specific kindergarten planning, which begins approximately 9 months before their child graduates from Walden. Nearly all Walden parents share the program's goal of arranging inclusive kindergarten placements, in order to secure continuing social learning opportunities. Of course, the level of support needed to ensure a child's success varies across individual children and across school systems. Staff members assist parents in planning their school contacts, and accompany parents on school visits as they make their final selection decisions. Receiving school administrators and teachers are invited to visit Walden, and most schools accept Walden's offer of intensive summer training for future teachers and classroom aides. Importantly, Walden provides a comprehensive evaluation report that includes current assessment information, written goals, and feasible objectives. Schools are likely to use the exit report because it is formatted in a manner that saves the receiving school time, in that it can be readily plugged into the child's formal Individualized Education Plan (IEP).

School Communication

The classroom maintains an open-door visitation policy. All children take home Daily Notes to inform parents of eating, napping, and instructional events, and these set the occasion for conversation about the child's day at school. Monthly classroom newsletters offer more detail on classroom activities (e.g., new vocabulary words, songs). Classroom coordinators allot time to be available to parents at arrivals and departures, and parents are made aware that senior project administrators are available for meetings on request.

Parent Information Seminars

Parents choose the topics and scheduling of group meetings. Some commonly selected seminar topics are Toilet Training, Selecting Toys, Balancing Personal and Parenting Time, and Promoting Good Behavior in Public Places. Guest speakers are sometimes invited to present (e.g., an attorney on disability law, or a speech–language pathologist on language milestones). At least half of the meeting topics are selected to have broad appeal to both parents of children with autism and those with typically developing children. Other meetings focus on information specific to autism and challenges faced by families of children with special needs. Grandparent information groups have also been helpful in enhancing family understanding and support.

Parent Participation

Parents of all children are encouraged to contribute enrichment activities to the classrooms. As in many good schools, Walden parents organize holiday parties and graduation, share cultural experiences and food, and inform children of their varied roles as community helpers (e.g., a nurse showed her medical supplies to her child's morning circle).

Social events are also arranged to provide all parents with opportunities to get to know each other and their children's teachers. Learning about the trials and tribulations experienced by parents of typical children helps parents of children with autism to put their child's development into perspective. Thus, parents are often reassured to learn that few young children behave well on long mall trips, or that restaurants can be an ordeal for all. It is also important for the parents of typical children to gain an understanding of the benefits of inclusion for their own children. Friendships formed between parents of typical children and parents of children with autism lay a foundation for community inclusion (e.g., birthday parties, weekend outings) both during and beyond their children's preschool years (Hall, 1987).

Synopsis of the Family Program Evolution

Over the years, Walden's Family Program has become increasingly intensive. Early on, a more laissez-faire approach gave parents a wide range of options regarding the level of parent involvement. However, data and experience proved that children's progress was directly related to parent participation (McGee et al., 1993). In addition, recognition that the number of hours of intervention was a critical variable related to child outcome made it necessary to add intervention time to the half-day center-based program for toddlers.

Parents of toddlers have been more than willing to commit to and fulfill the 10-hour per week home treatment requirement in the Toddler Center. This is the easiest period for a family to participate in intensive home treatment, because parents of all toddlers must constantly be with their children to keep them safe. Therefore, it is not viewed as a burden for a parent to teach while giving their child a bath, because the parent had to be present for custodial care anyway. By blending instruction into a family's normal home-living routines, with adjustments specific to the family and child's schedule, home teaching is able to occur consistently without disruption to the family household. Importantly, parents are able to become highly competent in the specialized skills needed to teach their child with autism while the child is young. The result is the prevention of the development of challenging behavioral routines in the home and parents are also prepared early on with the knowledge and skills to advocate for their child, which enables them to be assertive about their child's needs both at Walden and throughout his or her future.

Children's Outcomes

The group of 34 Walden graduates described in this chapter includes children who were enrolled in the original Preschool in Massachusetts, children who began in the Preschool after its relocation to Georgia, and the most recent graduates whose enrollment began in the Toddler Center and continued through the Preschool and Pre-Kindergarten. Therefore, the outcome data that follow represent the progress of a group of children with autism who entered treatment at younger and older ages. Previous research demonstrated that there was essentially no difference in the pretreatment social and language behaviors of children with autism who entered at younger versus older ages (McGee, Feldman, & Morrier, 1997). However, incoming data are showing that age of entry is a critical variable in children's social outcomes.

Verbalizations

Incidental teaching is a powerful method for promoting the development of functional, generalized language skills. All 34 Walden graduates acquired some functional words, and 30 of 34 graduated with meaningful verbal language (defined as more than 10 words and functional, unprompted speech).

Three of the four children who did not develop expressive language had documented neurological or sensory impairments, yet seven children who did develop language also had neurological impairments other than autism.

Language gains were supported by objective scoring of videotapes to assess the distribution of language use across the day. This measure provides a marker of how much of the time children were talking throughout preschool activities. The average level of verbalizations by the 30 verbal graduates with autism increased from 6% of observed intervals during their first 2 weeks in the program to 16% of time sampled during their last 2 weeks at Walden. The levels of verbalizations by the graduates with autism (who had developed meaningful language) compare favorably to the levels of verbalizations used by 5.5-year-old typical children at Walden (range 17% to 54%). Twelve of the 30 graduates with autism exited with verbalization levels in typical ranges for kindergarten entry. Corresponding to curriculum goals, major language gains tended to show up during children's first year of enrollment.

Peer Interactions

A measure of the distribution of receipt of social bids from peers provides a conservative marker of a child's social attractiveness. Social outcome data improved substantially as a function of expansions of the social curriculum. Thus, during the program's early years in Massachusetts, children with autism were receiving social bids from peers an average of only 4% (range 0% to 10%) of the classroom day at the time of their graduation. When the program moved to Georgia, curriculum changes included an increase in the ratio of typical peers to children with autism, as well as expansion of the amount of direct social instruction each day. Social intervention also began when children were younger and continued throughout their enrollment. Although the children in Georgia entered Walden with the same lack of social skills as the children in Massachusetts (i.e., at entry, both groups were scored for receipt of social bids an average of 3% of the preschool day), their social progress corresponded to programmatic adjustments. Thus, Walden graduates who participated in the expanded social curriculum exited the program receiving peer social bids an average of 11% (range 1% to 27%) of the preschool day. Overall, 17 of 34 children with autism exited the program receiving social bids from peers at levels within the ranges of 5.5-year-old typical children (range 6% to 39%).

It should be noted that even the children who showed little improvement on this measure of generalized and durable peer interaction skills had shown significant gains as a function of direct peer interventions. In other words, it is relatively easy to document social gains during a session in which social skills have been directly taught, but such findings can be deceptive. Transfer of social abilities to the daily lives of children with autism requires that children be provided with intensive social instruction that is spread across their days.

Future Placements

Early in the program's development, a team of experts (Sol Garfield, Todd Risley, and Beth Sulzer-Azaroff) was asked to review research measures to determine their suitability for future outcome studies. The team's conclusion was that the measures were solid, but that the ultimate outcome boils down to where children end up. We argued that future placements were politically contaminated. Virtually no children with autism were then being included in area schools. We later feared that political interference would be even worse in Georgia because, at the time the program relocated, the South had almost no inclusion of any children with disabilities. However, the bottom line was that it was necessary to track future placements if the goal was to prepare children for full community participation.

On this count, Walden has achieved striking success. Twenty-six of 33 (79%) Walden graduates with autism have been successfully included in regular kindergarten classes at their local public schools (full-year kindergarten placement information was not available for one child due to relocation). It must be qualified that the children exited with low, medium, and high treatment outcomes. In addition, varying levels of support have been provided. In some cases, transition assistance has included intensive preparation of a one-to-one classroom aide. For other children, especially those who entered treatment at young ages, no specialized support has been needed. Of the 7 children who were placed in special education classes, at least 3 were segregated because no support was available in their school's regular education classrooms (i.e., they were not "low functioning").

Inclusion placement outcomes were not only a matter of gradually preparing a school system to buy into inclusion of children with autism. To the contrary, the 26 Walden graduates who were successfully included went into 18 different school systems. Only 2 of the 26 children were enrolled in the same school. In nearly every situation, the Walden graduate was the first child with autism that the receiving school had placed in a regular classroom.

Informal follow-up has been accomplished via phone interviews with parents and annual reunion parties, which are well attended by children with autism and typical children. Although exact numbers are not available, most of the Walden graduates have continued to be included in regular classes through at least elementary school. Nearly all parents have reported continuing social and language advancement by the children who have been included in regular classes. Walden graduates participate in extracurricular activities such as judo, ballet, and soccer. Some have artistic talent, others are the neighborhood Nintendo champions, and one recent graduate was voted by his first-grade classmates to be the Student Council representative. To their parents' delight, there are many reports of invitations to birthday parties and visits to friends' homes. In short, the majority of Walden graduates with autism are successfully and fully participating in their schools and communities.

Future Directions

There is growing recognition that early behavioral intervention can radically alter the developmental course of autism, yet relatively few children with autism are receiving the treatment needed to fully realize their potential. The disparity between the treatment provided in model demonstration programs and the services available in most public educational systems persist due to (a) lack of controlled clinical trials that provide undisputed evidence of treatment efficacy, (b) complexity of social treatment protocols needed to effect lasting change, and (c) limitations on fiscal resources that drive educational policy and practice. Further, the ultimate proof of intervention efficacy may not be realized until there is a marriage between the biological and behavioral sciences.

Controlled Clinical Outcome Studies

Lovaas (1987) revolutionized the field of autism treatment with the discovery that early intensive intervention was significantly more effective that early nonintensive intervention. These findings have been subjected to attack due to various methodological and philosophical issues, yet varied demonstration models have provided indirect verification of the phenomena of early intensive intervention. The paucity of controlled clinical trials results from the nature of the intervention (i.e., it takes many hours and several years of intervention to accumulate data on individual children). Moreover, there are significant difficulties in obtaining legitimate comparison groups (e.g., ethics and federal law require referral of all young children for appropriate treatment, and there may be substantial differences in the families of children who pursue treatment in research-based programs and those who do not). At this point, it does not seem productive to quibble about the relative merit of various early intervention approaches. Rather, the time has come to devote serious effort to conducting well-designed and replicated studies of the results of early intensive autism intervention.

Complexity of Social Intervention Protocols

One of the limitations of current demonstration models is the issue of whether they are dependent on the clinical expertise of individuals or teams of investigators. This consideration is especially salient in the area of treatment of social irregularities, which are considered by many to be the core defining characteristics of autism. The science of social intervention is relatively new, and the procedures that have been effective are complicated to implement. Further, there is no formal professional training that adequately prepares a practitioner to intervene and improve social behavior. There is a pressing need for translation of research to practice in the form of practical materials and training sequences that prepare professionals and parents to better address the debilitating social needs of children with autism. More specifically, there is a need to develop and evaluate curricula that task-analyze developmentally linked social goals, and that delineate exactly how to teach social behaviors that will generalize from teaching conditions to use in children's daily lives.

In addition, there is a continuing need for research in the area of social knowledge for high-functioning people with autism, because most intervention research has been aimed at the basic foundations of social skills. In a sense, the high-outcome products of early intensive intervention may be likely to end up resembling adults with Asperger's syndrome. However, to date, few interventions are aimed at treatment of the developmental needs of the population we may be inadvertently expanding. We know very little about how to teach the complexities of social conversation, how to prepare children to respond to the subtleties of nonverbal expression, or how to help children cope with other residual aspects of autism that can lead to continuing discomfort. Given the high incidence of depression and other life difficulties that are reported in adults with Asperger's syndrome and high-functioning autism, our current autism treatment protocols remain incomplete in the area of preparation for long-term social success.

Fiscal Impediments to System Change

The findings and experience of virtually all demonstration programs for early autism intervention programs strongly suggest that intensity of treatment is an essential element of effective intervention. Simply put, more always turns out to be better than less. However, providing more hours of engaged time for a young child with autism translates to more money to buy supports to keep the child engaged. The fiscal realities of early intervention and educational systems are often at odds with the accumulating clinical evidence that early intervention for children with autism is not cheap. The result has been an unprecedented series of legal challenges, and the growing antagonism between researchers and educators can only widen the gap between research and practice. Although parents almost always win a lawsuit that enforces their child's educational rights, the vast majority of parents of young children have neither the knowledge nor the financial resources to pursue the full extent of these rights. Policy experts worry that systemwide accommodation of the needs of children with autism will open the floodgates for children with other disabilities, for whom it is unknown whether intensity of treatment will or will not make a difference. In the short run, voluntary or court-ordered school contributions will continue to subsidize the treatment needed by enough children to fill the nation's demonstration programs, but serious equity issues persist.

The Neuroscience of Behavioral Treatment

Ironically, the dramatic changes that appear to result from early intensive autism intervention have heralded return of discussion of "critical periods," which used to be in total contradiction to behavioral or learning theories of development. Tantalizing new technology exists that could theoretically answer questions regarding whether environmental manipulations can impact neurological functioning, yet to date the neuroscience technologies remain inaccessible to exactly the population of most relevance to autism intervention. Specifically, positron emission tomography (PET) studies cannot be done with very young children due to the need to use radioactive isotopes. Functional magnetic resonance imaging (functional MRI) studies are nearly impossible to conduct on young children with autism, who are unlikely to cooperate with tasks administered in conjunction with requirements to lie still in a tube while deafening noise pounds around their heads. However, technological advances are occurring daily, and the time may soon come when we are able to understand what neurological insults produce the behavioral symptoms known as autism. Even more exciting, it may soon be possible to determine whether the dramatic behavioral changes that are the result of early intensive intervention are associated with lasting neurological improvements.

Conclusion

We have found a comprehensive incidental teaching approach to be both socially palatable and empirically effective, for both children with autism and typical children. Unfortunately, combining incidental teaching and social inclusion in a manner that produces a maximally powerful program is not easy. High-quality education of any variety does not come naturally. Yet we believe that the venture has been worth the effort, given the mission of accomplishing fundamental, sweeping changes in outcomes for children with autism.

Regarding inclusion, it is clear that children with autism can be prepared for inclusion while they are included with normally developing peers. In fact, it is difficult to imagine how to build normalized peer interactions in the absence of normally developing peers. Inclusion has, in short, provided innumerable benefits to program development. Typical children have enjoyed the enriched education afforded by a lab-school, and children with autism have learned how to have friends in their classrooms and communities.

Finally, it seems worthwhile to note that this has been joyous work. Early intervention for autism is an exciting and rapidly progressing field. Yet there is much to be accomplished in an area where normalization of a severe disability is the goal, and approximations are not successes.

References

Allen, K. E., & Hart, B. M. (1984). *The early years: Arrangements for learning.* Englewood Cliffs, NJ: Prentice-Hall.

American Psychiatric Association. (1994). *Diagnostic and statistical manual of mental disorders* (4th ed.). Washington, DC: Author.

Baratta-Lorton, M. (1976). *Mathematics their way.* Menlo Park, CA: Addison Wesley.

Bayley, N. (1993). *Bayley Scales of Infant Development* (2nd ed.). San Antonio: Psychological Corp.

Carr, E. G., & Darcy, M. (1990). Setting generality of peer modeling in children with autism. *Journal of Autism and Developmental Disorders, 20,* 45–59.

Daly, T. (1991). *Social behavior and social understanding of mainstreamed and non-mainstreamed typical preschoolers.* Unpublished doctoral dissertation, University of Massachusetts, Amherst.

Devin-Sheehan, L., Feldman, R. S., & Allen, V. L. (1976). Theory and research on cross-age and peer interaction: A review of the literature. *Review of Educational Research, 46,* 355–385.

Dunn, L. M., & Dunn, L. M. (1981). *Peabody Picture Vocabulary Test–Revised.* Circle Pines, MN: American Guidance Service.

Dunst, C. J., Leet, H. E., & Trivette, C. M. (1988). Family resources, personal well-being, and early intervention. *Journal of Special Education, 22,* 108–116.

Gardner, M. F. (1990). *The Expressive One-Word Picture Vocabulary Test.* Novato, CA: Academic Therapy Publications.

Hall, L. J. (1987, May). An evaluation of parents' requests for assistance in an integrated preschool program. In G. G. McGee (Chair), *Advances in early social integration.* Symposium presented at the annual meeting of the Association for Behavior Analysis, Nashville, TN.

Hart, B. M., & Risley, T. R. (1968). Establishing the use of descriptive adjectives in the spontaneous speech of disadvantaged children. *Journal of Applied Behavior Analysis, 1,* 109–20.

Hart, B. M., & Risley, T. R. (1974). Using preschool materials to modify the language of disadvantaged children. *Journal of Applied Behavior Analysis, 7,* 243–256.

Hart, B. M., & Risley, T. R. (1975). Incidental teaching of language in the preschool. *Journal of Applied Behavior Analysis, 8,* 411–420.

Hart, B. M., & Risley, T. R. (1980). In vivo language intervention: Unanticipated general effects. *Journal of Applied Behavior Analysis, 13,* 407–432.

Hart, B. M., & Risley, T. R. (1982). *How to use incidental teaching for elaborating language.* Lawrence, KS: H & H Enterprises.

LeLaurin, K., & Risley, T. R. (1972). The organization of day-care environments: "Zone" versus "man-to-man" staff assignments. *Journal of Applied Behavior Analysis, 5,* 225–232.

Lord, C., Rutter, M., DiLavore, P., & Risi, S. (1999). *Autism Diagnostic Observation Schedule.* Los Angeles: Western Psychological Services.

Lord, C., Rutter, M., & LeCouteur, A. (1994). Autism Diagnostic Interview–Revised: A revised version of a diagnostic interview for caregivers of individuals with possible pervasive developmental disorders. *Journal of Autism and Developmental Disorders, 24,* 659–685.

Lovaas, O. I. (1987). Behavioral treatment and normal educational and intellectual functioning in young autistic children. *Journal of Consulting and Clinical Psychology, 55,* 3–9.

Mason, S. A., McGee, G. G., Farmer-Dougan, V., & Risley, T. R. (1989). A practical strategy for reinforcer assessment. *Journal of Applied Behavior Analysis, 22,* 171–179.

McGee, G. G., Almeida, M. C., Sulzer-Azaroff, B., & Feldman, R. S. (1992). Promoting reciprocal interactions via peer incidental teaching. *Journal of Applied Behavior Analysis, 25,* 117–126.

McGee, G. G., & Daly, T. (1999a). *Establishing use of child-culture conversational language by children with autism.* Manuscript submitted for publication.

McGee, G. G., & Daly, T. (1999b). Prevention of problem behaviors in preschool children. In A. C. Repp., & R. H. Horner (Eds.), *Functional analysis of problem behavior: From effective assessment to effective support* (pp. 171–196). New York: Wadsworth.

McGee, G. G., Daly, T., Izeman, S. G., Mann, L. H., & Risley, T. R. (1991). Use of classroom materials to promote preschool engagement. *Teaching Exceptional Children, 23*(4), 43–47.

McGee, G. G., Feldman, R. S., & Morrier, M. J. (1997). Benchmarks of social treatment for children with autism. *Journal of Autism and Developmental Disorders, 27,* 353–364.

McGee, G. G., Jacobs, H. A., & Regnier, M. C. (1993). Preparation of families for incidental teaching and advocacy for their children with autism. *OSERS News in Print, 5,* 9–13.

McGee, G. G., Krantz, P. J., Mason, D., & McClannahan, L. E. (1983). A modified incidental teaching procedure for autistic youth: Acquisition and generalization of receptive object labels. *Journal of Applied Behavior Analysis, 16,* 329–338.

McGee, G. G., Krantz, P. J., & McClannahan, L. E. (1985). The facilitative effects of incidental teaching on preposition use by autistic children. *Journal of Applied Behavior Analysis, 18,* 17–31.

McGee, G. G., Krantz, P. J., & McClannahan, L. E. (1986). An extension of incidental teaching procedures to reading instruction for autistic children. *Journal of Applied Behavior Analysis, 19,* 147–157.

McGee, G. G., Paradis, T., & Feldman, R. S. (1993). Free effects of integration on levels of autistic behavior. *Topics in Early Childhood Special Education, 13,* 57–67.

O'Brien, M., Porterfield, P. J., Herbert-Jackson, E., & Risley, T. R. (1979). *The Toddler Center Manual: A practical guide to day care for one- and two-year olds.* Baltimore: University Park Press.

Odom, S. L., & Strain, P. S. (1986). Peer social interactions: Effective intervention for social skills development of exceptional children. *Exceptional Children, 52,* 543–551.

Risley, T. R., & Favell, J. E. (1979). Constructing a living environment in an institution. In L. Hamerlynch (Ed.), *Behavioral systems for the developmentally disabled, Volume 2* (pp. 3–24). New York: Brunnel-Mazel.

Sanford, A. R., & Zelman, J. G. (1981). *The Learning Accomplishment Profile.* Winston-Salem, NC: Kaplin.

Schopler, E., Reichler, R. J., Bashford, A., Lansing, M. D., & Marcus, L. M. (1990). *Psychoeducational Profile–Revised.* Austin, TX: PRO-ED.

Schopler, E., Reichler, R., & Renner, B. R. (1988). *The Childhood Autism Rating Scale.* Los Angeles: Western Psychological Services.

Skinner, B. F. (1948). *Walden two.* New York: Macmillan.

Sparrow, S. S., Balla, D. A., & Cicchetti, D. V. (1984). *Vineland Adaptive Behavior Scales, Interview Edition, Survey form manual.* Circle Pines, MN: American Guidance Service.

Sulzer-Azaroff, B., Jones, E., & McGee, G. G. (1986, May). *The making of an integrated laboratory preschool.* Invited address presented at the annual meeting of the Association for Behavior Analysis, Milwaukee.

Thoreau, H. D. (1847). *Walden, or life in the woods.* New York: C. N. Potter/Crown.

Thorndike, R. L., Hagen, E. R., & Sattler, J. M. (1986). *The Stanford–Binet Intelligence Scale* (4th ed.). Chicago: Riverside.

Twardosz, S., Cataldo, M. F., & Risley, T. R. (1974). Open environment design for infant and toddler day care. *Journal of Applied Behavior Analysis, 7,* 529–549.

Behavior Analysis and Intervention for Preschoolers at the Princeton Child Development Institute

8

Lynn E. McClannahan and Patricia J. Krantz

F
ounded in 1970 as a private nonprofit agency, the Princeton Child Development Institute (PCDI) initially offered a special education program for children with autism. Today, PCDI's programs include early intervention for children under 3 years of age; a preschool and school; services to families; two community-based, family-style group homes; and career development and supported employment programs for adults. These programs are characterized by an applied behavior analysis approach and an emphasis on research as well as service.

In 1999–2000, tuition for the 10-month school year was $46,024 and tuition for the 5-week summer session was $7,159, a total of $53,183 per child. Tuition, paid by children's local school districts, covered approximately 90% of costs; the remainder came from grants from private foundations, and from the fund-raising endeavors of an active and committed governing board.

PCDI is not departmentalized; instead, all managers and supervisors participate in program administration, staff training, staff performance evaluation, and ongoing analysis and evaluation of people's progress. Thus, the Director of Adult and Community-Living Programs may conduct performance evaluations of Early Intervention Program personnel, the Director of Education Programs may review data on group home residents' progress, and all supervisors offer workshop training, provide instruction to novice home programmers, participate in ongoing review and revision of program evaluation procedures, and collectively determine training schedules and evaluation

Programming for children with autism has been a joint endeavor and an exciting journey undertaken with our long-time colleagues and friends, Edward C. Fenske and Gregory S. MacDuff.

Program Information: Princeton Child Development Institute, 300 Cold Soil Road, Princeton, NJ 08540; 609/924-6280.

191

assignments. This fluid organizational structure, supported by regular, ongoing exchange of data across all branches of the program, prevents disjunctions between policies and practices—for example, discrepancies between staff training goals and staff training procedures, between staff training and staff evaluation procedures, or between programs implemented in the school or preschool and those in the group homes or children's own homes. The absence of administrative, training, and evaluation "departments" also prevents inequitable distribution of program resources, and facilitates optimal deployment of training and evaluation services (McClannahan & Krantz, 1993).

Preschoolers

The first preschoolers were enrolled in 1975. In 1997, with the opening of the Early Intervention Program, services were extended to children younger than 28 months of age at referral. Of 41 children who entered intervention before 60 months of age, 8 are currently enrolled in the preschool or early intervention program, 14 have made successful transitions to public school classrooms (most in regular education), and 19 are enrolled in PCDI's school program. Of the 41 children, 5 are girls; 2 are African American, 2 are Asian, and the remainder are Caucasian. Their mean age at intake was 42 months (range 21 to 59 months).

Research on age at intervention and treatment outcome (Fenske, Zalenski, Krantz, & McClannahan, 1985) underlined the importance of early intervention and led to changes in intake policy. Thus, vacancies are created when (a) a toddler arrives at preschool age and moves from the early intervention program to the preschool, (b) a preschool- or school-aged child makes a transition to public school, (c) a youth completes his or her schooling, or (d) a child is withdrawn from the program. Virtually all vacancies are filled by toddlers or preschoolers.

A child is eligible for services if (a) a diagnosis of autism has been conferred by one or more persons or agencies beyond PCDI, (b) the child meets the criteria for autism designated in the *Diagnostic and Statistical Manual of Mental Disorders–Fourth Edition* (DSM–IV); American Psychiatric Association, 1994, and (c) direct observation based on PCDI's own assessment instruments supports a diagnosis of autism. IQ scores, skills or skill deficits, and severe behavior problems (e.g., self-injury) are unrelated to eligibility. At program entry, most children have little or no receptive or expressive language, are not toilet trained, do not visually attend to others at relevant times, do not imitate others, and engage in a broad range of stereotypies.

Because of board members' and administrators' belief in the efficacy of small versus large settings, the combined population of the early intervention program, preschool, and school is limited to approximately 32 children at any given time. As an alternative to an ever-expanding child population, technical assistance is offered to other agencies that wish to adopt PCDI's intervention model; this promotes the development of additional services for youngsters with autism while maintaining quality control. At this writing, four agencies are developing preschool and school programs similar to the PCDI model. They are Nassau Suffolk Services for Autism of Levittown, New York; New York Child Learning Institute of College Point, New York; Institute for Educational Achievement of River Edge, New Jersey; and Somerset Hills Learning Institute of Gladstone, New Jersey.

A formal contract with each of these agencies specifies that a successful program will produce several types of data: data to document that the curriculum is characterized by behavioral definitions, specified observation and recording procedures, defined intervention procedures, and specified procedures for summarizing data; data on the proportion of such intervention programs that produces favorable behavior change; and estimates of the reliability of these data. In addition, there will be data on staff members' skills and on the proportion of staff members whose skills are evaluated at least annually; programwide data on children's engagement with planned activities and materials; data demonstrating that services are delivered not only at school, but also in students' homes and other community settings; and data on the percentage of children who leave the program to enter regular schools as independent learners, not shadowed by aides.

Other data sets pertain to social validity; at a minimum, there must be consumer evaluation by the parents of enrolled children, by members of the governing board, and by intervention agents themselves, who evaluate the importance of target behaviors selected, the appropriateness of intervention procedures, and the social significance of behavior change (Wolf, 1978). Staff members' participation in consumer evaluation is of special importance because staff are uniquely positioned not only to evaluate the dimensions cited above, but also to evaluate staff training and evaluation procedures and administrative policies and procedures (McClannahan & Krantz, 1993). The data generated by the four young agencies are evaluated against benchmark data produced by the PCDI model year after year. Experience indicates that it takes a new program several years to produce a complete set of data in a given year. The development of new intervention resources for young children takes time.

Assessment Procedures

When children are enrolled, and at regular intervals thereafter, several formal assessments are administered. Since we began using the Checklist for Autism in Toddlers (Baron-Cohen et al., 1996), all of the enrolled toddlers have initially failed the three key items—protodeclarative pointing, gaze monitoring, and pretend play—that are indicators of autism. The *Early Language Milestone Scale–Second Edition* (Coplan, 1993), *Preschool Language Scale* (Zimmerman, Steiner, & Pond, 1979), *Peabody Picture Vocabulary Test–Revised* (PPVT–R; Dunn & Dunn, 1981), and *Vineland Adaptive Behavior Scales* (Sparrow, Balla, & Cicchetti, 1984) are also used. On first administration, most children do not achieve basal scores on the PPVT–R, and their Vineland scores are significantly below age norms. For example, Vineland composite age equivalent scores for the three children last enrolled in the preschool were 1-7, 1-10, and 2-6 at chronological ages 2-6, 3-4, and 4-4, respectively.

Staff, Staffing Patterns, and Staff Training

Most staff members have bachelor's or master's degrees in psychology or education; the number with educational certifications meets or exceeds the standards specified by the New Jersey Department of Education. Doctoral students from Queens College of the City University of New York, the University of Kansas, and other universities with applied behavior analysis graduate programs may occupy paid positions while completing their degree requirements. Stipends, awarded on a competitive basis, support 1- or 2-year residencies for young professionals who are preparing for careers in intervention and program administration. In addition, undergraduate interns from local and foreign colleges and universities earn academic credits by serving as data collectors and intervention trainees. In the preschool, the staff–child ratio is 1 to 1; in the school, the staff–child ratio is 1 to 1.5.

At the time of employment, most staff members do not have prior experience in providing intervention to people with developmental disabilities, and few are trained in applied behavior analysis. Preservice and inservice workshops are conducted to develop shared vocabularies and to build good relationships between trainers and trainees. However, data on trainees' pre- and postworkshop performances indicate that, although didactic training typically results in improved paper-and-pencil test scores, it does not enable trainees to display relevant intervention skills at criterion levels. Thus, most training is hands on—trainers accompany trainees to classrooms, playgrounds, or children's own homes; model the target skills; create supervised practice opportunities; and provide immediate positive and corrective feedback (McClannahan & Krantz, 1985). Typically, more hands-on training is delivered in a staff member's first 2 years than in subsequent years, but all teachers and therapists continue to receive such ongoing training throughout their employment at PCDI.

Much of the content of in vivo training is specified by a training protocol that includes observation and measurement of the trainee's use of behavior-specific (and contingent) praise, delivery of opportunities for children to respond, distribution of interactions across children, and number of incidental teaching episodes completed during designated times. Observational data are also collected on the engagement or on-task levels of children for whom the staff member is responsible. In addition, the protocol includes a series of behavioral checklists that assesses skill areas such as shaping; prompting and fading prompts; teaching language and social-competence skills; decreasing inappropriate behavior; using functional environmental design and classroom arrangements; maintaining the quality of the intervention environment; and building and maintaining positive relationships with children, colleagues, and trainers. Each of these content areas results in performance feedback to the trainee.

After 6 to 8 months of hands-on training, new staff members' intervention skills are evaluated. The evaluation protocol is identical to the training protocol, ensuring that precisely those skills that are trained are the skills evaluated; however, the evaluator is a supervisor or trainer who has not been the staff member's primary mentor. On the day of an evaluation, the evaluator observes 4 to 5 hours of the trainee's work with children, collects observational data, and scores the behavioral checklists. Verbal feedback, delivered at the end of the observation period, is followed within 30 days by extensive written performance feedback. Occasionally, a pair of evaluators assesses a teacher's or therapist's performance; this practice is used to train new evaluators, as well as to check interobserver agreement between experienced evaluators.

Training and evaluation procedures are designed to maximize staff members' successes. Hands-on training and evaluation continue throughout employment, the training protocol *is* the evaluation protocol, and evaluators' written recommendations are included in subsequent training plans. Further, children's, trainees', trainers', and administrators' outcomes are yoked. That is, trainees' skills are endorsed when direct observation and data on children's programs document that the children are receiving effective intervention; trainers' skills are recognized and appreciated when the majority of their trainees pass the evaluation; and administrators succeed when children, trainees, and trainers are successful. All staff members are evaluated at least annually, and passing the evaluation is a prerequisite for reappointment for the following school year.

Curriculum

The curriculum began in 1975 as a series of individualized programs developed to address the skill deficits and behavior problems of the children then enrolled. With the arrival of each new child, more programs were written and implemented. This ideographic approach to curriculum development resulted in a continuously expanding database that presently contains more than 600 programs relevant to early intervention, preschool, school, home, and community settings. Some illustrative content areas are community participation, expressive and receptive language, handwriting, keyboard skills, leisure skills, motor and verbal imitation, peer interaction, physical education, reading, self-care, social skills, and toileting. The curriculum reflects more than two decades of experience in programming for children with autism, and although some programs are suitable for many youngsters, most programs stored on disk are revised to reflect the learning characteristics and stimulus preferences of specific children.

Some instructional programs are based on commercially available curricula, such as the *Edmark Reading Program* (1992) and *The Sensible Pencil: A Handwriting Program* (Becht & Exley, 1989). Others are written with reference to our own or others' published research, such as using prepositions (McGee, Krantz, & McClannahan, 1985), using pronouns (Lovaas, 1977), verbally initiating to teachers (Halle, Baer, & Spradlin, 1981) and peers (Krantz & McClannahan, 1993), displaying appropriate affect (Gena, Krantz, McClannahan, Pelios, & Poulson, 1996), and reporting temporally remote past events (Krantz, Zalenski, Hall, Fenske, & McClannahan, 1981). Many programs, such as riding a tricycle, remaining in a designated play area, interacting with a sibling, and dressing oneself, are straightforward applications of behavioral technology.

As computer-based instructional programs became available, selected software was included in the curriculum (e.g., *First Words*, Wilson & Fox, 1991). However, because most commercially available software does not include the detailed task analyses, branch programs, or measurement systems that are important in intervention for children with autism, computers are more often used for reward activities, to teach leisure skills, to help children and youths acquire keyboard skills, and to edit videotapes that are used in instruction.

Children enrolled in PCDI's preschool do not occupy self-contained classrooms; instead, their daily schedules call for many transitions across rooms and activity areas, and across staff members. This strategy is used to promote the transfer of new skills. For example, an expressive language skill acquired during a verbal imitation session may be requested by a different teacher during outdoor play; lunch time may be an opportunity to probe peer initiations taught during the morning; counting responses that are the topic of a premath class may be targeted for incidental teaching during toy play; or a response that is incompatible with stereotypy may be measured and rewarded in the bathroom as well as the hallway. Stokes and Baer (1977) noted that "discriminated behavior changes may well be the rule if generalization is not specifically programmed" (p. 365); this observation is unquestionably relevant to children with autism. Scheduling children to enter multiple settings and to encounter multiple instructors creates many opportunities to assess and promote generalization across settings, persons, responses, and time. Children do not have the same schedules of activities. Instructional targets are selected with reference to each child's skills and skill deficits (Dunlap & Robbins, 1991), as well as with consideration for families' interests and concerns. For example, a child whose family values music may learn to play the piano, and a child whose parents enjoy athletic activities may learn to kick a soccer ball or play catch. Although individuality is emphasized, many youngsters' initial instructional programs share common features. Learning to follow simple directions (e.g., "come here," "look at me," "stand up," "sit down") is a necessary prerequisite to many other learning tasks. Acquiring motor and verbal imitation skills promotes repertoires that are incompatible with stereotypies, and contributes to the development of expressive language; in addition, establishing generalized imitation within and across motor and verbal response classes appears to facilitate later acquisition in many skill areas (Young, Krantz, McClannahan, & Poulson, 1994).

Since the first edition of this book, our intervention programming for young children has changed dramatically. Typically, early programming places special emphasis on match-to-sample tasks, and then on picture-object correspondence skills. When these goals are achieved, children learn to follow photographic activity schedules that enable them to independently work, play, change activities, and move across settings without verbal prompts from adults. Schedule-following skills are taught using graduated guidance, delivered from behind the child. Use of a most-to-least prompt sequence results in a relatively errorless teaching procedure, and prompts are faded as quickly as possible, from graduated guidance, to spatial fading (Cooper, 1987), to shadowing, to decreased proximity.

After a child learns to open his or her picture schedule book, point to a photograph, obtain the depicted materials, complete the scheduled activity, put materials away, and turn to the next photograph, pictures are resequenced to ensure that the child is not merely following a now-familiar routine, but is "reading" the pictorial cues. After a youngster achieves a high level of accuracy in following the frequently resequenced schedule, new photographs (of previously taught activities) are introduced (MacDuff, Krantz, & McClannahan, 1993). An initial photographic schedule for a preschooler might include photographs of a frame-tray puzzle, nesting cups, a picture-matching task, a stacking toy, and a snack; upon completion of the five depicted activities, the teacher provides praise and access to preferred stimuli. The length of the schedule is gradually extended, and the teacher's presence is gradually faded.

Photographic activity schedules (and written schedules, for children who are readers) provide an excellent framework for teaching youngsters to make choices among different activities and to manage changes in daily routine (McClannahan & Krantz, 1999). In addition, schedules promote generalization of new skills from the preschool to home and community settings (Krantz,

MacDuff, & McClannahan, 1993) and provide a vehicle for teaching social interaction in context.

Scripts embedded in activity schedules enable youngsters to experience the give-and-take of conversation, an experience that is difficult to achieve in a discrete trial paradigm. Children who are readers use written scripts that are gradually faded from end to beginning (Krantz & McClannahan, 1993, 1998); nonreaders use Language Master machines that play audiotaped scripts that are also faded from end to beginning (Stevenson, Krantz, & McClannahan, 2000).

For example, a schedule for a toddler who does not yet imitate verbal models may include photographs of social activities attached to Language Master cards. When he encounters such a card in his schedule, he runs it through the machine, hears an audiotaped cue such as "Pat-a-Cake" or "Ring Around the Rosie," and gives the card to an adult who engages in the social activity with him. Children who are acquiring verbal imitation skills learn to imitate audiotaped cues such as "Up," "Wagon," or "Swing." These initiations are followed by brief conversational comments by an adult and access to the target activity. Preschoolers with more language may imitate scripted phrases or sentences such as "Look, a top," "I like Pooh," or "Trucks are fun." Adult recipients respond with brief comments that model relevant language and that are of interest to children, but do not ask questions or give instructions, because this creates a discrete trial paradigm rather than an interaction that approximates typical conversation. Initially, most children echo the conversational partner's comments, but in later conversations the statements that were originally echoed reappear as spontaneous utterances, and are recombined with other scripted and unscripted statements in spontaneous and generative verbal productions (McClannahan & Krantz, 1999).

Photographic activity schedules that include social interaction tasks create a structure that supports the development of independence as well as conversational language; in addition, the prompt dependence that is often inadvertently engendered by discrete trial training is minimized. Through the use of scripts and script-fading procedures, youngsters learn to garner adult attention ("Look," "Watch me"); initiate interaction with peers ("Let's dance"); comment on next activities ("I'm going to paste"); and report on recently completed activities ("I did computer"). Scripts that provide multiple exemplars (e.g., "I colored," "Coloring is fun," "I like coloring") contribute to language variety, and young schedule followers learn to pursue some activities independently and to seek adult assistance when relevant ("It's time for reading"). An activity schedule may cue a child to independently complete matching tasks and then to seek out the teacher for discrete trial instruction on colors or shapes. Youngsters learn to sequence their own learning activities and to select their own reward activities. Thus, a child's schedule typically varies from day to day, and no two children's school schedules are the same.

Children's programs place strong emphasis on language development. PCDI does not employ specialists (e.g., occupational therapists, recreational therapists, speech therapists); instead, all intervention personnel are trained to implement children's individualized programs, and to teach receptive and expressive language skills in *every* activity. Thus, not only classroom activities, but also toilet training, outdoor play, and lunch times are occasions for expanding children's receptive and expressive language repertoires. In addition to the teaching procedures previously described, language instruction encompasses discrete trials, incidental teaching (McGee, Krantz, & McClannahan, 1985), time-delay procedures (Halle, Baer, & Spradlin, 1981), and video-modeling procedures (Charlop & Milstein, 1989; Krantz, MacDuff, Wadstrom, & McClannahan, 1991).

Of 41 children who entered the program before 60 months of age, 36 had *no* functional expressive language at program entry; presently, their performance ranges from the use of sounds as mands to age-appropriate verbal repertoires. Because most children develop speech, PCDI does not teach manual signing, which addresses specialized audiences; however, a few children use computerized communication devices while they are acquiring expressive language skills.

Toddlers and preschoolers who acquire necessary receptive and expressive language skills are quickly advanced to preacademic and academic programs. Reading receives special emphasis; development of textual behavior (Skinner, 1957) is viewed as an important part of a comprehensive program to promote verbal behavior. Art (e.g., coloring, cutting, pasting), arithmetic, handwriting, and social play skills are addressed as soon as children have achieved the prerequisite skills, in preparation for public school enrollment.

During the 1997–1998 school year, 217 individualized intervention programs were delivered to 8 early intervention and preschool children during their hours at PCDI; this represents a mean of 27 programs per child. Not all programs were implemented simultaneously; some were discontinued after children mastered the target skills and were supplanted by different programs. Of the 217 programs, 214 (99%) were skill acquisition programs and 3 were designed to decrease problem behaviors such as tantrums and stereotypy. Initially, all behavior problems are addressed via rich schedules of reinforcement. Children who engage in finger play or hand flapping are taught to carry toys and book bags and to put their hands in their pockets when not manipulating learning materials; children who display toe walking are rewarded for "heels down"; children who aggress or self-injure are rewarded for "hands down," "good sitting," and many other alternate responses; and children who engage in vocal stereotypy are rewarded for verbal imitation and verbal initiations.

Most unwanted responses decrease as a function of systematic and skillful shaping of relevant repertoires. However, when serious behavior problems do not respond to positive reinforcement procedures, other procedures (e.g., response cost, chair time-out, facial screening) are evaluated. Functional analyses are seldom used because they are typically unnecessary. But when severe behavior problems do not respond to intervention programming and functional analyses are conducted, we often find that self-injurious, aggressive, or destructive responses occur with comparable frequencies across all conditions. In these cases, programming based on clinical judgment, careful measurement, and tenacity is often successful, although not always rapid.

Assessing Progress

A written protocol used for training and evaluating staff members and evaluating intervention programming (McClannahan, MacDuff, Fenske, & Krantz, 1998) defines an individualized program as a document in a child's record that includes, at minimum, (a) a written response definition that provides an objective description of a target behavior, (b) a written description of a measurement procedure, (c) a written description of an instruction or treatment procedure, and (d) a graph or other form of data summary that displays levels of behavior over time. The protocol also defines four categories that are used to evaluate the effects of individualized programs: (a) behavior change in a desired direction, (b) no behavior change, (c) behavior change in an undesired direction, or (d) behavior change cannot be ascertained. In addition, the protocol defines current parental consent (consent given within the past 364 days or since a substantive program revision occurred) and assesses the frequency with which staff members obtain interobserver agreement on intervention data.

Institute staff members and their trainers regularly use this protocol, and the results are reported and discussed at weekly staff meetings. In addition, at the time of each staff member's performance evaluation, the evaluator uses the protocol to score all of the intervention programs for which that staff member is responsible, and the results are summarized as part of the trainee's postevaluation feedback. Finally, at the end of each program year, a behavior analyst who is an expert in autism intervention and who is not affiliated with PCDI is invited to use the protocol to evaluate intervention programs.

In the 1997–1998 program year, an independent evaluator reviewed 21% of 751 instructional programs (a sample drawn by the evaluator that included every child) and 100% of all behavior reduction programs. Of the early intervention and preschool programs reviewed, 100% were scored as meeting the criteria used to define an individualized program, 97% were scored as displaying behavior change in a desired direction, and 97% included current parental consent. Pairs of professionals, using this assessment procedure, have typically achieved appropriate levels of interobserver agreement. Repeated measures, representing successive years of assessment, now serve as benchmarks against which to compare the current year's data. On the basis of more than a decade of experience with this evaluation process, we expect that on each annual assessment at least 80% of all intervention programs will be scored as achieving behavior change in a desired direction.

Integration: A Complex Issue

All of the preschoolers served by PCDI have lived with one or both parents in apartments, condominiums, or single-family dwellings typical of the residences of other families in our state. A large majority of the children have nonhandicapped siblings, and virtually all of them are members of families who (like other families) enjoy visiting parks, local restaurants, community events, or the homes of friends and relatives. At the outset of intervention, parents' reports and our observations indicated that none of the children with autism displayed systematic visual attending to other children; none interacted appropriately with parents, grandparents, or other relatives; none shared toys or engaged in cooperative play with siblings; none imitated peers; and none participated in community outings without displaying behavior problems. Prior to intake, some of them attended local programs for typical children or children with special needs, but were disenrolled either because they did not progress or because program personnel were unable to manage their atypical performances. Behavioral repertoires associated with autism segregated them from others, including their own parents and siblings. Under these circumstances, PCDI's preschool program focuses on building skills that enable children to become participants in family life, and to transition to public school classrooms as soon as possible.

Specific behavioral characteristics are identified as prerequisites for transitioning to public school settings. These include exhibiting sustained engagement with learning and leisure materials; systematically following adults' instructions; responding favorably to delayed reinforcement procedures (e.g., behavioral contracts, home–school notes, allowances); displaying responses not specifically taught (e.g., generative speech or imitation of peers' play behavior); and generalization of new skills to other settings. In addition, very low or zero levels of inappropriate behavior (e.g., tantrums, self-injury, aggression, stereotypy) are viewed as a precondition for transition (Krantz & McClannahan, 1999).

Each of these prerequisite repertoires is systematically assessed. For example, engagement is measured as the percentage of momentary time samples at which a child is scored as appropriately participating with activities and materials, and children are considered to have achieved criterion performance when at least 80% of time samples are consistently scored for engagement. Discrete trial measures of following instructions first assess a youngster's skills in following single-step directions ("Come here," "Sit down") and later in following multiple-step instructions ("Get out your reading book and turn to page seven") and group directions ("Everyone go to the dining room and sit at the blue table"). There are specific response definitions and measurement procedures for each skill area.

Early in the process of preparing for transition, "safe" preliminary settings are identified. Summer day camps, church schools, neighborhood play groups, after-school recreation programs, gymnastics or dance classes, and similar activities offer opportunities to assess children's group participation and to design remedial programs without risking unsuccessful experiences in local school systems.

When a child achieves readiness for transition, parents, representatives of the local school district, and PCDI personnel meet to discuss placement options. Subsequently, visits are made to potential kindergarten, elementary, or special education classrooms. Whenever a child's skills permit, he or she is placed in a regular rather than a special education class and whenever possible classroom teachers are not informed of the diagnosis of autism (cf. Lovaas, 1987).

Efforts are made to select classrooms in children's own school districts on the bases of class size, teachers' skills, and teachers' willingness to participate in the transition process. It should be noted, however, that placement decisions ultimately rest with parents and public schools; PCDI personnel make recommendations and offer assistance but have no formal authority to determine placement arrangements.

After a public school classroom is identified, visits are made to observe the teacher's instructions and the children's activities and daily routines. Skills that will be called for in the target classroom are prioritized and taught before the transition begins. Typically, the curriculum used in the public school classroom is introduced to the child at PCDI, before he or she enters the new setting. In addition, the youngster is taught many specific responses that will be expected—how to request a bathroom pass; how to open a locker or use a cubby; how to correctly articulate the teacher's name; how to manipulate a book bag, pencil case, or gym bag; how to use classroom materials with which he or she may not be familiar; and how to put materials away in the manner expected by the new teacher. Concurrently, the child gains further experience with a home–school note or behavioral contract that mediates increasingly delayed rewards for appropriate performance.

When the transition begins, the child usually attends the target class for a few hours each day, and returns to PCDI for the remainder of the day, to rehearse new responses that are called for in the public school. Initially, the youngster is continuously accompanied by a PCDI staff member, who collects observational data that are used to structure teaching activities at PCDI, and consults with the classroom teacher about the child's academic work and use of the home–school note; this person's presence is faded as quickly as possible, first to the periphery of the classroom and then to the hall. As the child's time in attendance increases, the observation schedule gradually decreases to an aperiodic schedule of unobtrusive monitoring and, ultimately, to a schedule of telephone contacts with parents and the classroom teacher. Of course, the emergence of performance problems results in immediate adjustments in the classroom visit schedule and, in some cases, supplemental instructional sessions at PCDI.

Depending upon children's acquisition rates and characteristics of public school classrooms, transitions may extend over weeks or months. When children's full-time attendance in target classrooms is uneventful, follow-up contacts initiated by PCDI gradually decline to an annual schedule, but follow-up services remain available at the request of parents or school personnel. In some cases, no follow-up services are requested after transitions are successfully completed; in other cases, youngsters receive follow-up services over a period of years. Although there is no mandatory funding mechanism to support these services, some school districts pay for transition and follow-up programs.

Family Support

Occasional parent meetings are designed as social occasions that enable parents to meet other parents and to interact with PCDI staff members. Due to the diversity of children's repertoires, however, services to families are entirely individualized (McClannahan, Krantz, & McGee, 1982). Each family is assigned a home programmer (a teacher or therapist) who regularly visits the home; during the 1997–1998 school year, home programmers serving preschoolers averaged 84 visits per family.

In discussions with their home programmer, parents identify and prioritize their goals for their child. Subsequently, the home programmer and his or her trainer develop individualized programs to help the child acquire the target skills; these programs are initially implemented in the preschool, and parents are encouraged to visit, observe, and work with their child in that setting. When observational data indicate that the child is consistently displaying the desired behavior in the treatment setting, the program is introduced at home. The home programmer describes and models the intervention procedures and teaches the parents to use them at home.

Because children's programs are implemented in the treatment setting before they are implemented at home, and because generalization of new skills from the preschool to home is specifically programmed, parents achieve a high success rate. During the 1997–1998 school year, parents of five preschoolers implemented 55 home intervention programs, an average of 11 per family. An outside expert reviewed 51 of the 55 programs (a 93% sample drawn by the evaluator) using the evaluation protocol described earlier (McClannahan et al., 1998). Fifty of the 51 programs reviewed (98%) conformed to the definition of an individualized program, and 44 of 51 programs (86%) were scored as achieving favorable behavior change for children. These programs addressed toilet training, receptive and expressive language, play skills, direction following, dressing skills, interaction with family members, preacademic and academic skills, tantrums, and learning to follow photographic activity schedules that included a variety of social, self-help, and home living activities.

Because services to families are individualized, all participate at some level. Some families devote more time to home treatment than others (one preschooler had 3 home programs and another had 20); some are interested in data collection, and others are not; some acquire intervention skills more rapidly than others. If both parents are employed and hire a sitter, the parents and the surrogate may be taught to implement the child's home treatment programs. If parents enjoy participating in treatment but are uninterested in performance measurement, the home programmer may assume responsibility for data collection or may use a daily phone call to invite parents' reports on the presence or absence of critical responses.

The individualized services that facilitate parents' participation in treatment require a cadre of skilled home programmers. Thus, teachers and therapists receive specific training on how to provide family support. For example, they are taught how to build relationships with families and how to develop agendas for home visits. Novice home programmers are accompanied by trainers until they acquire the relevant skills. Subsequently, trainers review home programming agendas before each home visit, participate in revisions if necessary, and help home programmers rehearse requisite skills.

Treatment Outcomes

Of 41 children who entered the program before 60 months of age, 8 are presently enrolled in the preschool or early intervention program, 14 have made transitions to public schools, and 19 are enrolled in PCDI's school program. Because of the small number of children, the percentage of youngsters who enter intervention before age 5 and make successful transitions to public school classrooms varies considerably from year to year—from 42% to 67%. Calculation of the percentage of successfully transitioned children does not include children who were withdrawn from the program before an outcome was achieved, nor does it include children who are presently enrolled in the preschool and early intervention program.

Time in treatment for the 14 children who entered the program before 60 months of age and completed transitions to public schools ranged from 9 to 141 months (mean = 37 months). Eight of the 14 families requested and received follow-up services from PCDI after their children's transitions were complete, and 5 received follow-up services in the 1998–1999 school year. Two of the children are lost to follow-up contact because their families relocated and their current addresses are unknown.

The 11 males and 1 female still available for follow-up presently range in age from 6 to 26 years. Six have now graduated from high school, and 3 have completed college. Of the 12 young people, 9 were or are in regular education, and 3 were or are in special education classes; 1 of the 3 in a special education placement is now in a regular elementary school classroom but receives resource room assistance and twice-weekly speech sessions. Of the regular education students, 2 received special services in the form of individual or group counseling after their transitions to public school. All school-aged children continue to live at home with their own families. Two college graduates live away from home, and 1 recent graduate has been living on campus.

All 6 high school or college graduates are employed. One creates special effects for the television and movie industries, 1 does janitorial work, 1 is a therapist for youths with autism, 1 creates industrial and graphic designs, 1 works in a grocery store warehouse, and 1 does data entry. Some of these young adults reportedly have important relationships with opposite-sex peers; none is yet married. In 1994, when the Canadian Broadcast Company was filming a program on autism, the adult members of the follow-up group were invited to participate in videotaped interviews. Each of them declined, noting that they did not want their friends to know of their prior diagnosis.

Follow-up data have been gathered via mailed questionnaires or telephone interview. In 1997–1998, structured telephone interviews were conducted; on some items, parents were asked to respond to a 7-point rating scale with which they were familiar because it was used annually to obtain consumer input throughout the time that their children were enrolled. Twelve mothers participated in the structured interviews. After inquiring about the child's place of residence, school or college placement and grade level, employment status, and use of special services, the interviewer asked the parent to use the rating scale to respond to the following questions:

1. How satisfied are you with your child's current participation in your family and in family activities?

2. How satisfied are you that your child has been able to make friends and to participate in social activities with his or her peers?

3. How satisfied are you with your child's academic performance, that is, that he or she is doing as well as you feel he or she should?

4. How satisfied are you with your child's recreational activities, that is, that he or she participates in sports or hobbies, or finds other appropriate ways to use leisure time?

5. How satisfied are you with your child's self-care skills, and that his or her personal appearance is as good as other young peoples' of his/her age?

6. How satisfied are you with your child's present quality of life—that he or she is happy, well adjusted, and appreciated by others?

Responses to these questions are shown in Table 8.1.

On the 1997–1998 follow-up, satisfaction ratings were higher than when we last reported them; all ratings were *slightly satisfied* to *completely satisfied;* none of the parents assigned a rating below *slightly satisfied.* These data differ from our prior report, in which nine families gave eight ratings below *slightly satisfied* (McClannahan & Krantz, 1994). We speculate that this may be due to advances in intervention technology and to the expansion of transition and follow-up services. Parents in the follow-up group assigned the highest satisfaction ratings to items about their children's recreation activities, personal appearance, and quality of life.

We wondered how these ratings would compare with ratings by parents whose children never received a diagnosis of autism. Thus, we selected a purposive sample of 12 parents (friends, relatives, or acquaintances of PCDI staff members) whose typical children were of the same age and gender as the young people in the follow-up group. During telephone interviews, these parents were not given information about follow-up; they were simply asked to

Table 8.1

Satisfaction Ratings by Parents of 12 Children with Prior Diagnosis of Autism

Item	Number of Parents Assigning a Satisfaction Rating of:							Mean
	1	2	3	4	5	6	7	
1. Participation in family					1	6	5	6.3
2. Making friends					3	7	2	5.9
3. Academic performance[a]					2	3	1	5.8
4. Recreation activities					1	4	7	6.5
5. Personal appearance					2	2	8	6.5
6. Quality of life					1	4	7	6.5

Note. On this 7-point, Likert-type scale, 1 = *completely dissatisfied,* 2 = *dissatisfied,* 3 = *slightly dissatisfied,* 4 = *neither satisfied nor dissatisfied,* 5 = *slightly satisfied,* 6 = *satisfied,* and 7 = *completely satisfied.*
[a]n = 6. Six young people are no longer in school.

Table 8.2

Satisfaction Ratings by Parents of Children with Typical Development

Item	Number of Parents Assigning a Satisfaction Rating of:							Mean
	1	2	3	4	5	6	7	
1. Participation in family						3	9	6.8
2. Making friends					1	5	6	6.4
3. Academic performance[a]					2	2	5	6.3
4. Recreation activities					1	7	4	6.2
5. Personal appearance					2	2	8	6.5
6. Quality of life					1	3	8	6.6

Note. On this 7-point, Likert-type scale, 1 = *completely dissatisfied,* 2 = *dissatisfied,* 3 = *slightly dissatisfied,* 4 = *neither satisfied nor dissatisfied,* 5 = *slightly satisfied,* 6 = *satisfied,* and 7 = *completely satisfied.*
[a]$n = 9$. Three young people are no longer in school (more of the typical children attended or are attending college).

provide some information about their nondisabled children. Table 8.2 shows their responses to the same questions answered by the parents in the follow-up group. Like the parents of children in the follow-up group, the parents of typical children assigned ratings of *slightly satisfied* to *completely satisfied.* Parents of children with autism assigned 10 ratings of *slightly satisfied,* and parents of typical children assigned 7 ratings of *slightly satisfied.* Ratings of personal appearance were identical in the two groups, and the quality of life scores assigned by parents of children with autism and parents of typical children differed by only 1 rating. Parents of typical children were most satisfied with their children's participation in family life, quality of life, and personal appearance. On this ordinal scale, in which scale points are identified by words such as *completely dissatisfied* and *satisfied,* it is difficult to draw further conclusions. We leave it to the reader to assess the importance of other differences between the two groups' satisfaction ratings.

Future Research and Practice

Not long ago, autism intervention typically began at preschool age. A review of eight model programs, based on publications from 1984 to 1994, noted that the average age of children entering intervention was 3.5 to 4 years (Dawson & Osterling, 1997). Greater public awareness of autism and improved diagnostic indicators, however, have resulted in earlier diagnosis and intervention, and it is no longer unusual for toddlers to receive behavioral treatment, raising the possibility that in the future, the relationship between age at intervention and treatment outcome can be scrutinized in more detail. Such data may also be relevant to students of brain–behavior relationships, who hypothesize that there may be critical periods for intervention (see Schroeder, 1996).

Although funding for preschoolers with autism has been in place since the passage of the Education of the Handicapped Act Amendments of 1986, funding for children under the age of 3 remains problematic. School-based programs that report positive treatment outcomes offer preschoolers an average of 27 hours of intervention per week (Dawson & Osterling, 1997), but in many states, government funding for toddlers pays for as little as 2 hours of intervention per week. To assess whether intervention at very young ages enhances treatment outcomes for preschoolers, it will be necessary to achieve adequate funding of early, intensive intervention. Unfortunately, government funding agencies are often short-sighted; it has been estimated that, based on positive treatment outcomes for 30% to 40% of children with autism or pervasive developmental disorders, and using calculations that include inflation, government savings of $1.2 to $1.3 million per person would be realized by the time today's children reach age 45 (Jacobson, Mulick, & Green, 1998).

Age at intervention and intensive behavioral intervention appear to be predictors of treatment outcome, but after nearly 25 years of reviewing formal assessment data and observing and evaluating children who are entering intervention, we are no better at predicting individual treatment outcomes than we were at the outset. The data we obtain at the time of program enrollment indicate that scores (or lack of basal scores) on standardized instruments, presence or absence of speech, presence or absence of hyperlexia, presence or absence of motor and verbal imitation skills, and presence or absence of tantrums and stereotypy are negligible predictors. Perhaps the absence of indicators operates in favor of referred children, offering no reason not to enroll them in the order in which they are referred.

The data on acquisition of specific skills by individual youngsters, however, become predictive over time. Data showing that a child has acquired generalized motor and verbal imitation skills; displays spontaneous, generative language; engages in unprompted play with peers; and rarely engages in dysfunctional behavior become useful indicators of successful transition to regular education. Because of the practical importance of observational data on children's skills and skill deficits, we have systematically set increasingly stringent requirements for obtaining estimates of the reliability of clinical data, and have developed staff training sequences that are commensurate with these goals.

This endeavor has produced many positive side-effects. When trainers and trainees obtain independent measures of interobserver agreement, measurement problems and staff members' skill deficits become evident and can be addressed. In addition, interobserver agreement on observational data that document a child's skill acquisition helps to counteract the still all-too-common assertion that a youngster (previously mute, isolate, and engaged in high-rate stereotypy) who now engages in spontaneous conversation and garners adults' and peers' attention "was never really autistic" and the diagnosis of autism was erroneous.

We continue to believe that more data are needed on the relationships between known etiologies and treatment outcomes. Among the 19 children who enrolled in the preschool when they were less than 60 months of age and remain in treatment, there is 1 case in which autism is associated with tuberous sclerosis, 1 in which autism is associated with fragile X syndrome, 3 in which seizures appeared during childhood (see Gillberg, 1991), 1 in which there is a family history of Marfans syndrome, and 2 in which there is a family history of schizophrenia. Of the 14 children who made successful transitions to public school classrooms, only 1 has any such known etiologic factor (a family history of schizophrenia). Similarly, of the 14 children who attend or have graduated from public schools, only 1 has a sibling with a developmental disability, but 6 of the 19 children who remain in treatment have a sibling with a developmental disability.

Continuity of treatment is also an important issue. Most children who "age out" of PCDI's Early Intervention Program make seamless transitions to PCDI's preschool and continue to acquire target skills. Children who are unable to participate in public school classrooms at the end of their preschool years continue to receive systematic intervention in PCDI's school, and may later make transitions to their local school districts at the ages of 6, 7, or even (in one case) 15. Disjunctions in programming might impede these positive outcomes.

PCDI's continuing emphasis on home programming that enables parents to become partners in intervention is based on the assumption that, in the long term, babysitters, au pairs, and skilled behavior analysts will be less influential than parents who learn to manage day-to-day and minute-to-minute contingencies. Babysitters and professionals may come and go, but parent–child relationships usually persist. Although parents of children who do not meet the criteria for transition cannot, even with extraordinary effort, help them succeed in regular education, they can help them achieve "personal bests," such as improving social interaction skills, developing work skills, and eventually engaging in productive work in community settings. Also, parents of children who do acquire the skills necessary to make transitions to public schools can play key roles in children's educational placements and life paths.

During children's transitions from PCDI to public or parochial schools, we assess their performance along many dimensions, but the measures that we most often return to are (a) comparative observations of a target child's and typical classmates' engagement or on-task behavior vis-à-vis the teacher, other students, and designated learning materials, and (b) observations of a target child's rate of peer interaction in comparison with typical peers. These data often interact with decisions to intensify transition services or to diminish services and fade PCDI personnel from the integrated setting.

As noted previously, parents' ratings of their satisfaction with the performances of children who made successful transitions to public schools have improved over time and we hypothesize that this may be due not only to improved intervention technology, but also to the expansion of follow-up services. However, there is no dependable source of funding for follow-up treatment. Presently, such services are funded by some school districts (which are not obligated to do so), by parents (if able to pay), and by PCDI's fund-raising endeavors.

Follow-up assistance is most often requested during the first year after transition to public school, when life crises occur (e.g., separation or divorce of parents, death of significant others, loss of important friends), or during major life changes (e.g., family relocation, transition to middle school or high school). Many of these requests are satisfied by brief, time-efficient and cost-effective therapy. However, it is our impression that, although follow-up services may have a major impact on young peoples' current repertoires and future outcomes, requests for help are more likely to be received when funding mechanisms are in place and less probable when payment arrangements are absent. Thus, a key goal is identification of dependable sources of funding for follow-up services.

Applied behavior analysis continues to produce new, effective intervention strategies that are supported by research. Behavioral treatment of autism is no longer (or at least should not be) characterized by a single procedure, such as discrete trial instruction. Unfortunately, clinical practice does not always keep pace with science, and all too often we see toddlers or preschoolers who have already been exposed to treatment that is always delivered knee-to-knee, in sessions that occur in special "therapy rooms." Some of these youngsters have acquired receptive and expressive language skills that are only displayed when they are seated, facing a therapist, and when directions are given in a standard format. A growing technology deserves the attention of professionals and parents; although the discrete trial paradigm is unquestionably useful, so are incidental teaching, time delay, peer tutoring, photographic and written activity schedules, script fading, stimulus shaping, and video modeling procedures. We hope that the future will bring increasing attention to standards of best practice.

Finally, it seems important to note that age at intervention is not a perfect predictor of treatment outcome. At this writing, 35% of *all* children who received services at PCDI from 1975 to the present, regardless of age at enrollment, made successful transitions to public schools.

References

American Psychiatric Association. (1994). *Diagnostic and statistical manual of mental disorders* (4th ed.). Washington, DC: Author.

Baron-Cohen, S., Cox, A., Baird, G., Swettenham, J., Nightingale, N., Morgan, K., Drew, A., & Charman, T. (1996). Psychological markers in the detection of autism in infancy in a large population. *British Journal of Psychiatry, 168,* 158–163.

Becht, L. C., & Exley, J. (1989). *The sensible pencil: A handwriting program.* Birmingham, AL: Ebsco Curriculum Materials.

Charlop, M. H., & Milstein, J. P. (1989). Teaching autistic children conversational speech using video modeling. *Journal of Applied Behavior Analysis, 22,* 275–285.

Cooper, J. O. (1987). Stimulus control. In J. O. Cooper, T. E. Heron, & W. L. Heward (Eds.), *Applied behavior analysis* (pp. 298–326). Columbus, OH: Merrill.

Coplan, J. (1993). *Early Language Milestone Scale–Second Edition.* Austin, TX: PRO-ED.

Dawson, G., & Osterling, J. (1997). Early intervention in autism. In M. J. Guralnick (Ed.), *The effectiveness of early intervention* (pp. 307–326). Baltimore: Brookes.

Dunlap, G. D., & Robbins, F. R. (1991). Current perspectives in service delivery for young children with autism. *Comprehensive Mental Health Care, 1,* 177–194.

Dunn, L. M., & Dunn, L. M. (1981). *Peabody Picture Vocabulary Test–Revised: Manual for Forms L and M.* Circle Pines, MN: American Guidance Service.

Edmark reading program (2nd ed.). (1992). Bellevue, WA: Edmark Corp.

Education of the Handicapped Act Amendments of 1986, 20 U.S.C. § 1400 *et seq.*

Fenske, E. C., Zalenski, S., Krantz, P. J., & McClannahan, L. E. (1985). Age at intervention and treatment outcome for autistic children in a comprehensive intervention program. *Analysis and Intervention in Developmental Disabilities, 5,* 49–58.

Gena, A., Krantz, P. J., McClannahan, L. E., Pelios, L., & Poulson, C. (1996). Training and generalization of affective behavior displayed by youth with autism. *Journal of Applied Behavior Analysis, 29,* 291–304.

Gillberg, C. (1991). Outcome in autism and autistic-like conditions. *Journal of the American Academy of Child and Adolescent Psychiatry, 30,* 375–382.

Halle, J. W., Baer, D. M., & Spradlin, J. E. (1981). Teachers' generalized use of delay as a stimulus control procedure to increase language use in handicapped children. *Journal of Applied Behavior Analysis, 14,* 389–409.

Jacobson, J. W., Mullick, J. A., & Green, G. (1998). Cost–benefit estimates for early intensive behavioral intervention for young children with autism—General model and single state case. *Behavioral Interventions, 13,* 201–226.

Krantz, P. J., MacDuff, G. S., Wadstrom, O., & McClannahan, L. E. (1991). Using video with developmentally disabled learners. In P. W. Dowrick (Ed.), *Practical guide to using video in the behavioral sciences* (pp. 256–266). New York: Wiley.

Krantz, P. J., MacDuff, M. T., & McClannahan, L. E. (1993). Programming participation in family activities for children with autism: Parents' use of photographic activity schedules. *Journal of Applied Behavior Analysis, 26,* 137–139.

Krantz, P. J., & McClannahan, L. E. (1993). Teaching children with autism to initiate to peers: Effects of a script-fading procedure. *Journal of Applied Behavior Analysis, 26,* 121–132.

Krantz, P. J., & McClannahan, L. E. (1998). Social interaction skills for children with autism: A script-fading procedure for beginning readers. *Journal of Applied Behavior Analysis, 31,* 191–202.

Krantz, P. J., & McClannahan, L. E. (1999). Strategies for integration: Building repertoires that support transitions to public schools. In P. M. Ghezzi, W. L. Williams, & J. E. Carr (Eds.), *Autism: Behavior-analytic perspectives* (pp. 221–231). Reno, NV: Context Press.

Krantz, P. J., Zalenski, S., Hall, L. J., Fenske, E. C., & McClannahan, L. E. (1981). Teaching complex language to autistic children. *Analysis and Intervention in Developmental Disabilities, 1,* 259–297.

Lovaas, O. I. (1977). *The autistic child: Language development through behavior modification.* New York: Wiley.

Lovaas, O. I. (1987). Behavioral treatment and normal educational and intellectual functioning in young autistic children. *Journal of Consulting and Clinical Psychology, 55,* 3–9.

MacDuff, G. S., Krantz, P. J., & McClannahan, L. E. (1993). Teaching children with autism to use photographic activity schedules: Maintenance and generalization of complex response chains. *Journal of Applied Behavior Analysis, 26,* 89–95.

McClannahan, L. E., & Krantz, P. J. (1985). Some next steps in rights protection for the developmentally disabled. *School Psychology Review, 14,* 143–149.

McClannahan, L. E., & Krantz, P. J. (1993). On systems analysis in autism intervention programs. *Journal of Applied Behavior Analysis, 26,* 589–596.

McClannahan, L. E., & Krantz, P. J. (1994). The Princeton Child Development Institute. In S. L. Harris & J. S. Handleman (Eds.), *Preschool education programs for children with autism* (pp. 107–126). Austin, TX: PRO-ED.

McClannahan, L. E., & Krantz, P. J. (1999). *Activity schedules for children with autism: Teaching independent behavior.* Bethesda, MD: Woodbine House.

McClannahan, L. E., Krantz, P. J., & McGee, G. G. (1982). Parents as therapists for autistic children: A model for effective parent training. *Analysis and Intervention in Developmental Disabilities, 2,* 223–252.

McClannahan, L. E., MacDuff, G. S., Fenske, E. C., & Krantz, P. J. (1998). *Evaluation protocol* (rev. ed.). Unpublished manuscript.

McGee, G. G., Krantz, P. J., & McClannahan, L. E. (1985). The facilitative effects of incidental teaching on preposition use by autistic children. *Journal of Applied Behavior Analysis, 18,* 17–31.

Schroeder, S. (1996). *Cognitive and neurological importance of first and early experience.* Unpublished manuscript.

Skinner, B. F. (1957). *Verbal behavior.* New York: Appleton-Century-Crofts.

Sparrow, S. S., Balla, D. A., & Cicchetti, D. V. (1984). *Vineland Adaptive Behavior Scales, interview edition, survey form manual.* Circle Pines, MN: American Guidance Service.

Stevenson, C. L., Krantz, P. J., & McClannahan, L. E. (2000). Social interaction skills for children with autism: A script-fading procedure for nonreaders. *Behavioral Interventions, 15,* 1–20.

Stokes, T. F., & Baer, D. M. (1977). An implicit technology of generalization. *Journal of Applied Behavior Analysis, 10,* 349–367.

Wilson, M. S., & Fox, B. J. (1991). *First words* (2nd ed.). Winooski, VT: Laureate Learning Systems.

Wolf, M. M. (1978). Social validity: The case for subjective measurement or how applied behavior analysis is finding its heart. *Journal of Applied Behavior Analysis, 11,* 203–214.

Young, J. M., Krantz, P. J., McClannahan, L. E., & Poulson, C. L. (1994). Generalized imitation and response-class formation in children with autism. *Journal of Applied Behavior Analysis, 27,* 685–697.

Zimmerman, I. L., Steiner, V. G., & Pond, R. E. (1979). *Preschool Language Scale.* Columbus, OH: Merrill.

TEACCH Services for Preschool Children

9

Lee Marcus, Eric Schopler, and Catherine Lord

Division TEACCH (**T**reatment and **E**ducation of **A**utistic and Related Communication Handicapped **Ch**ildren) was founded in 1972 as a division of the Department of Psychiatry, University of North Carolina at Chapel Hill. TEACCH is a statewide, comprehensive, community-based program in North Carolina dedicated to improving the understanding and services for children with autism and communication disabilities, and their families. As of 1999, there were eight TEACCH centers distributed across the state, as well as an administration and research section, located in the School of Medicine in Chapel Hill, and a Community Living and Learning Center for adults, located near campus. TEACCH's services are both center and outreach based. There is one demonstration preschool classroom located in the medical school in Chapel Hill and one directed by the Asheville TEACCH Center; however, other educational services are provided within schools and programs in the communities in which the children and adults with autism live. Because one of the mandates of TEACCH is to provide services that best meet the needs of individual communities, these services range in conceptualization and focus. However, the overriding goal is to provide continuity of services from preschool and school age to adult life. In this chapter, we describe general characteristics of the services provided by TEACCH centers to preschool children across the state and, in some cases,

Program Information: TEACCH Services for Preschool Children, University of North Carolina, Department of Psychiatry, CB 7180 Medical School Wing E, Chapel Hill, NC 27599-7180; 919/966-2174.

offer specific examples from the Chapel Hill TEACCH Center to illustrate particular points.

North Carolina is predominately a rural state with several small to mid-size cities. TEACCH centers are placed in cities where branches of the University of North Carolina are located to provide TEACCH staff access to educational support while providing students and researchers access to TEACCH. Each center serves 6 to 28 counties. Educational and early intervention services for preschool children in these areas are funded primarily by state and county resources; school systems are now providing services for children down to age 3 years. TEACCH provides training and consultation for teachers and staff in these programs.

TEACCH receives state appropriations to help cover costs of all center and program activities. There are also several projects carried out through TEACCH jointly with the Autism Society of North Carolina and with state vocational rehabilitation services. Federal and state grants provide money for training; federal grants and funds from private foundations provide money for research. In addition, some of the activities of TEACCH are self-supporting, including teaching materials, conferences, and workshops.

About 290 new preschool children are seen at the eight TEACCH centers each year. This means that at any given time, about 650 to 700 preschool children are receiving TEACCH services. Most children receive a standard assessment, which is described later. However, this assessment and the kinds of services that the children receive are individualized according to families' needs and the services available in the community. TEACCH's goal is to provide appropriate services for every child with autism and related communication disabilities in North Carolina, regardless of his or her parents' ability to pay or to participate in particular clinical activities. Each TEACCH center has regular contracts with specific classrooms and programs offered by school systems and county agencies; TEACCH also "follows" children into other placements, which their parents have selected, for consultation. Because of the size of the TEACCH system and the fact that preschool children do not receive services separable in kind from older children, adolescents, or adults, it is not possible to provide an estimate of costs per preschool student per school year.

Autism/communication-disability is a classification recognized by the Department of Public Instruction in North Carolina. There is a specific mandate that up to 8 school-aged children in this category will be placed with a teacher and an assistant in a classroom designated for children with autism. For preschool children, guidelines are less specific, although in most instances, preschool classrooms average 5 to 6 children with a teacher and assistant. Preschoolers with autism in other classrooms (e.g. noncategorical) may be served with up to 10 to 12 other young children with developmental problems.

Population Served

Over 5,800 children and adults, and their families, have been served by TEACCH in the 26 years of its existence. By far, the majority of these children were first seen during the preschool years and have grown up with the program, although there are also children who were identified at later ages or who moved to North Carolina at older ages. One of the most important changes in TEACCH services over the last 15 years has been the decreasing age at which children are first referred. In the 1970s, children were most often seen entering or getting ready to enter kindergarten or first grade. Now, as early intervention and screening programs have become more active, the modal age for first referral is 3, with substantial numbers of 2-year-olds referred as well. TEACCH serves children who receive formal diagnoses of autism, as well as children with related pervasive developmental disorder (American Psychiatric Association, 1994) or severe communication disability, a category consistent with state educational regulations. The diagnoses are made at the TEACCH center, or increasingly by knowledgeable Developmental Evaluation Centers (DECs). In the 28 years TEACCH has been in existence, a variety of different diagnostic schemes have been proposed. All children are given *The Childhood Autism Rating Scale* (Schopler, Reichler, & Renner, 1988), and currently clinical diagnoses using the *Diagnostic and Statistical Manual of Mental Disorders–Fourth Edition* (American Psychiatric Association, 1994) and International Classification of Diseases–Tenth Revision (ICD–10) (World Health Organization, 1993) criteria are employed in the clinics. Children are not accepted or rejected into the program on the basis of formal diagnostic criteria. Once a child has been accepted for assessment, follow-up is available to any child and family for whom TEACCH is deemed to be the most appropriate agency to provide services; otherwise children are referred elsewhere.

Recent statistics suggest that over 80% of newly diagnosed children at TEACCH meet formal diagnostic criteria for autism (American Psychiatric Association, 1994; World Health Organization, 1993), with the majority of remaining children meeting criteria for pervasive developmental disorders or language disorders, with or without mental disability. However, the preschool age level presents some special diagnostic problems, as discussed later.

Ethnic distribution is equivalent to that of the state of North Carolina, with most recent estimates of the TEACCH population as 67% Caucasian, 29% African American, and 5% other ethnic groups. The estimated average IQ of the children under age 6 in all the TEACCH centers is 63 (range 10 to 122). For the Chapel Hill TEACCH Center, developmental quotients for children under 6 seen for initial assessment in the last 3 years averaged from 55 to 60 (range 10 to 146). These scores are generally based on the mental scale of the *Bayley Scales of Infant Development–Second Edition* (Bayley, 1993) or

performance tests such as the *Merrill–Palmer Scale of Mental Tests* (Stutsman, 1931). The gender ratio is 4 males to 1 female.

Assessment Procedures

The diagnosis of autism is somewhat more difficult at preschool ages than at
later ages. For example, social behaviors of both normal children and children
with mental retardation are relatively limited at very young ages. Moreover,
parents often develop repetitive routines such as Pat-a-Cake that can mask
the lack of spontaneous interaction. A parent's automatic response to a young
child's distress masks the extent to which a child does not seek comfort. Likewise, there is less language at an early age, even in normal children, so it
becomes more difficult to observe pronoun reversal; delayed echolalia; or
abnormal pitch, rate, and rhythm. Repetitive behavior also presents special
diagnostic consideration. Both normal and preschool children diagnosed as
mentally retarded have attachments to objects such as blankets. Therefore, at
the preschool level, special emphasis is given to diagnostic assessment, both
formal and informal.

　A standard structured diagnostic assessment is used across all of the
TEACCH centers; additional aspects of the assessment vary according to the
center and the individual child's needs. As an example, we describe the assessment procedure followed at the Chapel Hill TEACCH Center. When a child is
referred to the center, an appointment is scheduled for the child and parents
to meet with a staff psychoeducational therapist for a 1-hour intake interview or screening session. During this meeting, the therapist gathers information from the parents about their concerns, understanding of their child's
problems, identified resources, and expectations from our program. The therapist also spends time interacting informally with the child to gain an impression of the child's behaviors and developmental patterns. Service options are
discussed with the parents, who are told that following a staff referral meeting they will be scheduled for an evaluation or other relevant service. At the
referral meeting, the therapist reviews the main issues and points from the
intake interview and makes a recommendation for follow-up services. Typically, the next step is a full evaluation, unless there has been an adequate
prior evaluation and the family feels clear about the diagnosis and wishes to
get started with clinic teaching sessions.

　A standard assessment involves a team of five people: a clinical psychologist (the clinical director of the center), three psychoeducational therapists,
and a pediatrician. The clinical director coordinates the team and oversees the
evaluation; if standardized psychological testing is required, such as the *Wechsler Preschool and Primary Scale of Intelligence–Revised* (Wechsler, 1989), the
clinical director either does this testing or supervises a psychology intern or

practicum student. One of the therapists is responsible for doing the *Psychoeducational Profile–Revised* (PEP–R; Schopler, Reichler, Bashford, Lansing, & Marcus, 1990), a test that assesses developmental functioning in seven areas, provides opportunities for observing behaviors that can help in determining an autism diagnosis, and assesses potential teaching strategies. Some centers may also use the *Autism Diagnostic Interview–Revised* (Lord, Rutter, & LeCouteur, 1994) and the *Prelinguistic Autism Diagnostic Observation Schedule* (DiLavore, Lord, & Rutter, 1993), but as they offer much overlap with PEP-R information, they are not used at the Chapel Hill TEACCH Center. A second therapist conducts a detailed parent interview that covers parental concerns, patterns of behavior at home, adaptive skills as assessed with the *Vineland Adaptive Behavior Scales* (Sparrow, Balla, & Cicchetti, 1984), and observations of the child's behavior throughout the day using the *Childhood Autism Rating Scale* (Schopler et al., 1988). Prior to the evaluation, the parents have completed a history form that documents developmental and medical factors; a behavior checklist; and open-ended questionnaires that provide insight into the parents' concerns, a typical day, effects on the family, and hopes and expectations for the evaluation. These forms not only prepare the staff for the upcoming evaluation, but also help the parents anticipate the focus of what the staff will be looking for. The parent interview, in many respects, is built on these initial completed forms. The pediatrician reviews the medical history and conducts a medical screening. The third psychoeducational therapist does additional developmental testing as needed, using a test such as the *Bayley Scales* (Bayley, 1993) or *Merrill–Palmer Scale of Mental Tests* (Stutsman, 1931). Because the center is an integral part of the university, psychology interns and fellows and social work interns, as well as pediatric and other residents and fellows, actively participate in the evaluation process.

Following the prediagnostic staff meeting, the clinical director and staff therapists meet briefly with the family. The purpose of this meeting is to review the day's schedule with the family and find out from them what their primary questions are. After this meeting, the parent interview and PEP–R are conducted simultaneously, while the clinical director and others involved in the evaluation observe. Often, the child's teacher or others involved with the referral attend the evaluation, observe, and share their impressions. After the PEP–R and parent interview, each of the parents is asked to spend a few minutes playing with their child to see if the child responds to either parent differently or to allow a parent to demonstrate activity that might be useful to round out the assessment process. The medical screening is done next, followed by a lunch break and the second developmental testing session.

During the interview phase, the staff discusses the results of the various assessments, determines the diagnosis, reviews the questions presented by the parents, and considers next steps. The results of the afternoon testing session are then integrated into the case formulation, and the interpretative conference with the family and staff concludes the day. It is also helpful to refer to the parents' own estimates of their child's developmental function, which is usually quite accurate (Schopler & Reichler, 1972). During the conference, diagnosis is discussed openly and sensitively, individualized to the concerns and readiness of the parents to hear and process such information. In our experience, and as reported by parents, candidness about diagnosis, while sometimes painful to deal with, is far better for the parent than evasiveness or vagueness. Knowing the right diagnosis is necessary for knowing what to do about it. The conference also addresses whatever general or specific questions parents raise and recommendations for follow-up services through TEACCH or other agencies are discussed. Parents are sent written reports based on this conference as well as the testing sessions.

Teaching and Administrative Staff

Each TEACCH center has five to seven psychoeducational therapists. In most centers, one of the therapists is identified as the person who works with adults and adolescents, supervises job coaches, and consults with other programs and agencies working with this population. The remaining therapists serve as "generalists," taking on all the different roles of therapist and consultant. These therapists, in most cases, have master's degrees or bachelor's degrees and substantial amounts of experience with children with autism. They come from a range of disciplines, including special education, speech therapy, and social work. For individual treatment cases and assessments, therapists are often assigned to a particular child or placed in a particular role because of their expertise; however, the expectation is that each therapist will be able to work in a variety of different content areas with children of different ages and ability levels and to serve as a consultant to classrooms, as a support to parents, and to provide direct treatment to children and families. Each TEACCH center is headed by a clinical psychologist and is provided support by one or more secretaries. Most centers have graduate interns from psychology and social work, psychiatry and pediatric residents, and psychology and special education graduate students who rotate through practica. TEACCH also has a substantial number of international visitors who observe or come for internships.

Staff at TEACCH are hired through an intensive process in which they are asked, as part of the interview, to work with a child and to talk to a parent. Both situations are observed by the clinic staff from one-way mirrored observation rooms. Candidates are asked to formulate impressions of the child's learning problems and of the parents' primary concerns. They are asked to write a description of their brief interview, document their impressions and observations of the child, and then write a description of their experience. Even though psychoeducational therapists are required to have at least 2 years of experience working with persons with autism or a related disorder, this procedure allows staff to be selected on the basis of their flexibility and clinical skill to a degree not possible without this process. Using this mini-work sample provides a high degree of staff consensus for hiring decisions. Training of staff continues throughout all aspects of the job. For the first 6 to 12 months of employment, psychoeducational therapists are supported by another therapist or the clinical director in consultation, treatment, and work with parents. TEACCH is also involved in educational training for internal staff and others. Week-long summer training, day-long fall and spring workshops, a 2-day winter inservice, and a 2-day spring conference are part of the formal educational opportunities offered each staff member as well as teachers in TEACCH-affiliated community schools. Clinic and research staff are also encouraged to attend other conferences and meetings.

Curriculum

A long-established and central aspect of the TEACCH curriculum is structured teaching. It provides educational continuity from preschool age to adult years (Schopler, Mesibov, & Hearsey, 1995) and prevents many behavior problems. When we first showed that children with autism learned better in a structured rather than an unstructured learning situation (Schopler, Brehm, Kinsbourne, & Reichler, 1971), we also noted that children at earlier developmental levels needed structure more than children at higher levels of functioning. However, just as the diagnosis of autism is more obscure and requires more special consideration at the preschool age than at later ages, so does the use of structured teaching.

In addition to resolving diagnostic ambiguities, the preschool classes emphasize learning to be students and developing appropriate social and communicative behavior. Compared with school-aged children, preschoolers are exposed to a wider range of skills. Due to their shorter attention span, preschoolers' daily schedules are changed more frequently. Children spend more time learning in small groups, their fine and gross motor skills need more practice, and parents are more often involved in the classroom than in later grades. These activities contribute to the greater emphasis on the physical structure aspect of the curriculum and the layout of the classroom. An example of a preschool class layout is illustrated in Figure 9.1. In this figure, there are clear indications of where each activity will occur in order to help the student learn to stay in certain areas. Work tasks for teaching cognitive, fine motor, eye–hand integration, and organizational skills occur at the tables. Self-help skills such as toileting, eating habits, washing hands, wiping tables, and hanging up coats are taught in the lower left-hand corner. Expressive com-

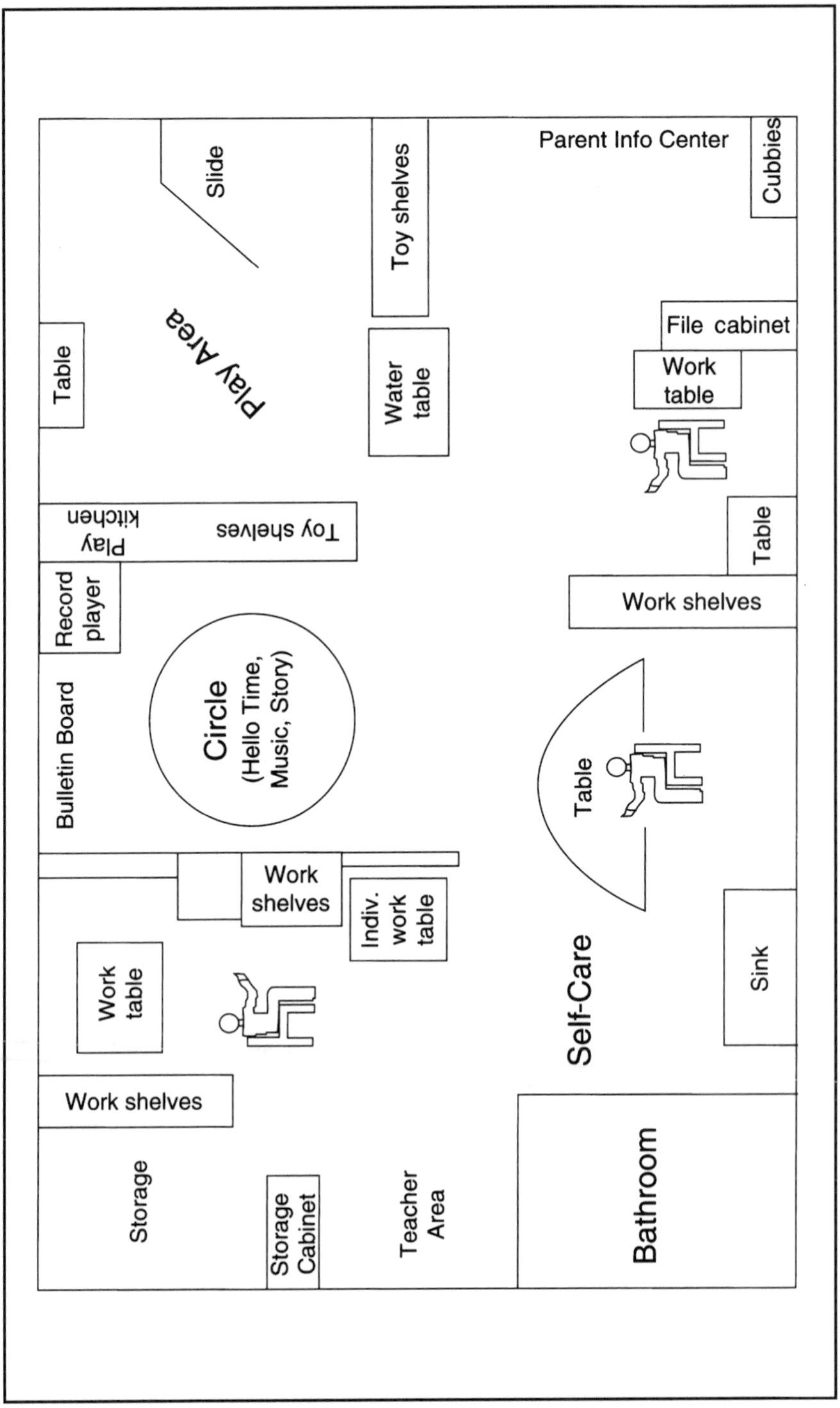

Figure 9.1. Example of a preschool class layout.

munication, receptive language, and social interaction are formally taught in another marked area, but also occur as part of other activities. Daily schedules clearly help the child learn directions, and those with better visual processing skills can be helped to understand schedules, such as those illustrated in Figure 9.2. Schedules can be adapted according to levels of communication and can help to prevent frustration and behavior problems.

The TEACCH philosophy (Schopler, 1997) includes the recognition that each family and each child with autism is unique and requires a continuum of services individualized for diverse family situations and differences in the cognitive, social, and language levels of each child. Very young children are reevaluated annually or on the basis of new concerns. Parents are offered a number of treatment options in the TEACCH centers and are encouraged to maintain some contact with TEACCH after an assessment, even if they do not participate in a formal treatment program.

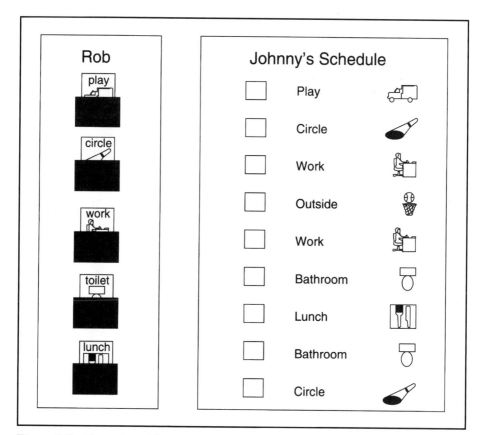

Figure 9.2. Examples of daily schedules.

Available to parents are "extended diagnostic" sessions in which parents return to the clinic for six to eight 1-hour sessions over the course of several months to work as co-therapists with their child on goals that they choose (e.g., anything from toilet training to increasing communication to creating activities for a child while a parent cooks dinner).

At the Chapel Hill TEACCH Center, parents of young children are encouraged to take advantage of several support programs: a mothers' group and a fathers' group, led by the clinical director, topically focused, with the main goal of information sharing in a supportive group atmosphere; a parent mentor program, in which a trained and experienced parent is assigned to a new parent and is available to help the new parent with information or simply to listen; a home teaching kit, more or less a starter set of materials, guidelines, and a list of teaching strategies and tasks; a six-session parent course co-taught by a TEACCH professional and veteran parent, covering such topics as home teaching and behavior management (based on Schopler, 1994, 1995); and parent workshops. Although most parents cannot participate in all of these programs, most are able to attend some of the meetings and begin to establish relationships with other parents, both experienced or new to autism like themselves.

Families are directed to family support groups, both specifically for autism, such as local chapters of the Autism Society of North Carolina, or for developmental disorders in general, such as Parent-to-Parent organizations run by local hospitals (Schopler, 1995). Each clinic also provides different support groups for parents, depending on the particular needs of the clients at the time.

Suggested teaching activities and strategies for parents and teachers are published in *Individualized Assessment and Treatment for Autistic and Developmentally Disabled Children, Volume 2: Teaching Strategies for Parents and Professionals* (Schopler, Reichler, & Lansing, 1980), and *Volume 3: Teaching Activities for Autistic Children* (Schopler, Lansing, & Waters, 1983). There is also a TEACCH communication curriculum that can be used both in school and at home (Watson, Lord, Schaffer, & Schopler, 1988). Two central aspects of each of these curricula are structuring the environment and facilitating independence at all levels of functioning. The importance of observing and assessing each child's current repertoire of spontaneous and practiced behavior is emphasized in order to design a truly individualized program that will facilitate the most rapid and generalizable progress.

Each TEACCH clinic has contractual relationships with a variety of educational programs. These contracts are not financial but consist of regular consultation provided to classrooms in return for school systems sending teachers to summer training and releasing them to attend inservice training and clinic-based assessments of their students during the year. In the Chapel Hill TEACCH Center catchment area, for example, there are seven categorical preschools for children with autism, including the TEACCH demonstration classroom; six of these, operated by the local public school districts, are in regular elementary schools. The majority of young children, however, are served in noncategorical preschools, which provide a lower ratio of teachers to students, but usually a wider range of students with developmental disabilities. Other youngsters are in normal preschools, often with technical assistance provided by the public schools as well as TEACCH consultation.

Older children with autism served by TEACCH centers participate in a similar range of placements although there are regional differences in what is available. Within each of these contexts, the primary role of the TEACCH consultant is to help teachers and other professionals understand the special learning needs associated with autism and individual children. This involves helping them distinguish between skills that can be taught directly and learning deficits that require environmental accommodation; the latter frequently require structured teaching and understanding of how structure reduces behavior problems. Consultation involves demonstration of appropriate teaching techniques and environmental manipulations appropriate for children at the preschool level. Consultants also support an emphasis on spontaneous communication and social skills, whether within an integrated situation or using reverse mainstreaming. Children are followed throughout the year with regular visits to their educational placements, and parents may elect to return to the clinic for follow-up sessions at any time.

Integration Versus Segregation

The TEACCH philosophy is that a continuum of services from complete inclusion to highly specialized, structured programming by teachers specifically trained in autism should be available. Families and professionals should be able to select the most appropriate service for each child from this continuum. Least restricted environments are supported, but there is also a commitment to providing highly structured intensive treatment for children who need this level of service. TEACCH attempts to support services developed in each community. In one community in which there are very good categorical classrooms for autism, TEACCH may provide consultation to preschool classes and serve as an advocate for reverse mainstreaming and a greater focus on spontaneous communication and social interaction. This important first phase of integration involves typical children coming to the TEACCH classroom to stimulate social interaction and communication. In another community, the TEACCH therapist may work with a group of mothers who are homemakers joining together in biweekly sessions with their children. The therapist may consult for an integrated day care center in the same community and have regular contact with public health and private speech–language pathologists who see children with autism.

Structured Teaching and Behavior Management

As discussed before, structured teaching provides the primary basis for educational continuity in the TEACCH Program. It can adjust to individual levels of communication and provides a continuum applicable for children with developmental impairments to children who are not disabled. Such structuring provides environmental accommodation to some of the primary learning deficits seen in children with autism. These deficits include problems with organization, memory of things other than special interests, difficulty with auditory processing, and making transitions from one topic to another. Conversely, children with autism tend to be relatively strong in visual processing, and special interests can be used for motivating learning.

By accommodating the learning environment to the deficits associated with autism, independent functioning of each student is gradually increased and many frustrations and behavior problems are avoided. Mild negative consequences (e.g., having a child sit in a chair in the corner for 30 seconds, removing a favorite object from the table for a minute) are employed, but the emphasis is much more on positive strategies and using structure to minimize difficulties before they occur. The prevention of behavior problems is difficult to study and, to date, we have not done so systematically. Nevertheless, clinical estimates suggest that appropriate structured teaching at home and at school can prevent most typical behavior problems associated with autism.

Various cognitive and behavioral interventions are also employed. This strategy of multiple approaches can be illustrated for one of the frequent preschool sources of behavior problems, the area of toilet training. Figure 9.3 presents an illustration using an iceberg metaphor. Above the water line are specific behavior problems such as soiling or wetting. Below the water line are listed explanatory deficits. By careful observation and parent interviews, an informal assessment is made of antecedent circumstances and behaviors. If, for example, a child soils himself, it may be that he or she does not understand the sequence of undressing, sitting on the toilet, wiping, and dressing. If this assessment is correct, the sequence can be taught separately. If the soiling discontinues, the assessment and intervention were correct. If soiling continues, alternative intervention efforts must be used. An indexed volume of successful behavior interventions used by parents is available (Schopler, 1995).

Parental and Family Involvement

Parents are seen as the first "generalists" in the treatment of their child and absolutely central to their child's progress. A unique emphasis of TEACCH is

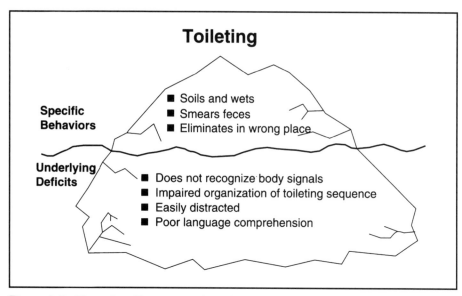

Figure 9.3. Metaphor illustrating the relationship between behaviors and deficits.

to provide services to parents who have varying amounts of time and degrees of commitment to working directly with their children. Home visits and joint school visits are an important part of the work with parents, as well as working with the Autism Society of North Carolina and its local units (currently 37 statewide) to provide advocacy and support. Every attempt is made to work around a family's particular needs and to work with the family to accomplish goals that are important to it, as well as goals identified by the TEACCH staff. For example, we have found that most families with newly diagnosed children benefit from a period of time in which caregivers carry out structured programming with their child in combination with regular contact with professionals who are concerned not only with the child's progress, but also with the desires and concerns of the whole family. The prototype of this process at TEACCH is the "extended diagnostic" session in which each parent works with the child on a set number of specific activities for about 15 minutes a day. These activities generally involve sitting at a table doing tasks such as matching, sorting, imitating, or working on receptive language and expressive language (Watson et al., 1988). The clinic team of parent consultant and child therapist helps the family develop the home program, encourages them to modify it to best suit their needs and the child's interests and abilities, and is available to discuss any other issues that arise.

Although this model is very successful with some families, others do not have the time, interest, or ability to carry out this kind of activity. In addition, while the process of learning to do structured programming may provide care-givers with invaluable general skills, often parents' greatest concerns have to do with managing specific behaviors (e.g., tantrums, spitting) or developing certain skills (e.g., toilet training). Thus, in addition to extended diagnostic sessions, the child therapist may visit the home and school and help design and monitor a toileting program. For parents with limited transportation, therapists may arrange a series of home visits or have the parent ride into school on the school bus and meet there. As an alternative to extended diag-nostic sessions, a therapist may accompany a parent on visits to possible preschool programs or respite centers or arrange a coffee hour for three moth-ers with similar concerns who are not yet interested in the larger parents' groups. Home programs may be developed for a grandmother or a babysitter, or, in families that have other children close in age to the child with autism, be carried out with siblings taking turns and playing together.

Outcome Measures

In general, outcome for TEACCH has been measured in terms of a very low rate of institutionalization of older children and adults (less than 8%). Recently, as a spin-off of a project on early diagnosis of children with autism referred to TEACCH, we have been able to document positive changes during the first few years after referral of a substantial number of very young chil-dren with autism and communication disabilities (Lord, 1991). Another fol-low-up study that included many subjects from TEACCH showed greater aca-demic achievement in high-functioning adolescents and adults than expected from earlier research (Venter, Lord, & Schopler, 1992). While these studies are not systematic tests of a particular intervention, they provide follow-up data of young children who received TEACCH services. A number of other follow-up studies have allowed us to trace the course of autism for young children first seen at TEACCH in the preschool years (Lord & Schopler, 1989). These studies have indicated that substantial increases in IQ scores are quite common in children first assessed at age 3 or 4, regardless of the inten-sity of treatment. For example, nonverbal 3-year-olds who received initial IQ scores between 30 and 50 showed a mean increase in IQ of 22 to 24 points by age 7 years; nonverbal 4-year-olds reassessed at age 9 gained an average of 15 to 19 points, although both groups remained in the range of mild mental disability. Gains in the preschool years were greatest for very young, nonver-bal children and for children who acquired language between the first and second assessment. The role of particular tests and the demands those tests place on children at different ages and developmental levels have also been documented (Lord & Schopler, 1989). Other formal and informal outcome evaluations have been reviewed by Schopler (1997).

Psychoeducational therapists keep records of each session, and teachers keep detailed notes concerning the outcome of educational programs for each child. School visits are also documented and a system of self-evaluation for teachers has been developed.

Major Issues for Future Effort

A number of philosophical and clinical issues confront the preschool services at TEACCH. First is the appropriateness of diagnosis of very young children, particularly nonverbal children age 3 years and younger. Although recent studies suggest that clinical diagnoses of these very young children may be quite stable (Gillberg et al., 1990), other studies suggest that there may be large differences in criteria and methods for diagnosis across samples and clinicians, and that this stability cannot be taken for granted (Knobloch & Pasamanick, 1975). It is also not clear, even if clinicians can judge if a child will have autism a year later, that they are necessarily using the same criteria by which autism is diagnosed in older children (Lord, 1991). Work is under way to define criteria and methods (and their limits) appropriate for the diagnosis of autism in very young children.

A question of intense interest is how to provide services to the increasing number of children and teachers serving young children with autism in integrated settings. In the past, TEACCH has been able to provide intensive training and support for teachers by centralizing resources for staff and children in self-contained classrooms for children with autism and communication disabilities. However, this is no longer feasible nor appropriate in all cases because many children are clearly benefiting from less restricted environments. The question remains how to train and provide support for teachers who have only one child with autism in their classrooms. While the teacher of a "TEACCH" self-contained classroom is expected to have attended 1 week of summer training before beginning the school year and 4 to 6 days of inservice training per year, the needs of a regular preschool teacher with one child with autism in his or her class or a teacher of a noncategorical preschool class are somewhat different. A TEACCH therapist typically visits a new teacher of a self-contained class for 6 children with autism once a week; if these 6 children all have different "new" teachers, weekly visits are not possible. How to maintain standards of training, support, and staff selection while providing each child an opportunity for education in the setting most appropriate for him or her is a question currently receiving much attention.

A related question is how best to structure programs for very young children, particularly children with autism with mental ages under 2 years of age. What does the concept of "structure," a conceptualization that underlies much of TEACCH training and consultation for older children, mean for children who are intellectually functioning as infants? How much of an emphasis should be placed on independence versus interactive learning? To what extent and how best can peers (i.e., classmates with autism, nondisabled models, or children with other disabilities) be used as a resource for children at this age? What type and intensity of one-to-one intervention is optimum for each child?

Another question concerns how services can be provided for all families of children with autism, not only families with extraordinary financial resources and energy. TEACCH is a state-funded agency mandated to work with all of the families of North Carolina and does not have the luxury of choosing only families who are willing and able to participate in highly intensive extra treatments. One question is whether such intensive treatments have results that are truly unique and, if so, how can families who are not able to carry them out be supported to do so? If such intensive treatments do not have unique results, what other factors determine positive outcome? In this same context, what demands are appropriate to make of school systems and state agencies providing early intervention? What is the critical mass of treatment, skill, and support that can be demanded of such agencies in order to ensure that the children with autism, reach their highest potential?

The 1990s were an exciting time for the field of autism with the advent of many new and creative approaches to treatment. A number of research achievements help us better understand the nature and course of autism (Lord & Rutter, 1994). However, it is not clear how much these exciting changes affect the daily lives of the preschool-aged children with autism for whom TEACCH is responsible. The TEACCH program originated as a service to help educate children with autism and provide their families with support. An essential component of the TEACCH model is to recognize that children with autism are individuals who are part of unique families and unique communities. Our goal is to use the resources available at each of these three levels (i.e., child, family, community) to facilitate the greatest independence and happiness for each child with autism in our program.

References

American Psychiatric Association. (1994). *Diagnostic and statistical manual of mental disorders* (4th ed.). Washington, DC: Author.

Bayley, N. (1993). *Bayley Scales of Infant Development–Second Edition*. San Antonio: Psychological Corp.

DiLavore, P., Lord, C., & Rutter, M. (1993). *Prelinguistic Autism Diagnostic Observation Schedule.* Unpublished manuscript, Division TEACCH, University of North Carolina, Chapel Hill.

Dunn, L. M., & Dunn, L. M. (1981). *Peabody Picture Vocabulary Test–Revised: Manual for Forms L and M*. Circle Pines, MN: American Guidance Service.

Elliott, C. D. (1990). *Differential Ability Scales*. San Antonio: Psychological Corp.

Gillberg, C., Ehlers, S., Schaumann, H., Jakobsson, G., Dahlgren, S. O., Lindblom, R., Bagenholm, A., Tjuus, T., & Blidner, E. (1990). Autism under age 3 years: A clinical study of 28 cases referred for autistic symptoms in infancy. *Journal of Child Psychology and Psychiatry, 21,* 921–934.

Hedrick, D. L., Prather, E. M., & Tobin, A. R. (1975). *Sequenced Inventory of Communication Development.* Seattle: University of Washington Press.

Knobloch, H., & Pasamanick, B. (1975). Some etiologic and prognostic factors in early infantile autism and psychosis. *Pediatrics, 55,* 182–191.

Lord, C. (1991, April). *Follow-up of two-year-olds referred for possible autism.* Paper presented at the biennial meeting of the Society for Research in Child Development, Seattle.

Lord, C., & Rutter, M. (1994). Autism and pervasive developmental disorders. In M. Rutter, L. Hersov, & E. Taylor (Eds.), *Child and adolescent psychiatry* (3rd ed.). Oxford, England: Blackwell Scientific Publications.

Lord, C., Rutter, M., & LeCouteur, A. (1994). Autism Diagnostic Interview–Revised: A revised version of a diagnostic interview for caregivers of individuals with possible pervasive developmental disorders. *Journal of Autism and Developmental Disorders, 24,* 659–685.

Lord, C., & Schopler, E. (1989a). The role of age at assessment, developmental level, and test in the stability of intelligence scores in young autistic children. *Journal of Autism and Developmental Disorders, 19,* 483–499.

Mullen, E. (1989). *Mullen Scales of Early Learning.* Cranston, RI: TOTAL Child.

Schopler, E. (1994). Behavioral priorities for autism and related developmental disorders. In E. Schopler & G. B. Mesibov (Eds.), *Behavioral issues in autism* (pp. 55–77). New York: Plenum.

Schopler, E. (1995). *Parent survival manual: A guide to autism crisis resolution.* New York: Plenum.

Schopler, E. (1997). Implementation of TEACCH philosophy. In D. J. Cohen & F. R. Volkmar (Eds.), *Handbook of autism and pervasive developmental disorders* (pp. 767–795). New York: Wiley.

Schopler, E., Brehm, S. S., Kinsbourne, M., & Reichler, R. J. (1971). Effect of treatment structure in autistic children. *Archives of General Psychiatry, 24,* 415–421.

Schopler, E., Lansing, M., & Waters, L. (1983). *Individualized assessment and treatment for autistic and developmentally disabled children: Vol. 3. Teaching activities for autistic children.* Austin, TX: PRO-ED.

Schopler, E., Mesibov, G. B., & Hearsey, K. (1995). Structured teaching in the TEACCH system. In E. Schopler & G. B. Mesibov (Eds.), *Learning and cognition in autism* (pp. 243–268). New York: Plenum.

Schopler, E., & Reichler, R. (1972). How well do parents understand their own psychotic child? *Journal of Autism and Childhood Schizophrenia, 2,* 387–400.

Schopler, E., Reichler, R. J., Bashford, A., Lansing, M. D., & Marcus, L. M. (1990). *Psychoeducational Profile–Revised.* Austin, TX: PRO-ED.

Schopler, E., Reichler, R., & Lansing, M. (1980). *Individualized assessment and treatment for autistic and developmentally disabled children: Vol. 2. Teaching strategies for parents and professionals.* Baltimore: University Park Press.

Schopler, E., Reichler, R., & Renner, B. R. (1988). *The Childhood Autism Rating Scale.* Austin, TX: PRO-ED.

Sparrow, S., Balla, D., & Cicchetti, D. (1984). *Vineland Adaptive Behavior Scales.* Circle Pines, MN: American Guidance Service.

Stutsman, R. (1931). Guide for administering the Merrill–Palmer Scale of Mental Tests. In L. M. Terman (Ed.), *Mental measurement of preschool children* (pp. 139–262). New York: Harcourt, Brace & World.

Venter, A., Lord, C., & Schopler, E. (1992). A follow-up study of high-functioning autistic children. *Journal of Child Psychology and Psychiatry, 33,* 489–507.

Watson, L., Lord, C., Schaffer, B., & Schopler, E. (1988). *Teaching spontaneous communication to autistic and developmentally handicapped children.* New York: Irvington Press.

Wechsler, D. (1989). *Wechsler Preschool and Primary Scale of Intelligence–Revised.* San Antonio: Psychological Corp.

World Health Organization. (1993). *Classification of mental and behavioral disorders: Diagnostic criteria for researchers.* Geneva: Author.

The Douglass Developmental Disabilities Center: Two Models of Service Delivery

10

Sandra L. Harris, Jan S. Handleman, Maria S. Arnold, and Rita F. Gordon

It has been 28 years since the Douglass Developmental Disabilities Center (DDDC) first opened its doors to school-age children with autism. The center, founded by the authority of the Board of Governors of Rutgers, The State University of New Jersey, has expanded steadily over the years and now has four separate divisions: the original Douglass School, Douglass Outreach, the Division of Adult and Transition Services, and the Division of Research and Training.

Both the Douglass School and Douglass Outreach serve preschool-age children, although each operates within a different service delivery model. Initially established for school-age children with autism, the Douglass School did not create a specialized preschool component until 1987 when the Small Group Preschool class and the integrated preschool class, which was named "Small Wonders," were opened. In 1990 a third preschool class, designated the "Prep" class, was introduced to offer a more complete continuum of services for preschoolers with autism. Douglass Outreach opened in 1994 to provide services to young children with autism who would benefit from an intensive home-based program, and additional hours of home-based instruction to supplement a day program, and to consult to school districts operating preschool classes. The parallel operation of a center-based school program and a home- or school-based consultation model has given us experience with both of these approaches to serving young children with autism.

Program Information: Douglass School, Douglass Developmental Disabilities Center, 25 Gibbons Circle, New Brunswick, NJ 08901-8528; 732/932-9137. Douglass Outreach, Douglas Developmental Disabilities Center, 30 Gibbons Circle, New Brunswick, NJ 08901; 732/932-3902.

Common Features

Although the Douglass School and Douglass Outreach operate from different models, they share a common philosophy of education. From its inception the DDDC has relied on the principles of applied behavior analysis as its primary technology for instruction. This includes a broad range of methods, including discrete trial instruction, functional assessment, functional communication training, and the use of naturalistic, incidental teaching strategies to ensure that the child is able to use his or her knowledge and skills in ways that appear spontaneous and appropriate. That behavioral commitment holds true for both the Douglass School and Douglass Outreach.

The funding mechanisms of the two units differ. The Douglass School is a state-operated program that serves individuals with autism from preschool through adolescence. The school offers a 10-month program with a seven-week extended school year. It is supported almost exclusively by tuition paid by local school districts for individual pupils unable to be served in their community schools. Tuition is determined annually with consideration given to the specialized needs of the autistic population and the mandates of state and local government.

Douglass Outreach uses a fee-for-service model. Outreach charges $70 per hour for a home-based program coordinator who oversees and manages the program; $45 per hour for a consultant/tutor who conducts therapy sessions in the home; $90 per hour for a speech–language therapist and $100 per hour for a consultant to school- and community-based programs. Psychoeducational evaluations are $1,800. A home-based program with a program coordinator providing 2 hours per week and a consultant/tutor providing 20 hours per week of therapy would cost $1,040 per week. A school consultation by a consultant once a week for a 6-month period costs $2,400. Fees for services come from a variety of sources, including school districts, early intervention services, and private insurance companies. However, most of the fees are paid privately by the individual child's family.

Population Served

Both programs serve children on the continuum of autism with a diagnosis of autistic disorder or pervasive developmental disorder–not otherwise specified as the most common categories, and a smaller number of children with Asperger's syndrome served primarily through Douglass Outreach. Consistent with the general literature (e.g., Lord & Schopler, 1987), most of the children admitted to the center are boys.

Teaching and Administrative Staff

The division directors of the Douglass School and Douglass Outreach are certified, master's level educators who have oversight responsibility for the management of their unit's daily operations, all educational, community, and related activities, and home programming. Each director collaborates with other division and agency directors in establishing agency policy, promoting program development, and providing a continuum of services. The division directors report to the director of the DDDC, who holds a doctorate in special education and is a certified principal. The executive director of the agency, the founder of the DDDC, and a clinical psychologist, in conjunction with the director, addresses administrative issues and supervises the delivery of services and activities by all divisions. All division directors consult with the director and executive director of the agency in planning and implementing major policy decisions.

The DDDC is a place where everyone is always learning. Professional development is encouraged in a variety of ways. Annual staff training occurs each September, with ongoing training through inservice presentations and required attendance at yearly conferences, including the annual statewide conference on autism sponsored by the New Jersey Center for Outreach and Services for the Autism Community (COSAC). The DDDC also sponsors a yearly conference for educators in New Jersey; many of our staff participate in this event and have also co-authored research papers and posters, and presented at other local, state, and national conferences.

Both the Douglass School and Douglass Outreach are located on the Douglass College campus of Rutgers University. Their close proximity to one another encourages the sharing of resources, including the services of the Division of Research and Training. The staff of that division, which include three clinical psychologists and five graduate students from the Graduate School of Applied and Professional Psychology and the Graduate Program of the Department of Psychology, offer behavioral consultation services, assistance with ongoing staff training, and the opportunity to participate in applied research. The programs also share a full-time nurse and a business manager. Each unit has secretarial staff.

Curriculum

The curriculum materials for both preschool programs are behaviorally based, developmentally organized, and language focused, and include the broad areas of attention, speech–language, cognition, fine and gross motor ability, socialization, self-help, and appropriate behavior. These are further delineated to address specific categories within each area. For example, goals and objectives in the area of cognitive development emphasize readiness skills, early concepts and reasoning, and skills through a kindergarten level, whereas those in the area of social development focus on affect, adult and peer interactions, self-concept, and play.

Curriculum planning progresses from relatively narrow and intensive fundamental skills training to instruction in all developmental areas. For example, initially a child is taught to attend to a task and comply with instructional demands. Once these skills are established, programming expands to emphasize language development, eventually including a balance of activities in all other curriculum areas. Table 10.1 provides examples of developmentally sequenced objectives in a variety of curricular areas.

Teaching materials include a blend of commercial offerings and teacher-made manipulatives, workbooks, activity sheets, and folders. For example, for language acquisition tasks we use a variety of products from Communication Skill Builders, such as Levine's (1988) *Great Beginnings for Early Language Training* and Ploudre's (1989) *CLAS Preschool*. In the area of concept formation, we use Earlley's (1986a, 1986b) AIMS Pre-Reading and Reading kits, the Attainment Company's (1993) *Life Skill Picture Cues,* Austin and Boeckmann's (1990) *Functional Word Series,* the Edmark Corporation's *Edmark Reading Program Level 1* (1992) and *Level 2* (1993), and the *PACE*-Math program (McClennen, 1991). In the fine motor area, we use *Handwriting Without Tears* (Olsen, 1998) and *The Sensible Pencil* (Becht & Exley, 1989). In addition, materials from a variety of publishers are used to supplement teacher instruction in order to meet the individualized needs of students, including the *Picture Exchange Communication System* (PECS; Frost & Bondy, 1994). Computer software from Laureate Systems, including Wilson and Fox's (1996) First Words and Semel's (1999) Following Directions Series: One and Two Level Commands, are used to supplement instruction and enhance concept development. At the Douglass School, Individualized Education Plans and quarterly progress reports are based on *The I.G.S. Curriculum* (Romanczyk & Lockshin, 1994).

Behavior Management

Both programs share the same philosophy of behavior management. On occasion, some children with autism pose challenging behavior problems, making it essential that we use the best of current behavioral technology to help them gain self-control. Behavior management policies reflect the broad spectrum of empirically based options. Our choices of specialized intervention strategies are consistent with the standards of appropriate clinical practice as determined by treatment effectiveness and the results of efficacy research. The ongoing monitoring and evaluation of these policies ensures adherence to changing professional and legal guidelines.

Table 10.1
Examples of Objectives from the Douglass
Developmental Disabilities Center's Developmental Curriculum

Objective	Age (in months)	Objective	Age (in months)
Language: Receptive		Identifies beginning or	
Turns head to name	12	end of book	48
Points to desired objects	12		
Identifies 2 or more objects		**Language: Use**	
or pictures from a group	12	Uses gestures communica-	
Imitates gross motor body		tively and starts to per-	
movements	18	ceive reactions (e.g., mak-	
Points to one body part	18	ing sure he or she has	
Gives or shows object		listener's attention prior	
on request	24	to continuing)	12
		Responding to pointing as a	
Language: Expressive		communicative gesture	
Babbles	12	(e.g., looks at direction	
Says 2 words besides		adult is pointing)	12
"Mama," "Dada"	18	Uses pointing to learn new	
Returns "Bye"	18	vocabulary	12
Imitates simple words		Makes up meanings of own	
on request	18	for vocalization (e.g.,	
Names 1 object	18	"ankle" for *blanket*)	12
Uses 3–20 simple words	18	Uses nonverbal communica-	
Asks for simple needs	18	tion to signify intent	24
Answers question		• to request, reaches for	
"What's this?"	18	the object	
Asks for more	18	• to draw attention to	
Says, "All gone"	18	the object, points or	
Identifies self in mirror	24	shows	
Refers to self by name	24	• to draw attention to	
		self, vocalizes	
Cognitive: Reading			
Enjoys having simple stories		**Socialization: Play and Peer**	
read	24	**Interaction**	
"Reads" on own initiative	24	Plays beside other child	18
Fills in the next word in text	24	Imitates other child at play	18
Reads along with adult	24	Initiates own play activity	24
Relates events in books to		Relates objects to self, indi-	
own experience	30	cating a pretend quality	24
"Reads" familiar books		Orients body to speaker	24
receptively	36	Establishes eye contact	
Uses pictures to read story	36	with peers	24

(continues)

Table 10.1 *Continued*

Objective	Age (in months)	Objective	Age (in months)
Socialization: Play and Peer Interaction *(Continued)*		**Gross Motor: Object Movement**	
		Grasps objects	3
Sustains own play activity	24	Drops objects	6
Pretends actions with inan-		Tosses objects	9
imate figures	30	Picks up ball/both hands	12
Repeats play in a ritualis-		Throws ball with both	
tic way	36	hands	15
		Stoops to pick up object	15
Fine Motor: Writing		Pushes and pulls objects	18
Holds pencil with fist	12	Pushes chair	18
Marks with pencil	12		
Scribbles	18	**Self-Help**	
Imitates horizontal and		Sucks food off spoon	3
vertical lines	18	Chews food	6
Imitates circle	24	Drinks from held cup	9
Imitates diagonal lines	24	Feeds self with fingers	12
Holds pencil or paintbrush		Uses spoon, with spilling	12
using pincer grip	30	Sits on small chair	12
		Takes off hat	12
		Takes off socks	12

As the field changes, policies regarding behavior management continue to evolve and are guided by current research and documented innovations in educational technology. For example, traditional techniques such as discrete trial teaching and systematic reinforcement are blended with incidental teaching, functional communication training (Durand, 1990), and community involvement experiences. Rigorous performance and procedural monitoring and close communication among staff, parents, and referring agencies promote accountability and treatment effectiveness.

Behavior reduction concerns are viewed within the context of a student's total educational program. The DDDC programs follow a strict protocol when developing and implementing behavioral interventions. Interventions are designed to address the individual needs of a student based on a thorough functional assessment. Accurate assessment of problem behaviors is essential in order to design effective interventions. In addition, a hierarchy of contingencies for addressing the challenging behaviors is considered from least to most intrusive. Reduction contingencies are always paired with positive approaches to ensure a rich schedule of reinforcement and functional alternative response training (e.g., social rule cards, social stories). We typically address challenging behaviors through minimally intrusive procedures (e.g., removal of attention, brief inclusionary time-out) and differential reinforcement. Table 10.2 outlines some of the considerations that highlight our guidelines for addressing challenging behaviors. Behavioral consultation services from the Research and Training Division are available to the Douglass School and Douglass Outreach.

Parental and Family Involvement

The DDDC's educational policy encourages the full involvement of families in the education of the targeted child. Parents are invited to be equal partners in the planning and evaluation of their child's curriculum, as well as participants in regularly scheduled meetings (called clinics) to evaluate the

Table 10.2
Douglass School Behavioral Intervention Guidelines

Protocol

1. Identify/specifically define problem behavior.
2. Submit request to initiate baseline to supervisor/behavioral consultation committee. Provide preliminary data.
3. Initiate baseline.
4. Design functional assessment (e.g., setting events, ABC data, motivation assessment).
5. Evaluate previous and current interventions.
6. Design intervention based on functional analysis. Include the following:
   a. Summary of assessment data
   b. Proposed intervention (with rationale)
   c. Differential reinforcement schedule
   d. Alternative response training
   e. Skill acquisition training
   f. Fading procedures
   g. Data collection procedures
   h. Reduction/review criteria

7. Submit proposed intervention for review/approval by:
   a. Supervisor
   b. Behavioral consultation committee
   c. Parents/guardians

Examples of Least to Most Intrusive Interventions

Level 1. Requires no physical intervention
Planned ignoring (Extinction)
Response cost
Verbal reprimand

Level 2. Requires minimal physical intervention
Inclusionary time-out
Brief restraint

Level 3. Requires intrusive physical intervention
Restitutional overcorrection
Positive practice

progress of their child. Parents are integral members of the therapy team and are encouraged to participate in all aspects of the program, including training, teaching, and educational decisions about their child's program. Parents are expected to participate in a workshop on applied behavior analysis, covering topics such as discrete trial instruction, reinforcement and motivational systems, prompting and data collection, and guidelines for increasing communication.

The Douglass School

The Douglass School preschool program has three classes. Our Prep class was created after we visited Ivar Lovaas at the University of California at Los Angeles (UCLA) in 1989 and observed the impressive progress he was making with preschool-age children. Following that visit we established a class that serves 6 children with autism and emphasizes one-to-one instruction during the initial phases of treatment. It provides 25 hours a week of center-based instruction, supplemented by an additional 10 to 15 hours of parent effort within the home and supported by home programming staff. The Prep program stresses an individualized curriculum and utilizes a variety of behavioral techniques to maximize effectiveness. Children move from individual to group work as they develop necessary skills. In theory, the next level in the continuum would be the Small Group Preschool followed by the Small Wonders class. However, in practice, movement is possible among any of the preschool classes, making both the Prep class and the Small Group class "feeders" to the Small Wonders class.

The Small Group class supports 6 children with autism, with an instructional ratio ranging from 2 children with 1 adult to 6 children with 1 adult leader, and the remaining staff called upon as needed to help the children maintain themselves in the group. On occasion, one-to-one interaction is provided to shape a student's group skills. This class uses a blend of discrete trial technology and incidental teaching. The preschool curriculum in this class meets the diverse needs of all the students by emphasizing the development of basic and more complex speech–language skills, play skills, social responsiveness, and academic readiness, and by promoting independence through structure and daily routines.

In the Small Wonders class the integrated class with 8 typically developing peers and 6 children with autism, instruction is provided in small and large group formats. There is an emphasis on normalization of the classroom structure. In this class, children with autism and their friends, who serve as social and language role models, are skillfully blended in the small and large group activities. A systematic program is used to encourage the development of social and play skills in all students. An important emphasis of this specialized programming is to teach the peers to persist in their efforts to interact with their often unresponsive classmates, and to teach the children with autism to spontaneously initiate interactions with their peers. Initial interactions between the children with autism and their typical peers may be deliberately structured, scripted, and reinforced; however, they usually become more natural as the peers become more adept social agents and as the children with autism acquire more social skills.

The intent for all children with autism admitted to the Douglass preschool program is to have them move through the continuum in 1 to 3 years. The physical and organizational structure of each of the three classes is uniquely designed to meet the needs of the children it serves. While the Prep model was inspired by Ivar Lovaas at UCLA, the Small Group and Small Wonders classes were envisioned as the result of a visit to Phillip Strain's integrated preschool program in Pittsburgh in 1986 (Strain, Hoyson, & Jamieson, 1985). Although we did not replicate a colleague's program, in either case, their achievements were an inspiration for our own. In addition, the philosophy and curriculum of the Douglass School provided the foundation for the Douglass Outreach approach to service provision.

Population Served

Since 1992 when we reported on our first 36 preschool students with autism, an additional 41 preschoolers have been enrolled in the Douglass Preschool program. Consistent with our previous report, the peers in the Small Wonders class continue to have no known developmental or behavioral difficulties, and our target students are referred to the center with a diagnosis of autistic disorder or pervasive developmental disorder–not otherwise specified. This diagnosis is made by the referring agency and is verified at the center by an experienced clinical psychologist using the most recent edition of the *Diagnostic and Statistical Manual of Mental Disorders*, currently in its fourth edition (American Psychiatric Association, 1994). We also use *The Childhood Autism Rating Scale* (CARS; Schopler, Reichler, DeVellis, & Daly, 1988). Generally, children are not accepted into the program unless they fall within the category of autism on the CARS. However, exceptions were made for 10 children who scored below 30 at intake. These decisions were made because documentation of the children's histories indicated an original diagnosis on the pervasive developmental disorders spectrum, and prior to coming to us, most of the children had enjoyed the benefits of a home-based program. These children have not been included in any of our published research. For the remainder of the children, the CARS scores to date have ranged from 30.5 to 42, with most children in the mild to moderate range.

Among the 41 children who have attended since 1993, 36 were boys, 5 girls; 36 were Caucasian, 1 Hispanic, and 4 Asian. Their age at admission ranged from 32 months to 74 months (mean = 47 months). Prior to 1993, IQ scores were based on the *Stanford–Binet Intelligence Scale–Fourth Edition* (Thorndike, Hagen, & Sattler, 1986); however, since 1993, the *Developmental Profile II* (Alpern, Boll, & Shearer, 1986) has been used as a broad measure of students' cognitive abilities. Speech–language assessments at admission, using the *Preschool Language Scale–Third Edition* (PLS–3; Zimmerman, Steiner, & Pond, 1992), has resulted in scores ranging from 7 months to 3 years 8 months (3-8) (mean = 2-1). Scores at admission on the *Peabody Picture Vocabulary Test–Revised* (PPVT–R; Dunn & Dunn, 1981) ranged from 1-1 to 5-3 (mean = 2-9).

Assessment Procedures

Children with autism are referred to the Douglass School's preschool program by child study teams, parents, physicians, or other professionals in related fields. In January and February of each year a projected number of preschool openings is determined. Following a review of each applicant's medical and educational records, children who appear suitable for admission are invited to the center for a screening (preliminary evaluation). During this visit parents who have not previously toured the preschool classes are encouraged to observe these classes so that they will be able to make an informed decision about whether an available opening is suitable for their child.

Initial screenings usually last 30 to 40 minutes, during which time 2 to 4 children with autism are observed in a semistructured setting by a multidisciplinary team of professional staff. Staff expose the children to a variety of social and academic stimuli and observe their responses. These preliminary screenings are helpful in ruling out children whose paper credentials sound consistent with the diagnosis of autistic disorder, but whose observed behavior is too social and responsive to support this diagnosis, or those whose profound degree of developmental delay makes a diagnosis of autistic disorder ambiguous.

After the screening, children who appear most appropriate to fill projected openings are invited to an in-depth intake evaluation. This evaluation includes a detailed interview with the parents by a clinical psychologist to obtain a developmental history, administration of the CARS, a classroom observation of the child with autism by a special education teacher, and administration of the PLS–3 by a speech and language specialist. At the conclusion of this assessment, the intake staff, which includes school administrators, supervisors, and educational and support staff, meet to decide whether any of our projected openings are suitable to the child's needs. A clear, confirmed diagnosis of autistic disorder, and a determination that at least one projected opening would be suitable, generally results in a favorable decision for admission. If more data are required for an accurate diagnosis or to determine placement suitability, the center's staff will visit the home, visit the child's present school placement, or speak with other professionals who have regular contact with the child.

Following admission, a child is evaluated by the special education teacher on the center's curriculum-based developmental assessment, the PPVT–R, and the *Vineland Adaptive Behavior Scales* (Sparrow, Balla, & Cicchetti, 1984). Preference assessments and functional analysis of challenging behaviors also provide information critical to the development of the child's individualized program. Videotaping may be used as well. Results from this assessment battery provide a profile of development in the major curriculum areas and a baseline against which to measure progress. Mastery, maintenance, and generalization data are charted on a daily, weekly, and quarterly basis to track a child's developmental gains.

Every child who is admitted must have a complete medical examination, and most children come to us with detailed pediatric and neurological evaluations, audiometric assessment, and other related tests.

Teaching and Administrative Staff

Each preschool class is staffed by a certified special education teacher, some of whom are also certified in early childhood, and full-time assistant teachers. The Prep class has five assistant teachers, and the Small Group and Small Wonders classes have three assistants each. In addition, each class is supported by a half-time speech–language specialist who provides individual and group therapy as well as consultation services to the preschool teachers. An adaptive physical education professional serves the preschool students one to three times a week and acts as the liaison for consulting professionals such as physical or occupational therapists.

We know our students are learning all day, not only in the classroom. Home-based learning must be planned as carefully as learning that occurs at the center. Our home programming staff assists teachers in promoting the generalization of acquired skills to the home and community environments. These home consultants help families establish priorities and develop and implement programs that address skill acquisition and challenging behaviors in the home and community. They go to each student's home twice a month and may provide crisis intervention as needed. In addition, home programmers provide technical support for using augmentative communication systems and related computer software; advise parents in implementing desensitization and behavior management programs; and assist parents in obtaining help from local and state agencies (e.g., recreation programs, New Jersey Division of Developmental Disabilities).

The Division of Research and Training assists the preschool teachers in training graduate and undergraduate students enrolled in special education, psychology, and a variety of other courses that may require field work experience. The school hosts as many as 50 field workers a semester. They work 1 full clinical day and attend a 90-minute seminar once a week. This very important source of person power provides each class with additional individualized tutors.

The educational staff members at the school are regularly supervised to ensure best practice service delivery to our students. Teachers are responsible for annually assessing students' skills, coordinating the development of educational plans with parents and child study teams, designing and implementing skill acquisition programs, monitoring student progress, organizing class and staff schedules, clinical training for field work students, and collaborating with other support staff. A certified supervisor of education and related services meets with new teachers twice a month, and more experienced teachers once a month. This supervisor does monthly classroom observations and attends student clinics throughout the year. The supervisor provides both formative and evaluative oral and written feedback to teachers, oversees the development of Individualized Education Plans and programming, monitors students' progress, and collaborates with the division director on policy, curriculum, and program development. In a similar role, the coordinator of speech and language services, a master's level person holding a certificate of clinical competence, oversees service delivery provided to students by speech–language specialists, coordinates speech–language programming, monitors students' progress, contributes to curriculum development, and maintains a library of augmentative communication systems.

Curriculum

Weekly schedules of classroom activities are determined by the classroom teacher and submitted to the supervisor of education and related services. Because the Douglass model has three distinct preschool classes arranged in a continuum of services, these schedules are quite different. For instance, the Prep class schedule provides intense individualized instruction throughout the day, whereas the Small Group class schedule includes both individualized and group instruction, and the Small Wonders class schedule has children working in small and large groups the entire day. Table 10.3 provides examples of the classroom schedule for each of the three classes.

Individual speech–language services are provided for all children with autism at least twice a week. During these sessions, each student's individual

Table 10.3

Examples of Douglass School classroom schedules

Time	Prep	Time	Small Group	Time	Small Wonders
9:15–9:30	Structured Play/ Toileting	9:15–9:40	Special Events/ Arrival/Free Play	9:15–9:40	Toileting/Free Play
9:35–9:45	Circle	9:40–10:00	Morning Group	9:40–10:00	Morning Group
9:45–11:15	Individual Work: Varied Programming	10:00–10:30	Work 1: Language Programs*	10:00–10:40	Fine Motor and Learning Centers 1. _____ 2. _____
10:00–11:00	Computer: 10 min each 1. _____ 2. _____ 3. _____ 4. _____ 5. _____ 6. _____	10:30–10:40	Language Group		3. _____ 4. _____ 5. _____ 6. _____
		10:40–11:10	Work 2: Cognitive Programs*		Spch. Spec: _____ Teacher: _____
		11:10–11:25	Circle	10:40–11:20	Play Centers— Blocks: _____
11:15–11:25	Music Group	11:25–12:00	Lunch		Games: _____
11:25–12:00	Lunch With Speech	12:00–12:15	Free Play		Sensory: _____ Computer: _____
12:00–12:30	Playground 2	12:15–12:35	Sensory Motor	11:20–12:05	Lunch
12:30–2:00	Individual Work: Varied Programming 1. _____ 2. _____ 3. _____ 4. _____ 5. _____ 6. _____	12:35–1:00	Gross Motor	12:05–12:40	Playground
		1:00–1:20	Play Centers— Game Team 1 Team 2	12:40–1:00	Circle
				1:00–1:30	Cognitive Learning Centers— 1. _____ 2. _____ 3. _____ 4. _____ 5. _____
		1:20–1:40	Work 3: Fine Motor Programs*		
		1:40–2:00	Snack		
		2:00–2:35	Centers— Art Audio Toys		Spch. Spec: _____ Teacher: _____
2:00–2:10	Snack	2:35–2:45	Afternoon Group	1:30–2:10	Play Centers— Blocks: _____
2:15–2:30	Art	2:45	Dismissal		Kitchen: _____ Art: _____
2:30–2:40	Story				Other: _____
2:45	Dismissal		* Vary Programming to increase motivation	2:10–2:20	Snack
				2:20–2:35	Story/Dismissal

communication needs are addressed and the speech–language specialist's assessment of progress is integrated into recommendations to the classroom teacher for comprehensive speech–language instruction in the classroom. The teacher and speech–language specialist form a team to provide the student with programming that is consistent from one setting to another. Goals for individual lessons, as well as for classroom programming, are determined according to the results of formal and informal assessment measures, classroom observation, and input from parents and other support staff. Instructional experiences are planned to capitalize on a child's strengths while addressing weaker areas of development. In addition to individual sessions, the speech–language specialists spend time in each preschool class, providing integrated speech services to support language instruction in a functional context, especially where opportunities arise for interaction between two children at play or within a group format. Beyond the obvious benefits derived from this integrated model, it also allows the teacher and assistant teachers to observe the specific instructional techniques of the speech–language specialists and thus enhances coordination among staff members.

Integration Versus Segregation

We believe that experiences that promote mainstreaming and inclusion are important components of educational programming for children with autism; however, an initially segregated experience may increase some children's ability to benefit from the subsequent integrated experiences. For all classes, objectives and activities are planned with the goal of teaching the fundamental skills that will eventually promote responsiveness to normalized and community-based living. This effort is most apparent in the Small Wonders class that provides daily opportunities for interacting with typically developing classmates. However, both the Prep and Small Group preschool classes employ educational strategies that are designed to promote the development of more advanced skills necessary for students with autism to be successful in integrated settings. Thus, there is a careful progression of skills that begins with mastering basic compliance, self-control, and attention to task, and advances to learning sensitivity to others and the ability to maintain oneself in a group. Although not all of the preschoolers will transition to less restrictive settings, our goal is for every child entering the program to work toward that transition. The DDDC's transition policy is guided by the highly individualized and increasingly complex curriculum that sets the framework for mainstreaming and inclusion efforts. This policy is also reflected in the consultation services provided by Douglass Outreach.

The actual transition process from the DDDC to another school is carefully planned and implemented in a highly systematic fashion. The Douglass School works cooperatively with parents and school district representatives to identify students who have the skills requisite for mainstreaming or inclusion in less restricted settings; most desirable placements would be regular education classes in a child's community school. Often, the process begins 9 to 12 months prior to a student's leaving our program so that all the "pieces" will be in place by the time a child leaves. For example, by initially visiting various public and private settings, the team can identify a preliminary student–placement match. After a comprehensive assessment of the skills needed in the new setting, requisite skills can be assessed and the child's existing deficits corrected. The team's assessment of the potential placement includes variables such as staff–student ratio, contingencies, school–life activities, and classroom structure. Our program efforts at the school are directed toward approximating the new placement in order to facilitate the student's optimal adjustment. Sometimes, this transition process is further enhanced by having the student attend the new school for increasing periods of time prior to enrollment. When this preplacement is not possible, we invite educational staff from the new school to visit a transitioning student in our program, thus allowing all staff to strategize and share ideas. The introduction of curriculum materials used in a student's anticipated school placement may also help to prepare a transitioning student. Formal follow-up services are offered after graduation.

Transition may present challenges for parents as well as for their children. The supports found in a specialized setting are often unavailable in more typical educational settings. To prepare the entire family for the transition to less intense support in other settings, we gradually fade our own level of home support. Parents are encouraged to become more independent problem solvers, strong advocates for their children, and full participants in the transition process by visiting prospective placements, making the decision about a preferred setting, and working at home to facilitate the process of change.

Parental and Family Involvement

After participating in parent training sessions when their child enters the preschool program, a family receives visits twice a month from a home programmer who provides ongoing support and training. These visits cover a broad range of parenting concerns and integrate the teaching of general psychological principles of child management with the specific ongoing needs of the child. For instance, the home programmer will help parents prioritize goals; develop skill acquisition programs; and define, chart, and address challenging behaviors in the home and community settings. Reference materials used to enhance home programming efforts include *Teaching Developmentally Disabled Children: The Me Book* (Lovaas, 1981), *Steps to Independence* (Baker & Brightman, 1989), *Children with Autism* (Powers, 1989), and *Behavioral Intervention for Young Children with Autism* (Maurice, Green, & Luce, 1996).

In the course of consulting about home programs, the home programmers are encouraged to be sensitive to the needs of the family as a system. For example, they look for constructive ways to engage older and younger siblings in home programming, encourage families to find equitable ways to distribute child care and other responsibilities, and in general try to be respectful of the family unit while helping families explore new ways to organize family routines. A continuing clinical challenge is that of meshing a behavioral approach with the complexities of the individual family structure. All parents are asked to do some work with their children in the home capitalizing on the many opportunities that arise throughout the day to teach self-help skills, socialization, and the ability to independently engage in functional activities.

In addition to home programming efforts, all three preschool classes invite parents to monthly clinics. A formal clinic is a forum for all persons who work with a child (educational, supervisory and support staff, and parents) to exchange ideas, problem solve, and observe each other implement programs. An observational clinic is a 30-minute period set aside for parents to observe their child in class once a month and then discuss the observation with the teacher or any other member of the team. The students in the Prep and Small Group preschool classes have one formal clinic and one observational clinic a month. New students in the Small Wonders class also have both a formal and an observational clinic for the first 3 months, and then only one observational clinic a month.

The formal clinic, which was inspired by our observations of Ivar Lovaas and his staff at UCLA, facilitates communication among the several people working with a child, ensures that everyone is requiring the same level of performance, and stimulates the development of new programming ideas. Home–school communication is also enhanced by regular phone contact and by a communication notebook that goes home daily with each student.

In addition to parent training and involvement of parents in the educational needs of the child, the center also provides support services for families. These include evening discussion groups, during which parents are encouraged to share with one another their feelings about the special stresses in their lives and methods of coping with these demands. For example, group members might discuss how they feel about their extended family's reaction to their child's special needs, the stresses they experience in their marriage, and so forth. These voluntary groups provide a useful source of support and often form the basis for new friendships among families. Similar age-appropriate support groups for siblings have also been a useful service. These sibling groups typically meet on Saturday morning or Sunday afternoon, combine play with discussion, and encourage children to share their experiences about growing up with a sibling with autism.

Approximately four times a year, parents at the center, including those with children in the preschool program, come together for an evening meeting. These meetings include an opportunity for parent–professional exchange, as well as the chance to discuss topics of concern with an invited speaker. We have addressed such topics as parent advocacy within the public school system, preparing wills and trusts to meet the needs of the child with autism, nutrition, and current topics in medical research.

Outcome Measures

We recently did a 4- to 6-year follow-up of 27 children with autistic disorder who completed our preschool program (Harris & Handleman, in press). Their mean age at time of admission was 49 months (range 31 to 65), and at follow-up 142 months (range 122 to 170). Their mean score on the CARS (Schopler et al., 1988) was 34.17 (range 30 to 40). The children's mean IQ on the *Stanford–Binet* (Thorndike et al., 1986) at intake was 59 (range 35 to 109).

In 1999 follow-up questionnaires were sent to the school districts and the parents of all children who had entered the preschool programs of the Douglass School between 1990 and 1992. We asked about whether the child was in a regular education class (with or without support), a special education class, or a combined model of regular and special education. Among the 13 children who began treatment at age 48 months or less, all but 3 were in regular education classes, while among the 14 who started at 50 months or older, all but 1 were in special education classes. If we look at those children from our program who entered before 48 months of age, outcome data are consistent with those of other researchers who report a favorable outcome following the use of applied behavior analysis treatment methods (e.g., Anderson, Avery, DiPietro, Edwards, & Christian, 1987; Birnbrauer & Leach, 1993; Lovaas, 1987; Sheinkopf & Siegel, 1998). Interestingly, in those other reports, the children also had a mean age below 48 months. By contrast, if we inspect the data for our older children alone, one would receive the misleading impression that our treatment methods were not as effective as those of our colleagues. At least for our program, and perhaps for those of our colleagues, age at time of admission is an important factor in outcome.

The IQs of children shortly after their admission to the school were also related to their later placement. Children who entered with higher IQs (mean = 81) were more likely to be placed in regular education classes at follow-up than those who entered with lower IQs (mean = 48). It is important to remember that children with lower IQs who went into special education settings still showed measurable gains in IQ from pre- to posttreatment. That group had a mean IQ of 46 at entry and of 59 at discharge. A 13-point increase in IQ is not minor. Their progress was not, however, sufficient to allow them to enter a regular education class. By contrast, the group of children who went in to regular classes made a 26-point gain in IQ, going from a mean of 78 at entry to 104 at discharge.

Our follow-up reveals that those children who started treatment before the age of 4 years had, as a group, a better placement outcome than those who started later. However, these data should not be taken to suggest that children 4 years of age and older do not benefit from intensive treatment. Their 13-point increase in IQ speaks to their capacity to make good progress.

We are presently analyzing follow-up data on the children who were enrolled in the Douglass preschool programs between 1993 and 1998. We anticipate that the results will be consistent with proven findings, and perhaps be even more impressive. It will be important to continue to follow up on all of these children as they encounter the challenges of higher grades.

Douglass Outreach

Douglass Outreach offers home-based services for preschool children with autism and has a small center-based component. The Outreach Division also offers extensive consultation services to public school programs and evaluates children with autism. In the present chapter we focus on the home-based services and school consultation services.

Population Served

Clients served by Douglass Outreach are referred with a diagnosis of autistic disorder, pervasive developmental disorder–not otherwise specified, or Asperger's syndrome (American Psychiatric Association, 1994), confirmed by an outside professional such as a neurologist, developmental pediatrician, or psychologist. Douglass Outreach has provided home-based services to nearly 300 clients since 1994 and is currently serving 82 clients; approximately 70 are receiving less than 30 hours per week and 12 are receiving 30 or more hours per week. The age range of the clients is 18 months to 12 years. To date, we have served as consultants to more than 160 school- and community-based programs and are currently serving 66 programs. These consultations focus on classes for students with an autism diagnosis using applied behavior analysis.

Assessment Procedures

Parents submit existing educational and medical records prior to the beginning of home-based services. The child's program coordinator completes the DDDC Preschool Checklist with input from parents and behavioral observations of the child in the home. In addition, the *Checklist of Learning and Lan-*

guage Behavior (Bangs, 1986) is administered to achieve a developmental age profile. Standardized videotape assessments are done every 3 to 4 months. The information from the initial assessment is used as a baseline to determine the client's progress. Progress is monitored daily via discrete trial data and summarized in quarterly progress reports. Checklists are updated regularly and probes are conducted monthly to ensure that skills are being maintained and generalized.

Teaching and Administrative Staff

Douglass Outreach has 92 employees; these include 8 full-time professional staff, 82 part-time staff, and 2 full-time office staff. All professional staff members have a minimum of a bachelor's degree in special education, psychology, or a related field, and at least 2 years supervised clinical experience. The office staff provides clerical support, and four full-time special education coordinators oversee home programs and consult to school-based programs.

The remainder of the Douglass Outreach staff, part-time employees called program coordinators and consultant/tutors, are certified special education teachers and assistant teachers. Special education coordinators supervise all program coordinators and consultant/tutors. Douglass Outreach also employs five licensed part-time speech pathologists for speech–language services. Consultant/tutors provide one-to-one instruction based on the client's individualized program, collect and record data for each therapy session, record anecdotal information about the therapy session, and attend regular meetings about their client's program. Consultant/tutors, who are supervised by a program coordinator, provide input for curricular issues as well as therapy support.

Curriculum

The Douglass Outreach home-based program includes intensive educational instruction organized by a program coordinator and the child's parents or caregivers. The home-based program provides continuous training and consultation for parents and assessment and goal development for the client. Topics such as instructional techniques, compliance training, reinforcement procedures and curriculum development are addressed through initial workshops and ongoing training.

After an initial telephone contact, a program coordinator visits the family to gather information about the child's needs and the family's resources. An individualized program is then designed based on the DDDC curriculum and typically begins with 10 to 20 hours per week of services. If a child is to receive a more extensive home program (30 to 40 hours per week) the curriculum reflects a broader scope but still focuses on the foundation skills necessary to build more complex skills. Consultant/tutors are assigned to work with the child, and the program coordinator sets up a weekly schedule for all team members. An initial program for a child could include the broad goals presented in Table 10.4. Specific behavioral objectives would also be developed by the team.

The child's progress through the curriculum is monitored by a program coordinator and evaluated frequently during regularly scheduled team meetings (clinics) that include all therapists and the parents. Programming progresses from least difficult to most difficult and from narrow fundamental skills to broader skills in all developmental areas. As an example, initially a child would be taught a variety of nonverbal skills progressing from gross motor imitation, to fine motor imitation, to oral motor imitation, to graphomotor imitation. An Educational Program Record (EPR) is supplied for every implemented program of the DDDC's curriculum. Figure 10.1 provides a sample of an Educational Program Record for Matching.

Curriculum planning proceeds from nonverbal imitation skills to beginning receptive language skills. Initially, programming focuses on following simple requests and commands, which might include sitting, coming when called, standing, walking to a person, or giving, getting, or touching common objects. As a child masters these initial receptive language skills programming moves to more advanced language skills such as labeling objects, pictures, actions, and people. More abstract concepts such as colors, shapes, use

Table 10.4
Sample Beginning Home Program

1. Sits appropriately

2. Establishes eye contact

3. Matches objects to objects (three-dimensional)

4. Performs nonverbal imitation

5. Follows one-step directions

6. Receptively identifies body parts

7. Plays with simple toys (stacking, nesting, pegboard)

8. Requests with a point or simple gesture

9. Toilet training

EDUCATIONAL PROGRAM RECORD

AREA: Cognitive—Matching

STUDENT: Susan R.   **COORDINATOR(S):** Tom

DATE INITIATED: 3/2/99   **DATE MASTERED:** 5/5/99

TARGET BEHAVIOR: Matches object to object

BEHAVIORAL OBJECTIVE: Susan will match identical objects within 3–5 seconds of stimulus presentation.

DESCRIPTION OF PROGRAM: Establish appropriate sitting and attending behavior.

Sd FOR TARGET BEHAVIOR: Teacher Says, "Match"

CONSEQUENCE: Reinforce correct response with behavior-specific praise. If student does not respond or responds incorrectly, provide appropriate prompt. Implement correction procedure and reinforce correct response with behavior-specific praise.

PROCEDURE:
Step 1: Present SD, "Match" and one object. Hand child the object to be matched. Child should place object on or next to target object.
Step 2: Present SD, "Match" and two objects. Hand child the object to be matched. Child should place object on or next to target object.
Step 3: Present SD, "Match" and three objects. Hand child the object to be matched. Child should place object on or next to target object.

PROMPT HIERARCHY:
Full Physical Prompt
Faded Physical Prompt
Gestural Prompt

GENERALIZATION: Mastery requires that you probe this skill varying the SD, if appropriate, and using at least two novel settings, sets of materials, and people. Criterion: 90% or above on at least two different days.

(continues)

Figure 10.1. Sample Educational Program Record for Matching.

SETS:

Set 1:	Bowls	Set 10:	Crayons (same color)
Set 2:	Cups	Set 11:	MIX
Set 3:	MIX	Set 12:	Balls
Set 4:	Spoons	Set 13:	MIX
Set 5:	MIX	Set 14:	Bubbles
Set 6:	Animals (identical)	Set 15:	MIX
Set 7:	MIX	Set 16:	Continue to add items that are familiar to the child.
Set 8:	Pens		(Always put in a mix after mastered in isolation.)
Set 9:	MIX		

MATERIALS: Variety of identical objects.

DATA: + correct answer
− incorrect answer
Take data on target set only.
Indicate prompt level.

TRIALS: 10–20 trials per day

CRITERION: 90% over two consecutive sessions

COMMENTS:

SUPPLEMENTAL COMPUTER SOFTWARE:

Figure 10.1. *Continued.*

of pronouns, spatial concepts using prepositions, discrimination of yes and no, and answering "wh" questions are introduced as the child progresses.

The curriculum emphasizes communication skills, including the acquisition of simple sentences such as "I want ___," "I have ___," and "I see ___," and teaching the child to describe his or her environment using more complex grammatical sentences. Engaging in reciprocal conversation and using language for social interactions are also emphasized. In addition, concepts, letters, and numbers, along with writing one's name, are introduced to prepare a child to enter a preschool program. The program coordinator and team members make recommendations about materials and help organize materials for use by team members.

All educational materials required to implement programs are supplied by the parents except for the program records and data sheets. An initial educational report is provided approximately 4 to 6 weeks after initiation of the home program and at 3-to-4 month intervals thereafter.

Program coordinators are prepared to assist families in their transition from a home-based program to a school-based one and offer help regarding skill development for academic programming, social skills training, communication and language training, and behavior management.

Integration

Initial programs for Douglass Outreach clients focus on skills preparing them to be integrated into community life and to transition to public educational settings where they have opportunities for peer interaction. Children are taught foundation skills, proceeding from simple skills to more complex ones, but always with the goal of teaching greater independence and social responsiveness.

An important strategy for integration involves play dates, and parents are encouraged to arrange these with a peer once their child has acquired basic play skills. As the child becomes more comfortable with the peer, parents increase the peer network by having several children join in a playgroup. The gradual expansion introduces the child to skills such as sharing, turn-taking, and waiting one's turn.

The program coordinator assists the parents in identifying appropriate community placements for their child and plans systematic transitions to the next environment. Initially, the program coordinator visits a potential placement to determine prerequisite skills for a successful transition and the home program continues to focus on deficit skills. The program coordinator also trains support staff, such as a shadow in the new school, for modifying curriculum, providing individualized support, implementing incentive systems, promoting peer interactions, and providing proper supports for modifying inappropriate behaviors. Coordinators monitor a child's transition from a home-based program to a school-based one and may be retained by a school district to provide services to that child in the new school setting. This model supports both the child and the family, with a continuum of services providing continuity of programming and emotional support.

Outcome Measures

The average time that a child remains in a Douglass Outreach home-based program is 1.5 years. Typically, services continue after a child has been placed in a community program, but on a reduced schedule. Currently 8 children who have been transitioned to school-based programs are receiving follow-up services through Douglass Outreach, and 5 school districts continue to request services from Douglass Outreach and are funding those programs.

School Consultation Program

Douglass Outreach provides consultation to community-based schools interested in implementing a behavioral program for students with autism. School-based consultations reflect the needs of the school district and focus on areas such as staff and professional training in applied behavior analysis, implementation of educational programs, integration and inclusion, functional assessment and behavior intervention plans, and social skills training. At the request of the district, Douglass Outreach will return on an annual basis to provide staff and professional training.

Consultation to community programs is based on the DDDC's many years of providing services to children with autism. Our model is adapted to the needs of public school programs in a variety of settings. A Douglass Outreach program coordinator is assigned as a consultant to work with the school in implementing the educational program. After the consultant meets with an administrator to outline goals and objectives for the consultation and to ascertain appropriate guidelines and schedules, the consultant conducts on-site visits approximately once per week and provides continuous supervision and monitoring with verbal and written feedback. In addition, consultants advise the schools about physical environments and assist in designing classrooms that address the needs of children with pervasive developmental disorders. For example, the consultant makes suggestions for individualized programming, group work, toilet facilities, and recreational facilities.

Douglass Outreach also assists schools in educational planning by being involved in training workshops, consulting to staff and administration, monitoring the educational program, sharing curriculum and other resources, and providing written feedback for each consultation. Professional staff training for a school district or private agency typically occurs during the summer months and in early fall, but can continue during the year on an as-needed basis. Table 10.5 outlines a sample workshop.

As with home-based programs, the DDDC curriculum is shared with the schools, with recommendations for individualized goals. Table 10.6 lists programming areas.

Major Issues for Future Effort

As members of a university-based facility, the staff of the Douglass School and Douglass Outreach, along with the staff of the other DDDC divisions,

Table 10.5
Sample Workshop for Staff

1. Teaching techniques
   a. Discrete trial instruction
   b. Establishing and strengthening behaviors
   c. Maintaining behaviors
   d. Discrimination, stimulus control, and generalization
   e. Incidental teaching
   f. Data collection and monitoring programs

2. Establishment of basic classroom behaviors
   a. Attending skills
   b. Imitative skills
   c. Independent work skills

3. Curriculum considerations

4. Scheduling classrooms

Table 10.6
Curriculum Content Areas

1. Language: Receptive and Expressive
2. Speech: Oral–Motor Development
3. Language Use
4. Cognitive: Academic, Conceptual, Reasoning Skills
5. Cognitive: Visual–Perceptual Memory
6. Auditory Memory
7. Auditory Perception
8. Auditory Closure
9. Cognitive: Matching, Counting, Reading
10. Fine Motor: Manipulation, Writing
11. Gross Motor Movement and Object Movement
12. Self-Help
13. Socialization: Play and Peer, Affect/Self-Concept
14. Adult Interaction/Classroom Behavior
15. Reduction of Inappropriate Behaviors

continue to be committed to ongoing program evaluation and development. This commitment has contributed to the evolutionary nature of the program and continues to result in innovations in programming for the range of children being served at the center. Current interests focus on issues related to the nature of autism and on programming strategies that address the specialized needs of these students.

Most recently, a review of our outcome data has revitalized our commitment to do long-term follow-up on our students who leave the preschool program and enter regular education. We hope to better understand the issues these students face in later years in order to continue to modify and refine our present program for future preschoolers. In addition, we are taking a critical look at a variety of methods for promoting skill acquisition; evaluating various behavioral strategies that show promise in the amelioration of challenging behaviors; assessing the influence of sensory experiences on learning; surveying the significance of compulsive behaviors as a characteristic of autistic disorder; and studying the variables that promote the development of spontaneous and sustained social interaction between typical preschoolers and their friends with autism within an integrated learning environment.

Since 1992, professionals in the field of autism have moved forward in their quest to further clarify diagnostic criteria and define and validate intervention strategies. However, a great deal remains to be learned about optimal educational strategies for young children with autism, making it essential that we renew our efforts to tackle complex questions through applied research.

References

Alpern, G., Boll, P., & Shearer, M. (1986). *Developmental Profile II*. Los Angeles: Western Psychological Services.

American Psychiatric Association. (1987). *Diagnostic and statistical manual of mental disorders* (3rd ed., revised). Washington, DC: Author.

American Psychiatric Association. (1994). *Diagnostic and statistical manual of mental disorders* (4th ed.). Washington, DC: Author.

Anderson, S. R., Avery, D. L., DiPietro, E. K., Edwards, G. L., & Christian, W. P. (1987). Intensive home-based early intervention with autistic children. *Education and Treatment of Children, 10*, 352–366

Attainment Company. (1993). *Life skill picture cues*. Verona, WI: Author.

Austin, P., & Boeckmann, K. (1990). *Functional word series*. Redmond, WA: Edmark Corp.

Baker, B. L., & Brightman, A. J. (1989). *Steps to independence*. Baltimore, MD: Brookes.

Bangs, T. E. (1986). *Checklist of Learning and Language Behavior*. Allen, TX: DLM Teaching Resources.

Becht, L. C., & Exley, J. (1989). *The sensible pencil: A handwriting program*. Birmingham, AL: EBSCO Curriculum Materials.

Birnbrauer, J. S., & Leach, D. J. (1993). The Murdoch Early Intervention Program after 2 years. *Behavior Change, 10,* 63–74.

Dunn, L. M., & Dunn, L. M. (1981). *Peabody Picture Vocabulary Test–Revised.* Circle Pines, MN: American Guidance Service.

Durand, V. M. (1990). *Severe behavior problems.* New York: Guilford Press.

Earlley, E. C. (1986a). *AIMS: Pre-reading kit.* Elizabethtown, PA: The Continental Press.

Earlley, E. C. (1986b). *AIMS: Reading kits 1 & 2.* Elizabethtown, PA: The Continental Press.

Edmark Corporation. (1992). *Edmark reading program, Level 1.* Redmond, WA: Author.

Edmark Corporation. (1993). *Edmark reading program, Level 2.* Redmond, WA: Author.

Frost, L., & Bondy, A. (1994). *The Picture Exchange Communication System.* Cherry Hill, NJ: Pyramid Educational Consultants.

Grumblatt, L., & McClennen, S. (1991). *PACE-Math. Cognitive skills for community living.* Austin, TX: PRO-ED.

Harris, S. L., & Handleman, J. S. (in press). Age and IQ at intake as predictors of placement for young children with autism: A four to six year follow-up. *Journal of Autism and Developmental Disorders.*

Levine, L. (1988). *Great beginnings for early language training.* San Antonio, TX: Communication Skill Builders.

Lord, C., & Schopler, E. (1987). Neurobiological implications of sex differences in autism. In E. Schopler & G. B. Mesibov (Eds.), *Neurobiological issues in autism* (pp. 191–211). New York: Plenum.

Lovaas, O. I. (1981). *Teaching developmentally disabled children: The me book.* Baltimore: University Park Press.

Lovaas, O. I. (1987). Behavioral treatment and normal educational and intellectual functioning in young autistic children. *Journal of Consulting and Clinical Psychology, 55,* 3–9.

Maurice, C., Green, G., & Luce, S. (1996). *Behavioral intervention for young children with autism.* Austin, TX: PRO-ED.

McClennen, S. E. (1991). *Cognitive skills for living: Teaching students with moderate to severe disabilities.* Austin, TX: PRO-ED.

Olsen, J. Z. (1998). *Handwriting without tears.* Potomac, MD: Handwriting Without Tears.

Ploudre, L. (1989). *CLAS Preschool.* San Antonio, TX: Communication Skill Builders.

Powers, M. D. (1989). *Children with autism: A parents' guide.* Bethesda, MD: Woodbine House.

Romanczyk, R. G., & Lockshin, S. (1994). *The I.G.S. Curriculum.* Vestal, NY: C.B.T.A.

Schopler, E., Reichler, R. J., DeVellis, R. F., & Daly, K. (1988). *The Childhood Autism Rating Scale.* Los Angeles, CA: Western Psychological Services.

Semels, V. (1999). *Following directions series: One and two level commands.* Winooski, VT: Laureate Learning Systems.

Sheinkopf, S. J., & Siegel, B. (1998). Home based behavioral treatment of young autistic children. *Journal of Autism and Developmental Disorders, 28,* 15–24.

Sparrow, S. S., Balla, D. A., & Cicchetti, D. V. (1984). *Vineland Adaptive Behavior Scales, Interview Edition, Survey form manual.* Circle Pines, MN: American Guidance Service.

Strain, P. S., Hoyson, M., & Jamieson, B. (1985, Spring). Normally developing preschoolers as intervention agents for autistic-like children: Effects on class deportment and social interaction. *Journal for the Division of Early Childhood,* 105–115.

Thorndike, R. L., Hagen, E. R., & Sattler, J. M. (1986). *The Stanford–Binet Intelligence Scale–Fourth Edition.* Chicago: Riverside.

Wilson, M. S., & Fox, B. (1996) *First words.* Winooski, VT: Laureate Learning Systems.

Zimmerman, I. L., Steiner, V. G., & Pond, R. E. (1992). *Preschool Language Scale–Third Edition.* San Antonio: Psychological Corp.

About the Editors

Jan S. Handleman earned his doctoral degree in special education from Rutgers, The State University of New Jersey, in 1977. He is currently director of the Douglass Developmental Disabilities Center of Rutgers University and professor of psychology for the Graduate School of Applied and Professional Psychology. He and the Center recently celebrated their 27th anniversary. Dr. Handleman is the author of a number of books, book chapters, and articles and has widely presented at national and international conferences. He serves on numerous editorial boards and boards of agencies serving individuals with autism.

Sandra L. Harris earned her doctorate in clinical psychology from the State University of New York at Buffalo in 1969. She is presently professor and dean of the Graduate School of Applied and Professional Psychology at Rutgers, The State University of New Jersey. Dr. Harris is executive director of the Douglass Developmental Disabilities Center, a Rutgers University program for children and adolescents with autism that she founded in 1972. She is the author of several books and numerous book chapters and journal articles concerning the needs of children with autism and the special needs of families that include a child with autism. Dr. Harris is nationally and internationally recognized for her work in this area and gives lectures around the world on her research. She is a fellow of the American Psychological Association, the American Psychological Society, and the American Association of Applied and Preventive Psychology. She is a past editor of *The Clinical Psychologist,* and serves on several editorial boards. Her book *Siblings: A Guide for Parents of Children with Autism* won the 1995 Autism Society of America's Literary Achievement Award. Her most recent book, written with Mary Jane Weiss, is titled *Right From the Start: Intensive Behavioral Intervention for Young Children with Autism.* It is a guide for parents seeking behavioral treatment of their preschool child.